WJEC Level 1/2 Vocational Award

Hospitality & Catering
(Technical Award)

Study & Revision Guide
2nd Edition

Anita Tull

Illuminate
Publishing

British Library Cataloguing in Publication Data

A catalogue record for this book is available from the British Library

ISBN 978-1-913963-32-3

Produced by DZS Grafik, Printed in Slovenia

Impression 3
Year 2023

Publisher: Claire Hart

Editor: Geoff Tuttle

Design and layout: Nigel Harriss

Cover image: Shutterstock.com/goodluz

Acknowledgements

Reproduced with kind permission of Nisbets Plc:

p38 chopping boards; **p38** chopping boards and knives; **p39** knife set; **p40** cleaning products; **p58** slip-on shoes, chain mail glove, freezer gloves; **p61** anti-fatigue mat; **p65** anti-fatigue mat, trolley; **p66** slicer with safety guard, deep fat frying machine, knife wallet; **p165** blast chiller; **p168** bottles, mousse ring, plating wedge, tweezers; **p169** chip scoop

p64 DRIP allergen menu, reproduced with the kind permission of DRIP restaurant, Bury

p60 sit-stand stool reproduced with the kind permission of LOTZ Lagertechnik GmbH, Germany

p119 graphs contain public sector information licensed under the Open Government Licence v3.0.

MIX
Paper | Supporting responsible forestry
FSC™ C104740
FSC
www.fsc.org

CONTENTS

You will find suggested answers to Knowledge check, Practice exam questions and Stretch and challenge questions at: www.illuminatepublishing.com/srghosp&cateranswers2ed

Introduction

This study and revision guide has been written to help you get ready for the online e-assessment in Unit 1 (this can also be taken as a written examination) and the controlled assessment task that you will do for Unit 2 in the WJEC Vocational Award in Hospitality and Catering Level 1/2 qualification.

The student textbook gives you more information about the types of questions you may be asked in the Unit 1 written exam and the Unit 2 controlled assessment task.

How to use this study and revision guide

Unit 1: The Hospitality and Catering Industry

How much of the qualification is this worth?	40%

Unit 1 covers the following topics:

- Topic 1.1 – Hospitality and catering provision
- Topic 1.2 – How hospitality and catering providers operate
- Topic 1.3 – Health and safety in hospitality and catering
- Topic 1.4 – Food safety in hospitality and catering

What do you have to do?

Answer questions on a variety of topics in a written examination.

Unit 2: Hospitality and Catering in Action

How much of the qualification is this worth?	60%

In **Unit 2**, you will learn about and apply your learning to:

- Topic 2.1 – The importance of nutrition
- Topic 2.2 – Menu planning
- Topic 2.3 – The skills and techniques of preparation, cooking and presentation of dishes
- Topic 2.4 – Evaluating cooking skills

What do you have to do?

Apply what you have learned to a Learner Assignment Brief, which will give you a scenario that you have to answer. You will write an account of what you have done and take a practical cooking assessment to show your skills.

Good luck on your course. We hope that you will enjoy learning about hospitality and catering, and will develop your skills and confidence as you progress through the course and possibly on to further training and a career in this industry.

Features to help you

Throughout this book, there are a number of features to help you to study and progress through the course, which are shown below.

Specification stems (see pages 96-98) indicate that questions on certain topics will need to be answered in a particular way:

> …know
> …know and understand
> …be aware of
> …be able to

Activity

A range of activities are given throughout the book. They are designed to help you learn a topic more thoroughly and practise answering questions.

Key terms

These give you the definitions of the key terminology (words) in each of the topics that you need to know and use.

Knowledge check – can you remember…?

These are end-of-topic questions that are designed to help you remember key points when you are revising for the Unit 1 Assessment.

Practice exam questions

These are end-of-topic questions, written in different styles and with a range of command words. They are designed to give you the chance to practise and improve the way you answer questions.

Scenario

These are activities that use realistic situations/proposals/problems that occur in hospitality and catering. You are asked to consider and make suggestions as to how these situations would be dealt with and/or suggest a suitable option for hospitality and catering provision, and/or suggest solutions to the problems presented.

Stretch and challenge questions

These are activities/questions in which you will need to find out more about a topic and practise answering questions at a higher level, showing your detailed knowledge and understanding.

Photographs and drawings: there are many of these throughout the book. They are included to help you further understand and visualise a topic.

Unit 1: The Hospitality and Catering Industry

Topic 1.1 Hospitality and catering provision

Hospitality and catering providers

Key learning and terms you should try to include in your answers

The hospitality and catering industry is one of the biggest employers in the UK. It uses many outside agencies, businesses and people to supply it with everything it needs.

Hospitality means providing people with a place to stay (accommodation), meals, drinks and entertainment in a variety of places.

Catering means providing people with a food and drink service in a variety of places.

Caterers supply businesses and places with food that is made in a central kitchen/factory, then delivered to order.

The structure of the hospitality and catering industry

 *... know and understand*

Hospitality
Somewhere to stay (accommodation), food, drinks and entertainment

 +

Catering
Food and drinks

Where?

Hotels, guest houses, Airbnbs, bed and breakfasts, inns, pubs, farmhouses, holiday camps and parks, family cabins, lodges, pods, luxury camping (glamping) sites, cruise ships, long-distance trains, airlines, motorway services, hostels

 Where?

Restaurants, bistros, dining rooms, canteens, cafés, tearooms, coffee shops, takeaway and fast food outlets, pubs, bars, clubs, casinos, street food stalls, pop-up restaurants, mobile/roadside food vans, motorway services, visitor and tourist attractions (theme parks, museums, zoos, etc.), sport stadiums, concert/gig venues, hospitals, schools, prisons, care homes, customers' homes (parties, funerals, etc.)

Suppliers provide:
Agency staff/employees (temporary and permanent)
Cleaning materials
Drinks
Equipment
Flower arrangements
Food
Furniture
Laundering services (washing and drying clothes and bed sheets, etc.)
Tableware – knives, forks, spoons, glasses, plates, etc.
Uniforms
Waste disposal
etc.

The commercial sector of the H&C industry

...know and understand

What do you need to know?

- Types of hospitality and catering places that provide services for different customers
- Types of services provided
- Job roles.

Commercial sector hospitality and catering businesses aim to make a profit.

They can be places where people stay in the accommodation provided (residential).

They can be places where hospitality and catering services are provided, but there is no accommodation for people to stay in (non-residential).

Residential commercial sector

Places

- Hotels
- Motels
- Guest houses
- Airbnbs
- Bed and breakfasts
- Inns
- Pubs
- Farmhouses
- Holiday camps and parks, lodges, pods
- Glamping (luxury camping) sites
- Cruise ships
- Long-distance trains
- Motorway services
- Hostels

Customers

Individuals and groups:

- Business conferences and meetings
- Family events
- Guests at a social event
- Tourists
- Participants in leisure activities
- Student field trips
- Travellers breaking a journey
- Passengers on a journey

H&C services

- Accommodation
- Housekeeping
- Turn down bed
- Room food and drinks service
- Packed lunches
- Formal meals
- Study and training facilities
- Conference rooms
- Internet access
- Transport catering service
- Rooms: single, double, king, family, en suite
- Leisure facilities: spa, gym, swimming pool
- Function facilities: e.g. weddings, parties, etc.

Job roles

- Managers
- Administrators
- Receptionists
- Porters
- Security
- Kitchen brigade
- Waiting staff
- Baristas
- Bartenders
- Housekeeping
- Room attendants
- Maintenance staff
- Conference staff

Non-residential commercial sector

Places

- Restaurants
- Bistros, cafés
- Dining rooms
- Canteens
- Tearooms, coffee shops
- Takeaway and fast food outlets
- Pubs, bars
- Clubs
- Casinos
- Street food stalls
- Pop-up restaurants
- Mobile/roadside food vans
- Motorway services
- Visitor and tourist attractions (theme parks, museums, zoos, etc.)
- Sport stadiums
- Concert/gig venues
- Vending machines
- Airlines

Customers

- Individuals, families, groups of different ages
- Tourists
- Visitors
- Workers on regular hours and shift workers

H&C services

- Eat in or takeaway food and drinks
- Private rooms for business or celebrations
- Training facilities
- Meeting rooms
- Internet access

Job roles

- Managers
- Administrators
- Security
- Kitchen brigade
- Receptionists
- Waiting staff
- Baristas
- Bartenders
- Housekeeping
- Maintenance staff

The non-commercial sector of the H&C industry ◁ ...know and understand

What do you need to know?

- Types of hospitality and catering establishments that provide services for different clients
- Services provided
- Job roles.

Non-commercial sector hospitality and catering businesses are non-profit making.

They can be places where people stay in the accommodation provided (residential).

They can be places where hospitality and catering services are provided, but there is no accommodation for people to stay in (non-residential).

Residential non-commercial sector

Establishments

1. Health and welfare:
   - NHS hospitals
   - Hospices
   - NHS nursing and care homes
   - Emergency services
   - Prisons
2. Education:
   - Colleges/universities
   - Boarding schools
3. Armed forces:
   - Army/Navy/Air Force
4. Other:
   - Hostels/shelters
   - Private nursing and care homes

Clients

1. Staff, patients, elderly people, people with disabilities, mental health patients, visitors, prisoners
2. Students, school children, visitors, staff
3. Armed forces personnel (all ranks), special events visitors
4. Homeless people, people with personal problems, elderly people, people with disabilities, people with mental health issues, staff

Job roles

- Managers
- Administrators
- Receptionists
- Porters
- Security
- Kitchen brigade
- Food counter staff
- Housekeeping/ maintenance staff
- Volunteers

H&C services

- Accommodation
- Food and drinks throughout day and night

Non-residential non-commercial sector

Establishments

1. Workforce catering:
   - Subsidised canteens
   - Dining rooms in factories, construction sites, shops, etc.
2. Voluntary sector/Health & welfare:
   - Senior citizen luncheon clubs
   - Charity food providers, e.g. soup vans, food banks and cafés
   - Day-care centres
   - Food delivery service, e.g. Meals on Wheels
3. Education:
   - Childcare day nurseries
   - School holiday clubs
4. Public sector catering:
   - Schools
   - Colleges and universities

Clients

1. Staff from all levels and departments
2. Elderly people, people with disabilities, people with mental health issues, staff
3. Babies, pre-school and school-age children and teenagers
4. School-age children, teenagers, students, lecturing staff, technicians, administration and other staff

H&C services

- Food and drinks

Job roles

- Managers
- Administrators
- Porters
- Security
- Receptionists
- Kitchen brigade
- Food counter staff
- Dining room manager
- Maintenance staff
- Volunteers

Types of food service systems

...know and understand

What do you need to know?

- How food is served to people in different ways (food service systems) in different places (establishments)

Counter service

- Customers choose food from a display
- Customers queue to pay before they eat the food – queue may be lengthy at busy times, e.g. at lunchtime
- Food can be eaten in the place or taken away

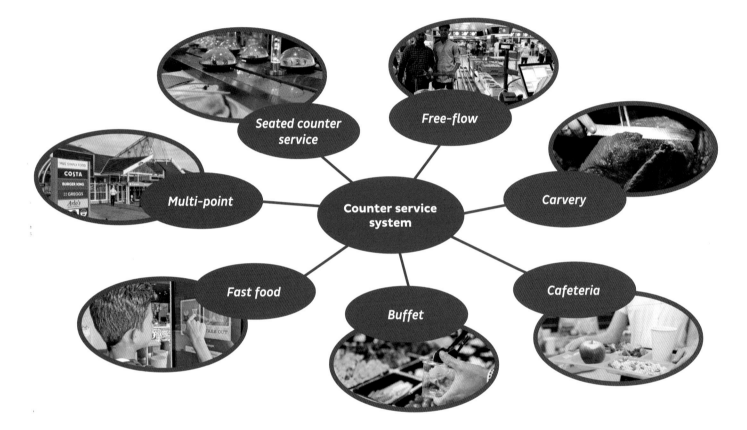

Table service

- Waiting staff take food orders and serve customers seated at a table
- Large restaurants divide tables into areas called stations
- There are different types of table service:
  - Plate service: food is placed on a plate in the kitchen, then served at the table by a waiter
  - Family-style service: all the food is put in dishes on the table for customers to serve themselves
  - Silver service: food is served by a waiter to each customer from a serving dish (traditionally made of silver) at the table. Each part of the meal is eaten with separate cutlery in a particular order.
  - Banquet service: is for large occasions where many people are served meals, e.g. a wedding reception. The food could be served as a buffet, plate service or silver service.
  - Gueridon system (trolley/moveable) service: food is prepared/cooked at the table to entertain customers.

Food being flambéed by the waiter

Transport catering

Careful planning is needed to make sure that:

- Food is kept safe to eat
- Different customer needs are catered for:

  Trains
  - Restaurant carriages on some long-distance trains
  - Takeaway cafeteria or trolley service available

  Aeroplanes
  - Frozen or cook-chilled meals provided on long-distance flights – heated by microwave
  - Trolley drink and snack service available on many short-distance flights

  Ships
  - Cruise ships provide a variety of food service options
  - Ferries usually have a cafeteria service

Food trolley service on a Japanese train

Vending system

- Vending machines sell hot and cold meals, snacks and drinks in a variety of places
- A team of people is needed to service them and maintain their stocks

Personal service

- Online food-delivery service companies collect customers' ready-to-eat food orders from restaurants and takeaway businesses and deliver them to customers in their homes.
- Other food-delivery companies deliver frozen or long-life ready-made meals to customers, including elderly or disabled people, for them to store and heat at home when required.
- Ready-to-eat (hot) food-delivery companies have to deliver the food quickly to the customer, so that it does not cool down and lose its freshly cooked flavour and texture.

Hospitality and catering standards and ratings ◀ ...know and understand

What do you need to know?

- A hospitality and catering business with a high rating will attract more customers
- Ratings give customers an assurance of a high standard of service
- The following charts show how ratings are awarded in the hospitality and catering industry:

Hotels and guest houses

Who does the inspections?	Type of rating awarded	What is being inspected?
Organisations, e.g.: AA/RAC Tourist Boards Visit Britain **Customers on social media, e.g.:** Facebook Twitter TripAdvisor Google Booking.com	**Stars:** ★ ★★ ★★★ ★★★★ ★★★★★	Open times, (i.e. all year or seasonal) Number of guest rooms En suite facilities Reception facilities Customer care Environment (noisy/quiet, friendly, relaxing, clean?) Facilities/accessibility for people with disabilities Staff Catering standards Insurance cover Healthy and safety Security Maintenance of facilities Extra facilities, e.g. gym, swimming pool, internet availability, TV, etc. Car parking Licence for sale of alcohol

Restaurants

Who does the inspections?	Type of rating awarded	What is being inspected?
Organisations, e.g.: AA The Good Food Guide Michelin Guide	AA: 1–5 rosettes The Good Food Guide: Score 1–10 Michelin Guide: 1, 2 or 3 stars	Type/range of food Quality of food and ingredients Where food comes from (provenance) Standard of cooking, flavour, presentation, quality How skilful and creative the chefs are

Food hygiene

Who does the inspections?	Type of rating awarded	What is being inspected?
Organisations, e.g.: Food Standards Agency and Local Authorities in England, Wales and Northern Ireland Food Hygiene Information Scheme in Scotland Environmental Health Officers	Food Hygiene Rating 0–5 Food Standards Agency **FOOD HYGIENE RATING** ⓪ ① ② ③ ④ **5** VERY GOOD	How hygienically the food is handled during preparation, cooking, reheating, cooling, storage, presentation Cleanliness and condition of kitchen and buildings Pest control Ventilation Hand-washing and toilet facilities for staff Training of staff in food safety How food safety is managed – HACCP (see pages 69–72)

Environmental sustainability

Who does the inspections?	Type of rating awarded	What is being inspected?
Organisations, e.g.: The Sustainable Restaurant Association	Percentage (%) score for how much the H&C provider meets the 10 standards set: Less than 50% = 1 star 50–69% = 2 stars More than 70% = 3 stars	Ten standards: 1–4: Where food is sourced: • Locally? • Less meat and dairy foods – more plant foods? • Sustainably caught fish? • Support for farmers and fair trade? 5–6: People: • Are employees treated equally and fairly? • Can employees develop their skills? • How involved is the business in the local community? 7–10: Care of the environment: • Healthy, balanced meals produced? • Energy-efficient equipment used? • Water not wasted? • Food waste reduced? • Materials recycled where possible?

Knowledge check – can you remember ... ?

1. What 'hospitality' means?

2. What 'catering' means?

3. Five types of place where hospitality is provided?

4. Five types of place where catering is provided?

5. Five things that suppliers provide the hospitality and catering industry with?

6. Three different ways in which food is served to customers in different places?

7. Three hospitality and catering services provided by residential commercial businesses?

8. Three hospitality and catering services provided by non-residential commercial businesses?

9. Two hospitality and catering services provided by residential non-commercial businesses?

10. One hospitality and catering service provided by non-residential non-commercial businesses?

11. Three things that are inspected in hotels and guest houses when they are given a rating?

12. Three things that are inspected in restaurants when giving them a rating?

13. Three things that are inspected during food hygiene checks in catering businesses when they are given a rating?

14. Two things that are inspected during environmental sustainability checks in catering businesses when they are given a rating?

15. Why it is good for a hospitality and catering business to be given a high rating.

Practice exam questions

Short-answer questions

1. Hospitality and catering businesses provide a range of services.
   List four services provided by each of the following:
   a) A large inner-city hotel *[4 marks]*
   b) A family holiday park *[4 marks]*
   c) A cruise ship *[4 marks]*

2. Food is served to customers in a variety of different food service systems.
   Describe how customers receive their food in the following systems:
   a) Cafeteria *[2 marks]*
   b) Buffet service *[2 marks]*
   c) Table service *[2 marks]*
   d) Seated counter service *[2 marks]*

Stretch and challenge question

A restaurant has been taken over by a new management team. The restaurant is located in the centre of a small country town that attracts many tourists. It has previously received only average ratings for its food, customer service and food hygiene standards.

The new management want to improve these ratings.

Suggest a variety of ways in which the management could help the restaurant to score high ratings for:

a) The food they offer *[4 marks]*
b) Food hygiene standards *[4 marks]*
c) Customer service *[4 marks]*

Key learning

There are many different types of job in the hospitality and catering industry, especially part-time and temporary (seasonal) jobs.

There are lots of opportunities for people who are willing to work hard to build a career.

At busy times of the year (e.g. summer holiday season, Christmas and New Year), the hospitality and catering industry hires seasonal **workers**.

Many hospitality and catering workers come from different countries around the world.

You can train to get a job in the hospitality and catering industry by:

● Doing some work experience

● Going to college when you leave school to take a course

● Working and training as an apprentice.

Key terms you should try to include in your answers

Employee – someone who works in the industry and has an employment contract

Employer – someone who owns a business and pays an employee to work there

Worker – someone who works in the industry but does not have an employment contract

What type of person do you need to be to work successfully in the hospitality and catering industry?

(What *personal attributes* do you need to have?)

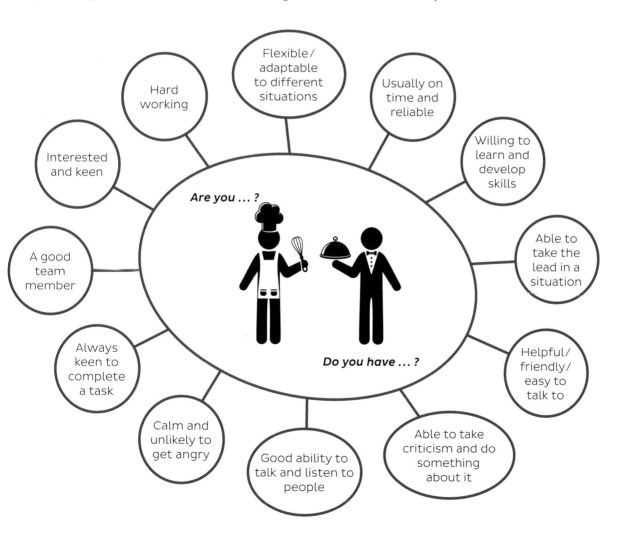

Job roles in the hospitality and catering industry ...know and understand

What do you need to know?

The different types of jobs in the hospitality and catering industry

Managers

Examples in a hotel:

General Manager

Finance Manager

Sales and Bookings Manager

Head Receptionist

Human Resources (staff) Manager

Restaurant Manager (also called the Maitre d'hotel or Maitre d')

Conference Manager

Head (Executive) Chef

Head Housekeeper

What are they responsible for?

The smooth running of the business

Finances

Security

Employment/dismissal of staff

Staff training and development

Customer satisfaction

Business development and planning

Health, safety and welfare of customers and staff

Cleaning and maintenance of buildings

Making sure the business follows health, safety and employment laws

Sorting out problems and complaints

Administrators

Examples in a hotel:

(usually only in large businesses)

Secretary

Assistant/Deputy Managers

Accountant

Cashier

What are they responsible for?

The smooth running of the business

Organising the Manager's diary

Sending letters and emails, making phone calls

Typing, filing, organising staff and customer details, bookings, taxation, etc.

Ordering and paying for supplies, e.g. cleaning materials, food, drinks

Managing events

Organising ICT support

Marketing to promote the business

Front-of-house staff

Examples in a hotel:

Receptionists

Waiting staff

Valets (park cars for customers) and drivers

Bartenders

Cashier

Concierge (assists guests/customers)

What are they responsible for?

Representing and promoting the business

Working directly with customers and back-of-house staff

Taking bookings

Checking customers in and out of the building

Dealing with customer questions and problems

Assisting customers to their rooms

Setting up meeting rooms

Back-of-house staff

Examples in a hotel:

Stockroom Manager

Kitchen brigade (all the people who work in a kitchen – see facing page)

Maintenance team

Gardeners/Groundskeeper

Security guards

Cleaners

Guest room attendants (used to be called chambermaids)

What are they responsible for?

Buying and organising supplies

Storing, preparing and cooking food

Storing and organising drinks

Ensuring all areas of the buildings (premises) are regularly cleaned, tidy, safe, comfortable and pleasant

Ensuring all areas outside are well maintained and working properly

Maintaining security

In each sector of the hospitality and catering industry, the jobs are put into an order (called a **hierarchy**), according to the number of people and activities each job role is responsible for. The person at the top of the hierarchy has the most responsibilities. For example, in a restaurant/catering kitchen, the Head Chef is at the top and has responsibility for:

- The activities, behaviour and welfare of all the people who work in the kitchen
- Hiring new staff to work in the kitchen
- Planning and writing the menu
- Choosing, buying and storing the food
- Food hygiene and safety
- Personal safety
- The kitchen equipment
- The production of the food
- Managing the costs of running the kitchen
- Organising and maintaining the kitchen.

The hierarchy in a catering kitchen is called the **kitchen brigade**.
The kitchen brigade is shown in detail below.

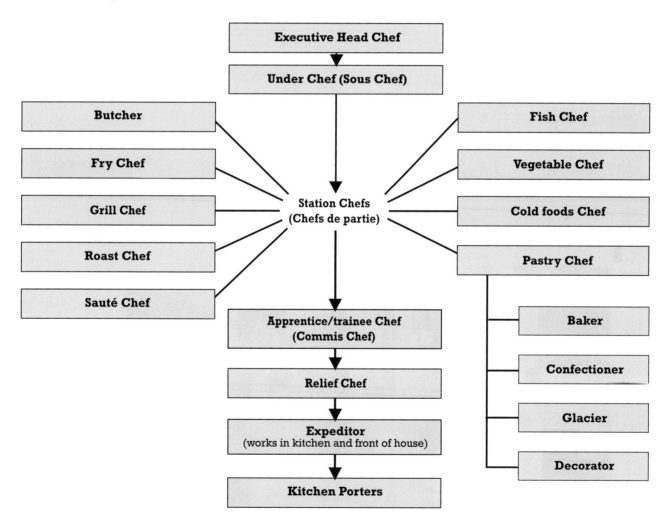

The hierarchy in a catering kitchen

Activity: Job roles and responsibilities

Match each job role/responsibility to the right member of staff in a hotel:

Job role/responsibility

Finances; security; health, safety and welfare of customers and staff; customer satisfaction — A

Buy and organise supplies; store and organise drinks — F

In charge of entire kitchen: ordering, menu development, supervision of kitchen staff — B

Park customers' cars — G

Prepare hot appetisers, soups, vegetables, pastas — C

Pass orders from dining room to chefs; ensure food reaches diners properly — H

Order supplies; ICT support; manage events; typing; filing; Manager's diary — D

Work directly with customers; check customers in and out of building; take bookings — I

Ensure all areas of the hospitality and catering premises (buildings) are well maintained and working properly — E

Prepare all baked items, pastries and desserts — J

Which member of staff?

5 Manager

8 Executive Chef

1 Valet

3 Stockroom Manager

6 Pastry Chef

9 Vegetable Chef

2 Maintenance team

4 Expeditor (food runner)

7 Front-of-house receptionist

10 Administrator

What do you need to be able to do and know for different jobs?

...know and understand

What skills and knowledge do you need to work in the hospitality and catering industry?

Here are some examples:

	What does a person need to be able to do and know for this job (which skills and knowledge should they have)?
Hotel receptionist 	*A hotel receptionist needs to have:* • Good personal communication and customer service skills • Good computer skills • Good local knowledge to answer customer questions and provide advice and information • Good knowledge of the business and how it is run • Good organisational skills. *A hotel receptionist needs to be able to:* • Do more than one thing at a time (multi-task) • Deal with any problems that happen.
Chef in a restaurant 	*A chef needs to have:* • A wide range of good practical cookery skills • A good knowledge of food • A good knowledge of food safety and hygiene • Good organisational skills. *A chef needs to be able to:* • Present food creatively • Use a variety of tools and equipment • Multi-task.
Barista in a busy coffee bar 	*A barista needs to have:* • A good knowledge of coffee and other drinks • A good knowledge of food safety and hygiene • Good organisational skills. *A barista needs to be able to:* • Present drinks creatively • Use a variety of tools and equipment • Multi-task.
Stockroom manager in a large kitchen 	*A stockroom manager needs to have:* • Good computer skills • A good knowledge of food safety and hygiene • Good organisational skills.

Activity: Skills and knowledge needed by hospitality and catering employees

Fill in the chart to show which skills and knowledge you think each of the following **employees** in the hospitality and catering industry needs.

Job role in the hospitality and catering industry	What does a person need to be able to do and know for this job (which skills and knowledge should they have)?
A maintenance team member 	A maintenance team member needs to have: A maintenance team member needs to be able to:
A hotel housekeeping team member 	A housekeeping team member needs to have: A housekeeping team member needs to be able to:
A restaurant waiter 	A restaurant waiter needs to have: A restaurant waiter needs to be able to:
A hotel concierge  CONCIERGE	A hotel concierge needs to have: A hotel concierge needs to be able to:

There are rules and laws about how people work:

... be aware of

Rule	Which law?	What does it mean?
Number of working hours in a week	Working Time Directive	A worker cannot be expected to work for more than 48 hours a week (but can choose to work longer if they want to).
Age	Working Time Directive	A worker under 18 years of age cannot work more than 8 hours a day, or 40 hours a week.
Days off/rest breaks	Working Time Directive	A worker must have one day off each week. If they work 6 or more hours a day, they must have a rest break of at least 20 minutes.
Earnings	National Minimum Wage	The minimum amount working people are paid each hour, for most workers over school-leaving age.
	National Living Wage	The minimum amount all working people aged 25 years and over should earn.

There are different types of employment contract:

... know and understand

Type of contract	Hours/start and end times	Sick pay?	Holiday pay?
Full-time – **permanent** or **temporary** employee	Written down in the contract	Yes	Yes
Part-time – permanent or temporary employee	Written down in the contract	Yes	Yes
Casual worker – contract from an agency	Vary according to what is needed	Yes	No
Zero-hours worker	No set hours or times – a worker may or may not accept work offered to them by an **employer**	Yes	Yes

A **wage** is the amount of money someone is paid for each hour they work.

A **salary** is a fixed amount of money someone is paid each year in return for the work they do for an employer.

There are **extra payments** that people may earn:

... be aware of

Tips – money given to a worker by a customer to say thank you for good service (tips may be shared out between staff).

Service charges – an amount of money added to a customer's bill to reward the employees who have given the customer a good service.

Bonus payment – given by some employers to reward their staff for their hard work during the year that helped to make the business successful.

Key terms you should try to include in your answers

Permanent contract – one that lasts indefinitely. If the worker decides to leave, they must give the employer enough notice.

The employer can cancel the contract if the person does something wrong or does not do their job properly.

Temporary contract – this means that the worker is only employed for a set amount of time, and the date the contract ends must be given in the contract.

Pension

A pension is a way of saving money while someone is working, for when they retire from work.

A **state pension** is a regular payment of money that most people in the UK can claim when they reach state pension age. The amount they receive depends on how many National Insurance payments they made when they worked.

A **workplace pension** is arranged by an employer. Each time a worker is paid, some of their pay is automatically put into the pension scheme. Many employers add extra money to the pension scheme for their workers.

All employers must, by law, provide a workplace pension scheme for workers who:
- Are 22 years or older, but not yet at state pension age
- Earn at least £10,000 a year
- Usually work in the UK.

Knowledge check – can you remember…?

1. What a seasonal worker is?
2. Five things (personal attributes) a person needs to be/have to work successfully in the hospitality and catering industry?
3. Three types of skill/knowledge a hotel receptionist needs?
4. Three types of skill/knowledge a chef needs?
5. Three types of skill/knowledge a barista needs?
6. Three types of skill/knowledge a kitchen stockroom manager needs?
7. The maximum numbers of hours a week a person can be expected to work?
8. What the National Minimum Wage means?
9. What a tip is?
10. What a service charge is?

Practice exam questions

Short-answer questions

1. There are many different types of job in the hospitality and catering industry.
    a) List four personal attributes that someone needs (what type of person they need to be) to be able to work successfully in the hospitality and catering industry. *[4 marks]*
    b) List three things a person needs to be able to do or know for each of the following jobs:
        i)   Head Chef *[3 marks]*
        ii) Front-of-house Manager in a hotel restaurant *[3 marks]*
        iii) Night porter in an inner-city hotel *[3 marks]*

Key learning

The success of a hospitality and catering business is affected by:

Money – what it costs to run the business and how much money it makes (profit).

Employees – do they work well together to help the success of the business? Are they well trained and happy?

Customer service and satisfaction – do customers like the service they get? Do they come back again?

Trends – is the business keeping up to date and always trying to improve what it does?

Competition – are there similar businesses nearby which compete for customers?

Money

...know and understand

To run a hospitality and catering business, money is needed for many things, including:

Food/ingredients

Equipment

Health and safety

Staff wages, pensions and National Insurance payments

Cleaning materials and equipment

Waste and waste disposal

Pest control

Administration (paperwork): insurance, licences, printing, advertising, phone bills, taxes, ICT support, etc.

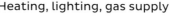

Heating, lighting, gas supply

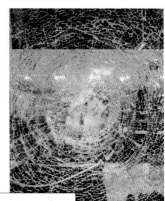

Breakages and repairs

Maintenance work, gardening, decorating

Making a profit

...know and understand

Key terms you should try to include in your answers

Gross profit – the difference between how much the ingredients in a menu item cost and how much it is sold for

Net profit – the profit made once all the costs of running a restaurant have been taken out

Overheads – the additional costs of running a hospitality and catering business (apart from the cost of ingredients), including staff wages, electricity and gas, cleaning, rent, council tax, etc.

To successfully continue in business, it is important to make a profit.

A **profit** is the amount of money made from selling something, after all the costs of making and serving it to customers have been taken out.

For example, in a restaurant, the profit for a menu item is worked out like this:

Menu item:

Fried fish and chips, with mushy peas – one portion

Cost of ingredients: £2.25

\+

Overheads:	£8.30
Total costs:	£10.55 (cost of ingredients + overheads)
Price:	£11.95

Gross profit: = selling price – cost of ingredients:

£11.95 – £2.25 = **£9.70**

Net profit: = selling price – total costs:

£11.95 – £10.55 = **£1.40**

The amount of profit that a hospitality and catering business makes is affected by a variety of things:

What affects how much profit is made?	Why does it affect the amount of profit made?
Ordering ingredients and materials	Ordering the right amounts prevents wastage and loss of profits
Wastage	Wasted ingredients and materials have to be paid for, so the money they cost to buy is lost if they are thrown away
A trained and skilled workforce	Trained and skilled workers are less likely to waste ingredients or materials
Popular menu choices	Customers will buy these menu items, so the food used to make them will not be wasted

What affects how much profit is made?	Why does it affect the amount of profit made?
The range of services provided	Some services cost more than others to provide or can be sold for a higher profit
Breakages and repairs	Breakages have to be replaced or repaired; both of which cost money
Planning for events	Carefully planned events are less likely to lose money than badly planned events
Feedback/reviews from customers	Good feedback and reviews will encourage new and returning customers to use the business
How well the economy of the country is doing ...*be aware of*	If the country's economy is struggling, people have less money to spend, fewer tourists visit and spend money, and the cost of things such as electricity and gas, food and materials may increase. These can all affect the amount of profit a business can make.

Customer service and satisfaction ...*know and understand*

Good customer service skills and satisfaction are an essential part of the image and success of a hospitality and catering business, and they should be of a high standard in all of the services that the business provides. If customers are happy and satisfied with the service they have received, they will tell other people about it and recommend the business to them. They are also likely to come back and become regular customers.

What makes a customer in a hotel or restaurant happy?

A business that provides an efficient and well-run service

A business that takes action on customer feedback

Staff who listen to customers and answer their questions

Staff who understand customers' needs and wants

A business that provides what customers expect

Staff who are well trained, helpful, cheerful, smiling and friendly

Staff who aim to solve customer complaints promptly and politely

Trends ...*know and understand*

A **trend** means the ways in which something is developing or changing and becoming well known and/or popular. Hospitality and catering businesses should be aware of and keep up with trends which will affect their success. An example of a trend which continues to affect the success of businesses in all industries is **information and computer technology (ICT)**, and there are some important trends that are used to attract customers to hospitality and catering providers and improve their experience of the service:

Satellite technology and beacons – these show people on their mobile phones their location or the directions to another location. They are also used by businesses to:

- Find would-be customers and show them nearby restaurants, hotels, bars, etc.
- Give customers links to the services provided so they can choose what to eat or drink.

Customer Relationship Management systems (CRMs) – these enable customers to make online bookings, order food and drinks, etc. directly with a hospitality and catering business. A restaurant, for example, then knows how many customers are expected and can manage its kitchen, ordering and customer needs more efficiently.

Apps (ICT applications) – these are downloaded to a mobile phone or tablet to allow customers, workers, managers, etc. to perform specific tasks in a convenient and efficient way.

Social media – this enables businesses to receive feedback (good and bad!) from customers who write reviews and send photographs or videos of their experiences to other people.

Smartphones and smart devices – devices such as smart watches linked to smartphones use apps to monitor things and allow people to send requests or instructions to other devices. Hospitality and catering businesses are using this technology to enable customers to:

- Place orders for food, etc. when they are elsewhere
- Check in to hotels online
- Unlock their hotel room door
- Control their TV, hotel room heating, lighting, etc.
- Make contactless payments for goods and services instead of using cash.

Key card access for guests to open doors to their rooms and specific areas in a building (e.g. the gym in a hotel), for improved security and customer convenience.

Digital menus to allow customers to order food from a restaurant and have it delivered to their home, or from a restaurant table directly to the kitchen; food deliveries by drone.

Kitchen and food technology – e.g. digitally operated or controlled equipment, food storage, food service, hygiene and food safety procedures.

Environmental sustainability ...be aware of

Another trend that affects the success of hospitality and catering businesses is environmental sustainability. Research shows that the following things all have a big impact on the environment:

- Food production (especially meat, poultry, eggs and dairy foods)
- The production and use of packaging materials (especially plastics)
- Refrigeration and food transport (especially using lorries, ships and aeroplanes).

In order to reduce their impact on the environment, help save money, save space and give them a good reputation with their customers, many hospitality and catering businesses are being encouraged to become more **environmentally sustainable** by doing things such as:

- Using renewable energy, e.g. solar from solar panels
- Using automatic switches to control lighting and air conditioning
- Using water-saving washing machines and dishwashers
- Reducing, reusing and recycling any waste they create.

Reducing the use of:
- **Food packaging**
  - Buying food with minimum amounts of packaging
  - Buying food with biodegradable packaging that will naturally break down in the soil
  - Not using individual sachets/packets of sauces, sugar, butter, etc.
- **Food waste**
  - Reducing portion sizes served to customers
  - Providing containers for customers to take left-over food home to eat later
  - Passing on good-quality left-over foods to food charities to make into meals for people who do not have enough money for all the food they need
  - Turning food waste into compost to grow vegetables and herbs
  - Making stock from vegetable peelings and poultry and meat off-cuts and bones
  - Storing food correctly so that it stays safe to eat and is not wasted.

- **Disposable items**
  - Not using disposable plastic cutlery and drinking straws
  - Not using paper or plastic plates, dishes, serviettes, tablecloths, etc.

Reusing:

- **Left-over foods** to make new dishes, e.g. left-over vegetables can be turned into soups; left-over cooked meat can be used in pies
- **Packaging and containers** – some are reusable. Some empty containers can be used to store other ingredients (they must be clearly labelled to say what is in them).

Recycling:

- Left-over used **cooking oil** can be recycled into biofuel to run machines and vehicles
- Many plastics, glass, aluminium foil, paper and card can be recycled
- Products made from **recycled materials** can be bought and used, e.g.:
  - Paper hand towels and toilet rolls from recycled paper
  - Plastic chairs and containers from recycled plastics
  - Bottles and glasses from recycled glass.

Recycled paper products   Recycled plastic chairs   Recycled drinking glasses

Competition with other businesses   ...know and understand

There is a lot of competition between hospitality and catering businesses to attract and keep regular customers. The chart below shows some of the ideas that hospitality and catering businesses can try in order to keep up with the competition:

What does the hospitality and catering business want to do?	Examples of products and services that could be offered to help the hospitality and catering business be successful	How a hospitality and catering business can show would-be customers that it is a good choice for them

Offer a range of different products and services to attract customers and compete with other similar local businesses	Wedding fairs, ceremonies and receptions
	
	Birthday and celebration parties (e.g. bar/bat mitzvahs, wedding anniversaries, company dinner and dances)
	
	School and college proms
	
	University graduation ceremonies
	
	Conferences and training courses
	
	Quiz nights and other competitions
	
	Special food events, e.g. curry nights; Christmas meals; food, beer and wine festivals
		The business should:
		Reply to customer enquiries and give them a price quote within 24 hours
		Make sure the business has a detailed, reliable, user-friendly and regularly updated website
		Carry out market research to find out the number and types of other businesses that it will compete with
		Find out about the local population:
		  – How many people are there?
		  – What are their age groups?
		  – What are their lifestyles?
		  – What are their needs and wants?

Craft fairs and other community events

Special sports events viewing and celebrations, e.g. national and international rugby games, world athletics events, etc.

Offer a range of catering services, menus and cultural food events

The business *could*:

Advertise in different ways and places, using good-quality images and clear explanations of the services on offer and the prices

Offer competitive prices, group discounts, customer loyalty schemes (e.g. collect tokens to earn a free meal)

Offer meal deals, e.g. discounts for pensioners, free bottle of wine with a meal, buy two meals and get a third one free

Offer competitive/discounted accommodation for guests

Policies, laws and regulations

...be aware of

Policies, laws and regulations are made by the government, and many of these affect the success of hospitality and catering businesses. Some of the laws and regulations and what they cover are outlined below.

Licensing laws for selling alcohol

- A hospitality and catering business must have a licence to sell alcohol
- Alcohol can only be sold at certain times of the day
- Alcohol can only be sold to people who are 18 years old or older

Employment laws

- Health and safety regulations
- Pension and National Insurance contributions
- Working hours and holiday entitlement
- Gender, age, religious, disability and racial anti-discrimination laws
- Income Tax and insurance
- Childcare
- Sick pay
- Redundancy and dismissal
- Employment contracts
- Trade unions
- Employment of overseas workers

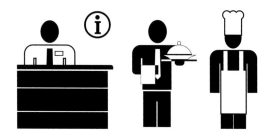

Health and safety (customers and workers) laws

- Fire regulations — to avoid fires starting; to be able to put them out with fire blankets and extinguishers, and to make sure people can escape from a burning building
- Building regulations — e.g. to make sure all electrical equipment is safe to use; there are emergency escape exits; the building is well ventilated
- Use and storage of chemicals, e.g. for cleaning and maintenance
- Tobacco and e-cigarette smoking regulations
- Food Safety Act and other regulations to make sure that food and drinks are safe to consume
- Public liability insurance cover to claim from if there is an accident

Tax collection laws

- Income Tax – paid by employees to the government
- Value Added Tax (VAT) – collected by businesses from goods and services that customers buy; paid to the government

Businesses need to:

- Be aware of all the regulations and laws that will affect them
- Make sure that they have the appropriate checks carried out and up-to-date certificates to prove that they have complied with the law.

If it is proved that a business has not obeyed laws or regulations, it can be prosecuted and made to pay a large fine (money) or have an aspect of its licence to trade taken away. This will seriously affect the business's reputation and profits.

Media

 ... know and understand

It is important for hospitality and catering businesses to advertise and promote their products and services by using social media, television and films, magazines and other printed media.

Social media is used by millions of businesses and followed by billions of people across the world. It can have positive and negative effects on the success of a hospitality and catering business.

Positive effects of social media on hospitality and catering businesses	Negative effects of social media on hospitality and catering businesses
A very large number of customers (a customer base) can be contacted easily and cheaply.	Hospitality and catering employees who use social media may say something negative about the business, which will rapidly reach many people through retweets, comments, likes and shares. This may damage its reputation (and the employee may lose their job!).
Specific customer groups can be targeted with advertisements and special offers, e.g. young adults, families with young children, business customers.	Negative feedback and complaints from customers about the service they have received will reach a lot of people who may then decide not to use the business.
Customers feel they have a personal connection with a business, which many people like. They are more likely to trust the business.	If messages and statements (e.g. confidential information about the business) are sent by mistake on social media, they will spread very rapidly and are almost impossible to correct.

Knowledge check – can you remember...?

1. Three things that affect the success of a hospitality and catering business?
2. Five things that a hospitality and catering business needs money for?
3. What a gross profit is?
4. What a net profit is?
5. Five things that affect how much profit a hospitality and catering business makes?
6. Four things that make hotel or restaurant customers happy?
7. Two trends in computer technology that will attract customers to a restaurant?
8. Two ways in which hospitality and catering businesses can become more environmentally sustainable?
9. Two ways in which hospitality and catering businesses can reduce their use of food packaging?
10. Two ways in which hospitality and catering businesses can reduce food waste?

11. Two ways in which hospitality and catering businesses can reduce their use of plastics?

12. Two products made from recycled materials that a hospitality and catering business could use?

13. Four products/services that a hospitality and catering business could offer to help make it successful?

14. Three things a hospitality and catering business *should* do to help make it successful?

15. Three things a hospitality and catering business *could* do to help make it successful?

16. Two ways in which social media can have a positive effect on hospitality and catering businesses?

17. Two ways in which social media can have a negative effect on hospitality and catering businesses?

Practice exam questions

Short-answer questions

1. The amount of profit that a hospitality and catering business makes is affected by a variety of things.

   State one reason why each of the following affects the amount of profit made:
   a) Wasted food *[1 mark]*
   b) Feedback and reviews from customers *[1 mark]*
   c) The range of services provided *[1 mark]*

2. There is a lot of competition between hospitality and catering businesses to attract and keep regular customers.

   Suggest four ways in which a hospitality and catering business can attract people to become regular customers. *[4 marks]*

3. There are different groups of people who use the services that hospitality and catering businesses provide.

   For each of the following groups of people, identify two ways in which a hospitality and catering business can provide their needs and wants:
   a) Families with young children *[2 marks]*
   b) Business customers *[2 marks]*
   c) Travellers and tourists *[2 marks]*

Stretch and challenge question

A new bar and restaurant is opening in a city centre in which many people in the millennials age group live and work.

The management want to provide services that will appeal particularly to this group. Suggest three services they could provide, giving details and reasons for your answers. *[4 marks for each suggestion = 12]*

Topic 1.2 How hospitality and catering providers operate

The operation of the front and back of house

Key learning

In this section you will learn about the operation and activities that take place in the front and back of house:

The **front of house** means the place where customers first arrive when they visit a hospitality and catering business e.g. the reception in a hotel or entrance / bar area in a restaurant.

The **back of house** is where food, drinks and other materials are stored and prepared ready for customer service, i.e., a catering kitchen and storage area.

Key learning for the front of house

Front of house means all the areas where customers go in a restaurant: reception, dining area, bar, waiting area, cloakrooms, toilets.

In a hotel, the front of house is the **reception**, where customers are greeted and check in when they arrive, and check out when they leave.

The front of house needs to have a suitable layout so that a good **workflow** can be set up.

Workflow in a restaurant means how quickly and well meals come from the kitchen and are served to customers, and how drinks are served to them from the bar.

Food safety has a high priority in the operation of the front of house.

The **safety and security** of employees in the front of house is very important.

It is important to organise and carefully manage all the **materials**, **equipment** and **paperwork** that is needed in the front of house.

Front-of-house staff should wear appropriate clothing, as required by the hospitality and catering business they work for.

Key terms you should try to include in your answers

Materials – the range of items and products that are needed to run a H&C business, besides equipment and ingredients.

Stock – the name for all the materials, ingredients and equipment that are in use in the front and back of house.

Workflow – the way that food and drinks pass through the front and back of house from delivery of ingredients/ materials to service to the customer.

Activities in the front of house and where they take place in a restaurant

...be aware of

Which area?	Activities	Why the activities and the quality of the area are important for the success of the hospitality and catering business
 **Entrance /reception area**	To welcome customers and take them to a table. It is important that staff in the front of house smile and are polite and helpful to customers.	A customer's first impression of a restaurant is really important. • Does it (and the staff who work there) look welcoming, clean and tidy? • Is there a menu to look at before the customer goes into the restaurant? • If the customer has a disability, can they get into the restaurant easily?
Waiting area	A place where customers wait for a table to become ready for them.	The customers will be happy to wait if: • The waiting area is comfortable and welcoming • They are given menus so they can choose their meal • They are offered drinks while they wait.

 **Counter service/bar area**	The place where customers have a drink and meet people before they have their meal.	The customers will feel relaxed before they go to their table.
 **Dining area**	Customers are served with their meal. The dining area is usually divided into sections (called stations). Each station has one or more waiter(s) who serve customers at a set number of tables. This means that those customers will be served as soon as possible, because the waiter(s) are concentrating only on them and not the whole restaurant.	The dining area should be a place that customers recommend to other people and want to come back to another time. It should: • Be a comfortable place to sit – not too hot or cold, with good chairs, etc. • Be a pleasant place to be in, e.g. nice decorations, plant/flower displays, background music, pictures on the walls, not too noisy, etc. • Be away from strong smells and fumes from the kitchen • Have enough space for customers and waiting staff to move around freely • Have a menu that suits people's different needs and wants • Welcome disabled customers and their assistance dogs.
 **Cloakrooms/toilets**	For customers to use to make their stay more comfortable. People with disabilities should be able to use the cloakrooms and toilets easily.	If these are clean and regularly checked, customers will be pleased.

Workflow and layout of the front of house in a restaurant

...be aware of

The front of house in a restaurant needs a good workflow, especially when it is busy with lots of customers. Here is an example of the workflow in the front of house of a busy restaurant:

CUSTOMERS COME INTO RESTAURANT ← **END OF WORKFLOW**

Greet customers and take them to a table	Give customers the dessert menu	Take customer orders for desserts and send to kitchen	Re-set table ready for next customers
↓	↑	↓	↑
Give customers a menu	Clear table Take used plates and cutlery to kitchen	Serve desserts	Customers leave restaurant
↓	↑	↓	↑
Take customer orders for drinks and serve them	Check customers are happy with their meal	Clear table Take used dishes and cutlery to kitchen	Take payment for the meal
↓	↑	↓	↑
Take orders for food and send to kitchen	→ Serve meals to customers	Take orders for coffee and other drinks →	Give customers the bill for their meal

The layout of a restaurant

A good restaurant layout should:

- Be easy for staff and customers to move around in – not too many tables and chairs
- Be easy, pleasant and comfortable to work and eat in
- Have clearly signposted toilet facilities, access for customers with disabilities, and emergency exits.

Front-of-house equipment

...be aware of

There are seven groups of equipment used in the front of house in a restaurant:

1. Table top

Examples of equipment:

Table covers and napkins
Menu holders
Salt and pepper mills
Table signs and numbers
Knives, forks, spoons
Place mats
Glasses

2. Food service

Examples of equipment:

China plates, dishes, serving dishes
Stainless steel bowls and plates
Wooden platters
Cups, saucers
Individual oven-to-table dishes, e.g. pie dish

3. Waiting at table

Examples of equipment:

Trays, tray stands
Serving spoons and tongs
Bottle openers
Customer order notepads and pens
Computer-generated customer ordering equipment,
  e.g. smart pad or tablet
Candle lighter

4. Customer seating

Examples of equipment:

Chairs, stools
Benches
Picnic tables and benches
High chairs for babies
Booster seats for children
Armchairs and sofas
Sun shades and garden seats

5. Organisation

Examples of equipment:

Rope barriers for queueing
Direction signs
Menu posters and blackboards
Cutlery storage trays
Wine racks and glass holders
Cupboards and drawers

6. First aid and safety

Examples of equipment:

First aid kit
Safety and emergency exit signs
Fire extinguishers
Smoke and gas alarms
Safety lighting

7. Bar area

Examples of equipment:

Drinks measures
Refrigerators, e.g. glass and drinks chillers
Ice bucket and tongs
Bottle openers
Food blender/juicer
Coffee machine
Panini maker
Frappuccino ice maker (often in
coffee shops)
Glasses
Washing up equipment
Till

Materials

... be aware of

Materials that are used in the front of house in a restaurant include:

Types of materials	Examples
Cleaning materials	Detergents for cleaning glasses, etc. at the bar Washing up cloths, floor cloths, mops, dustpans and brushes, brooms, buckets, etc. to clean the tables, bar area, floor, toilets and waiting area
Materials for food service	Serviettes, napkins Packets and pots of sauces, salad dressings, seasonings, sugar, milk, cream, jam, marmalade, butter, vegetable fat spread, etc. Candles and table decorations, e.g. fresh flowers
Waste disposal materials	Waste bags and bins Recycling bags and bins
Employee welfare materials	First aid materials Hand-wash liquid Paper towels/hand driers Toilet paper Feminine hygiene disposal bags
Maintenance materials	Replacement filters for extractors, coffee machines, etc. Replacement light bulbs, batteries, till rolls Replacement of broken equipment, e.g. glasses, china plates, etc.

Stock control

... know and understand

It is necessary for good **stock** control systems to be in place, especially as the front of house uses expensive products such as wines and spirits. There should be one or more people who look after the stock and keep records of what is bought, what is used and what needs to be re-ordered (see also page 40).

Clothing for the front of house

... be aware of

The dress code for staff in the front of house varies, depending on the hospitality and catering business.

What the front-of-house staff wear is important because:

- It gives customers an important first impression – smart-looking staff give a good impression of the business
- A uniform sets a standard and avoids staff working in unsuitable clothes
- It makes the employees feel part of a team
- It encourages staff to take care and pride in their work
- Customers will know who is a member of staff if they need to ask them something.

Activity: Dress code in the front of house

There are rules about wearing a front-of-house uniform. Fill in the table below:

Dress code rules in the front of house		Explain why each rule is necessary and important
1. Uniform should be worn by front-of-house staff		
2. Front-of-house staff should change into their uniform at their workplace and should not wear their uniform in public areas such as on buses and trains		
3. The uniform should be changed every day and washed and ironed before it is worn again.		
4. False nails, nail polish and false eyelashes should not be worn		
5. Strong scents and after-shave lotions should not be worn		

Safety and security in the front of house   ...know and understand

CCTV camera in a restaurant

People who work in the front of house need to be aware of possible safety and security issues, most of which are the same as in a catering kitchen (see page 45).

There may also be security issues when dealing with possible drunk and/or aggressive customers, or customers who argue with the staff about a problem, e.g. with their bill or the quality of the food.

The management of the business should make sure that staff are trained to deal with problems and that security systems are in place, e.g.:

- Security guards
- Closed-circuit television (CCTV) cameras
- An emergency button to alert the police if there is a problem.

Knowledge check – can you remember...?

1. Three main activities that happen in the front of house in a restaurant?

2. Three important points for the design and layout of a restaurant?

3. How the dining area in a restaurant is divided up?

4. Three things that make a dining area a pleasant place to be in?

5. Why it is important that front-of-house staff smile and are polite and helpful to customers?

6. Five groups of equipment that are used in a restaurant, with three examples for each group?

7. Three types of materials that are used in a restaurant?

8. Three reasons why front-of-house staff wear a uniform?

9. Four rules about wearing a front-of-house uniform?

10. Two possible security issues in a restaurant?

Practice exam questions

Short-answer questions

1. The front of house area in a hotel or restaurant is divided up into areas where different activities take place. For each of the following areas, give one activity that takes place and one reason why the quality of the area is important for the success of a hospitality and catering business:
   a) Entrance/reception area *[2 marks]*
   b) Bar area *[2 marks]*
   c) Dining area *[3 marks]*

2. The safety and security of the staff and customers are important in the front of house. For each of the following situations, suggest one way in which the management of a hospitality and catering business could help to prevent or manage the risks:
   a) A customer in the bar area drinks too much alcohol and starts shouting and behaving in an aggressive manner *[1 mark]*
   b) A customer has their mobile phone stolen while they are eating their meal *[1 mark]*
   c) The fire alarms go off in a restaurant and the customers and staff all have to leave the building by the emergency exits *[1 mark]*

Key terms you should try to include in your answers

Materials – the range of items and products that are needed to run a hospitality and catering business, besides equipment and ingredients

Stock – the name for all the materials, ingredients and equipment that are in use in the front and back of house

Workflow – the way that food and drinks pass through the front and back of house from delivery of ingredients/materials to service to the customer.

Key learning for the back of house

There are **four** main activities that happen in a catering kitchen:

- **Storing** equipment, **materials** and food
- **Preparing** food ready for cooking
- **Cooking** and presenting food
- **Cleaning** and maintaining the kitchen and equipment.

The kitchen needs to have a suitable layout so that a good **workflow** can be set up.

Good-quality **kitchen equipment**, **ingredients** and **materials** are essential for the efficient and safe production of food.

Food safety is the most important priority in the operation of a catering kitchen.

To make sure the business makes a profit, it is important to have good **stock control**.

It is important to organise and carefully manage all the **paperwork** that is needed in a catering kitchen.

Chefs/cooks working in a catering kitchen must wear clean **protective clothing**.

The **safety and security** of employees in the kitchen is very important.

Workflow and layout of a catering kitchen   ...be aware of

A catering kitchen is divided into areas where different activities take place:

Storage of personal belongings, toilet and hand-washing facilities

Dry area for canned and packaged foods

Cool, dry area for freezers and refrigerators

Staff rest area

Storage area

Hot, dry area for grilling, roasting, frying, baking, microwaving

Catering kitchen

Preparation and cooking area

Hot, wet area for steaming, boiling, poaching

Wet area for preparing fish, meat, vegetables and cold dishes

Washing up/ cleaning area

For waste food, rubbish, washing up

Serving area

For plating up and presenting food

The way that food passes through the kitchen from delivery to the customer (in the front of house) is the workflow:

FOOD AND INGREDIENTS IN

END OF WORKFLOW

The layout of a catering kitchen

...be aware of

A good catering kitchen should:
- Be easy, pleasant and comfortable to work in
- Have a low risk of cross-contamination by bacteria.

The kitchen should be designed so that:

There is plenty of storage space for food

Equipment, ingredients and water supply are within easy reach for the chefs

It is well lit, not too hot and always has plenty of fresh air

The washing up/cleaning area is well away from food preparation areas

Steam, fumes and heat are extracted from the kitchen

It is easy to clean and maintain

Kitchen equipment

...be aware of

There are five groups of equipment used in a catering kitchen:

Large equipment

E.g. ovens, cooking ranges, walk-in freezers and refrigerators, steamers, grills, floor-standing mixers and processors, deep-fat fryers, blast chiller, hot water urn, bain marie

Mechanical equipment

E.g. mincer, food processor, mixer, vegetable peeler, dough mixer, dishwasher

Small hand-held utensils and equipment

E.g. bowls, jugs, pans, whisks, spatulas, knives, chopping boards, sieves, food temperature probes

First aid and safety equipment

E.g. first aid kit; safety and emergency exit signs; fire extinguishers; smoke, gas and carbon monoxide alarms; safety and emergency lighting

Food safety equipment

E.g. colour-coded chopping boards, knives, tongs, food labels, food temperature probes, etc. to prevent cross-contamination

Activity: Food safety equipment

Which board should be used for the following foods?
Match the correct colour board to the correct foods.

Colour	Food
Green	Raw meat and poultry
Yellow	Dairy and bakery
White	Vegetables
Red	Raw fish
Brown	Fruits and salad vegetables
Blue	Cooked meat, poultry and fish

When choosing equipment for a catering kitchen, several points should be considered, including:

The size

Where it will go in the kitchen

How much noise it makes when being used

How easy it is to clean and maintain

How easy it is to use

How safe it is to use

How well it is made

How many different jobs it can do

How much energy/water it uses

How long the manufacturer's warranty lasts

Activity: Equipment: name the knives

The pictures below show a variety of kitchen knives that are used to prepare different foods.
Match the correct knife to its name and the description of the foods it is designed to be used for:

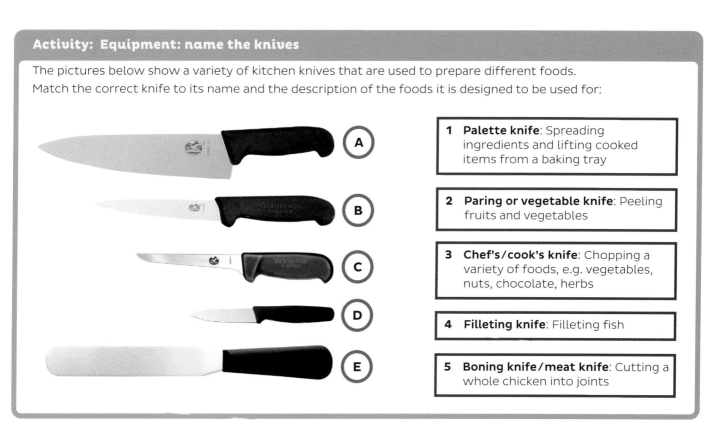

A

B

C

D

E

1 **Palette knife**: Spreading ingredients and lifting cooked items from a baking tray

2 **Paring or vegetable knife**: Peeling fruits and vegetables

3 **Chef's/cook's knife**: Chopping a variety of foods, e.g. vegetables, nuts, chocolate, herbs

4 **Filleting knife**: Filleting fish

5 **Boning knife/meat knife**: Cutting a whole chicken into joints

Materials

Materials that are used in a catering kitchen include:

Cleaning materials
- Detergents for washing dishes, cutlery, etc.
- Detergents for washing clothes, dishcloths, oven gloves, etc.
- Scourers, washing up cloths, floor cloths, mops, dustpans and brushes, brooms, buckets
- Chemicals to clean walls, equipment, toilets and floors

Food preparation materials
- Kitchen paper, foil, baking paper
- Food labels
- Food storage boxes and bags
- Cloths for dishwashing and cleaning, oven gloves, disposable gloves

Waste disposal materials
- Waste bags and bins
- Recycling bags and bins

Employee welfare materials
- First aid kit
- Hand-wash liquid
- Paper towels / hand driers
- Toilet paper
- Feminine hygiene disposal bags
- Fire extinguishers and smoke/gas alarms

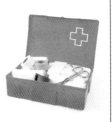

Maintenance materials
- Filters for extractors
- Oil for greasing machines
- Light bulbs and batteries

Stock controlling systems

All the materials, ingredients and equipment that are in use in a catering kitchen are known as 'stock'. A good stock control system needs to be in place to prevent stock running out or being wasted (which would mean loss of profit for the business). There may be one or more employees who look after the stock and keep accurate records of what is purchased, what is used and what needs to be reordered.

Stock control systems have been made much easier and quicker to run and keep up to date by computer technology.

These are the actions that need to take place in a stock control system:

Order ingredients, materials and equipment

Know how much stock has been bought and how much has been used

Keep a list of current prices for all stock

Keep all receipts, delivery notes, emails from suppliers, etc. in order

Store stock (especially food) correctly and use older stock first before new stock (FIFO – First In, First Out)

Make sure there is always enough stock available

Prevent stock being damaged by pests (e.g. insects), water, heat, etc.

Prepare and send out orders for each department in the business

Keep a detailed list of the stock in the business. There are a number of stock control apps that can be used to make the process more efficient and accurate

Here is an example of part of a stock control sheet that is used in a large high-street bakery, where all the items for sale are made on the premises:

Stock item + purchase unit	Amount in stock + date	Amount taken out of stock + date	Amount ordered + date	Amount delivered into stock + date	Amount in stock + date	Signed
Plain flour 16 kg sack	1/5/21 5 sacks	2/5/21 2 sacks	3/5/21 5 sacks	4/5/21 5 sacks	4/5/21 8 sacks	A. Person
Self-raising flour 16 kg sack	1/5/21 5 sacks	2/5/21 3 sacks	3/5/21 5 sacks	4/5/21 5 sacks	4/5/21 7 sacks	A. Person
White bread flour 20 kg sack	1/5/21 5 sacks	2/5/21 4 sacks	3/5/21 8 sacks	4/5/21 8 sacks	4/5/21 9 sacks	A. Person
Wholemeal bread flour 20 kg sack	1/5/21 4 sacks	2/5/21 3 sacks	3/5/21 5 sacks	4/5/21 5 sacks	4/5/21 6 sacks	A. Person
Caster sugar 25 kg sack	1/5/21 4 sacks	2/5/21 2 sacks	4/5/21 3 sacks	7/5/21 3 sacks	7/5/21 5 sacks	A.N. Other
Eggs Box of 10 dozen (120 eggs)	1/5/21 10 dozen (120 eggs)	2/5/21 8 dozen (96 eggs)	2/5/21 10 dozen (120 eggs)	3/5/21 10 dozen (120 eggs)	5/5/21 12 dozen (144 eggs)	A.N. Other
Butter 1 kg pack	1/5/21 20 kg	2/5/21 10 kg	2/5/21 10 kg	4/5/21 10 kg	4/5/21 20 kg	A. Person

Paperwork in a catering kitchen

...know and understand

There are many forms and pieces of information that need to be completed, signed and dated, and kept in a catering kitchen. Many of these are required by law, e.g. gas and fire safety certificates and accident reports.

Keeping documents in a well-organised way is important, as it helps to maintain good organisation and the safety of workers and customers, and ensures that bills are paid on time.

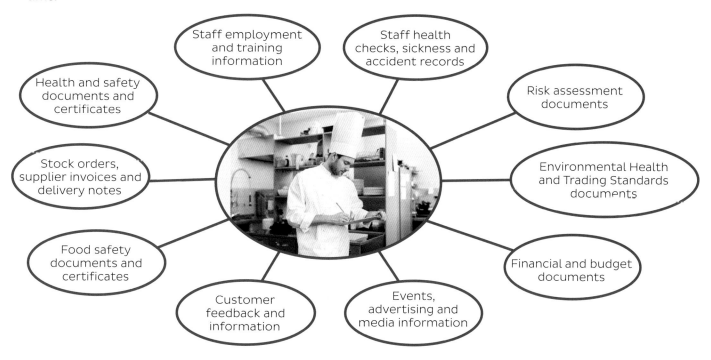

On the following pages, there is an example of a Control of Substances Hazardous to Health (COSHH) form, followed by an example of an accident report form.

COSHH Risk Assessment

A Local Restaurant

Location of activity/process:	Date:
	Signed:

Description of activity/process:

- How often carried out
- How long for
- How much substance is used
- Which substance(s) is/are being used (give brand name, manufacturer and provide product safety sheet)

Who is at risk?

Employee	Customer	Contractor	Supplier
☐	☐	☐	☐

Category of danger

Flammable	Explosive	Toxic	Corrosive	Environmental hazard	Biohazard
☐	☐	☐	☐	☐	☐

Type of hazard

Gas	Fumes	Vapour	Mist	Dust	Solid	Liquid	Other?
☐	☐	☐	☐	☐	☐	☐	☐

Exposure to which part of the body?

Lungs	Eyes	Skin	Digestive system	Other?
☐	☐	☐	☐	☐

Risks to health

ACCIDENT REPORT FORM (example)

Instructions: All work-related accidents MUST be reported within 24 hours of an accident occurring. This form must be completed, signed and dated and handed to the Manager.

I am reporting an accident that occurred in the workplace on the following:

Date:	Time:

Name of person who had the accident:		

Your name and job title:	Line manager name:	Date of report:

Location of accident:

Name(s) of any witnesses:

Describe, in detail, what happened to cause the accident (attach extra pages to this form if necessary):

What injuries has the person received due to the accident?

Did the injuries require medical treatment? If yes, where did this treatment take place?

Employee signature:	Date:	Manager signature:	Date:

Protective clothing

The cook's/chef's uniform is a well-known symbol of the catering industry.

Wearing the uniform shows that the cook/chef represents a hospitality and catering business and is professional, clean and smart.

There are several parts to the uniform. Each part has a special purpose:

Hat
- Protects hair from smoke and oil
- Lets air cool the head
- Stops hair falling in food

Some chefs wear a cotton necktie to absorb sweat.

A long-sleeved, double-breasted, cotton jacket
- Protects body from burns and heat from ovens and grills
- Makes a clean barrier between the chef and the food
- Absorbs sweat

Knee-length cotton apron
- Protects lower body from burns

Patterned or plain cotton trousers
- Comfortable to wear in a hot kitchen

Strong, well-fitting, slip-resistant shoes, with toe protectors and low heels
- Protect feet from burns and falling objects
- Help prevent slips and falls

There are rules about wearing a chef's uniform

Change into the uniform at work

Do not wear jewellery (plain wedding rings are allowed)

Change the uniform for a clean one every day

Do not wear heavy make-up, false nails, nail varnish or false eyelashes

Wash and iron the uniform regularly

Do not wear strong scents (affects the taste and smell of food)

Do not wear the uniform in public places to prevent contamination by microbes

Wear a hairnet if hair is longer than the collar and/or a beard net (if necessary)

Safety and security in the front and back of house   *... know and understand*

People who work in the front and back of house need to be aware of possible personal safety and security issues in a kitchen, e.g.:

Possible personal safety issues:

- Risk of fire or electrocution

- Risk of trips, slips and falls

- Risk of injury from machinery, e.g. electric food slicer; steamer

- Risk of cuts, burns and scalds

- Risk of heavy stored items falling from shelves or cupboards

Possible security issues:

- Stealing personal items from staff area
- Stealing money, equipment, e.g. knives, small electrical items and utensils from the business

- Stealing stored ingredients, alcohol and materials from the business

- Vandalism (deliberate damage) of buildings

- Arson (deliberately setting fire to a place)

- Problems with alcohol and drug misuse (a common problem in the hospitality and catering industry)

Knowledge check – can you remember...?

1. Three main activities that happen in a catering kitchen?
2. What the most important priority is in a catering kitchen?
3. The names of three areas of a catering kitchen and what happens in them?
4. What 'workflow' means?
5. Three important points for the design of a catering kitchen?
6. Four groups of equipment that are used in a catering kitchen?
7. Five points to consider when choosing equipment for a catering kitchen?
8. Three types of materials that are used in a catering kitchen?
9. Three jobs that a stock controller has to do?
10. Four types of information that have to be completed, signed and dated, and kept in a catering kitchen?
11. Two reasons why a chef wears a uniform?
12. Two reasons why a chef should wear a hat?
13. Two reasons why a chef should wear a cotton jacket?
14. One reason why a chef should wear an apron?
15. Two reasons why a chef should wear sturdy, well-fitting shoes?
16. Five rules about wearing a chef's uniform?
17. Three possible safety issues in a catering kitchen?
18. Three possible security issues in a catering kitchen?

Practice exam question

Short-answer question

1. Catering kitchens are divided up into areas where different activities take place.
   a) Give two reasons why good organisation in a catering kitchen is important. *[2 marks]*
   b) List three things that a stock controller has to do in a catering kitchen. *[3 marks]*

Stretch and challenge questions

An inspection of a hotel kitchen by Environmental Health Officers has revealed the following personal safety and food hygiene problems:

1. Several chefs not following the rules of food hygiene practice
2. Faulty refrigerators that are not keeping food cool enough
3. Evidence of insect and mouse infestation in the kitchen and storerooms
4. Detection of gas leaking from a pipe from one of the cookers
5. Not enough smoke alarms in the kitchen
6. Very few hygiene and safety warning signs displayed in the kitchen
7. Torn vinyl flooring in various places in the kitchen

For each of the problems above, list the documents and pieces of information (e.g. certificates) that hospitality and catering businesses are required to keep and which the Environmental Health Officers will demand to see, to check whether or not the hotel managers have been complying with health and safety and food safety laws. *[7 marks]*

Customer requirements in hospitality and catering
(including hospitality and catering provision to meet specific requirements)

Key learning

Customers have a variety of **needs** and **wants** when they visit a hospitality and catering business.

Customers **expect** hospitality and catering businesses to provide certain services.

If a hospitality and catering business provides for their customers' needs and wants well, it will be successful.

A hospitality and catering business can find out what customers need and want by doing **market research**, e.g. surveys, online reviews and feedback, talking to customers, reading industry magazines and searching the internet.

Customers have certain **legal rights** when they use a hospitality and catering business.

Customer needs, wants and expectations ◀ *...know and understand* ▶

There are three levels for what customers need, want and expect to be provided by a hospitality and catering business:

1. Essential: things that a customer would expect from a restaurant or hotel, e.g.:

In a restaurant
- A variety of menu choices
- Information about the ingredients used (e.g. for people with food allergies)
- Toilets and hand-washing facilities
- Access and facilities for people with disabilities
- Internet availability

In a hotel
- A bar or vending machine serving hot and cold drinks
- Food available at different times of day
- Help with carrying luggage to room
- Lifts to upper floors
- Access and facilities for people with disabilities
- Internet availability

2. Desirable: things that it would be nice to have, e.g.:

In a restaurant
- Some foods (appetisers) to eat before the meal, e.g. olives, nuts, flatbread, etc.
- A mint chocolate or biscuit to go with a cup of coffee
- A choice of cream, ice cream, yogurt or custard to go with a chosen dessert
- A children's play area or table activities to occupy young children, e.g. colouring book and crayons

In a hotel
- A range of toiletries (e.g. shampoo, shower gel, soap) in the en suite bathroom
- A refrigerator to keep drinks, etc. cold
- Air conditioning
- Facilities to make hot drinks in the room
- A hairdryer
- A television or radio

3. Extras: things that customers do not expect or desire but are happy to be given, e.g.:

In a restaurant
- Vouchers for a free meal next time
- A free bottle of wine with their meal
- Free coffee refills at the end of the meal

In a hotel
- Free transport to and from an airport or train station
- Money-off vouchers for a future stay at the hotel
- Free bottle of water, packet of sweets, nuts or biscuits in customer's room

Accessible hotel bathroom for customers with disabilities

Customers want **consistent** (the same all the time), **good-quality** service from all parts of a hospitality and catering business, including:

- The **environment** of the business, which should be comfortable, warm, friendly and accessible to people with disabilities.
- The **ingredients** and **materials** used, which should include good-quality food, toilet and bathroom facilities, comfortable furniture and beds.
- The **opening hours** of the business, which should suit a wide range of customers who want to eat, drink and socialise at different times of the day.
- The **customer service**, which should be provided by well-trained, helpful, polite, efficient and welcoming staff.
- There should be accessibility, equality and inclusion for all customers, especially people with disabilities and those with assistance dogs.

Providing good-quality customer service has many benefits:

...*know and understand*

- Customer satisfaction and loyalty
- More customers
- Staff feel more confident and happy
- Staff enjoy their job
- Fewer staff leave the job
- Fewer complaints from customers.

Customer needs, wants and trends   *... know and understand*

There are more goods and services available than ever before, so businesses have a lot of competition and need to stay up to date in order to attract customers. The ways in which people choose and use hospitality and catering products and services include:

- **Self-service**: e.g. buying food and drinks from a vending machine or drive-through food outlet
- **Online services**: that are instant/fast/user-friendly/up to date with information technology (ICT), e.g. for ordering takeaway meals to be delivered to their home
- **Social media/messaging** (texts, emails, Twitter, Facebook, WhatsApp, etc.): for finding out and sharing information about hospitality and catering businesses, e.g. to comment on or review the products and services provided. Businesses also use these to attract and hold on to their customers.

Customers also expect:

- **Businesses to be available all the time**: e.g. to order takeaway food online for delivery at any time of day or night
- **A personalised service**: e.g. being able to find the type of restaurant they like, close to where they are, on their mobile phone
- **Dietary information**: e.g.:
  - Nutritional information about meals – available on menus and/or online
  - Food allergy and intolerance information to be shown clearly on the menu
  - Whether menu choices are suitable for particular dietary needs, e.g. vegetarian, vegan, dairy free, low salt, etc.
- **Environmentally sustainable and ethically conscious products and customer services**: businesses need to be aware of this for their customer service
- **Well-trained staff**: e.g. who understand dietary requirements and are able to answer customer questions about them.

Drive-through food outlet

Food blogger using smartphone to write a review

Ordering food by smartphone

Activity: Customer dietary requirements

Menus should show a range of dietary information so that customers are informed when they choose their food.

On the menu below, show where the following customer information (using the codes in the tables after the menu) should be printed, e.g.:

Wholewheat pasta with pesto and parmesan cheese:
> Allergy advice: contains: G, N and L
> Suitable for: V

Menu

Starters

Wholewheat pasta with pesto and parmesan cheese

Spicy lentil and tomato soup with flatbread

Garlic prawns with mayonnaise and salad

Main courses

Roasted vegetable tart with new potatoes and crisp green salad

Grilled chicken with peanut sauce, served with sweet potato wedges and peas

Cauliflower cheese with seasonal vegetables

Shepherd's pie with cheesy potato crust, sweetcorn and peas

Desserts

Panna cotta with fresh fruits

Rich chocolate mousse

Sticky toffee pudding with pecan fudge sauce

Lemon meringue pie

1. Allergy advice:

Key	Contains foods/ingredients known to cause allergies or intolerance
G	Gluten (wheat, barley, oats, rye)
N	Nuts/tree nuts/peanuts
C	Celery
F	Fish/shellfish/crustaceans (prawns, lobsters, etc.)
E	Eggs
L	Lactose (dairy foods – milk, cheese, cream, butter, yogurt)
S	Seeds (sesame, pumpkin, poppy, etc.)
B	Beans (soya beans, kidney beans, etc.)

2. Suitability:

Key	Suitable for
V	Suitable for vegetarians
VG	Suitable for vegans

The hospitality and catering industry is a major part of the leisure industry, which includes sports activities, holidays, tourism and outdoor activities (walking, water activities, etc.). The two areas work together very closely to provide customers with what they need, want and expect.

Customer needs and wants   ...know and understand

There are different groups of people who use the services that hospitality and catering businesses provide. The chart below shows that each group has different needs and wants, and a successful business will provide services for these in order to attract customers.

Type of customer	Examples of their needs and wants	Examples of how a hospitality and catering business can provide for their needs and wants
Couples and small groups who want a leisure visit for two or three days	Short leisure breaks Reasonably priced accommodation	Special hotel 'packages' at quiet times of year, e.g. 'out of [holiday] season' or in the winter, offering reduced price accommodation and including one or two evening meals as well as breakfast
	Leisure facilities	Swimming pool, gym, beauty therapy, spa
Families with young children	Value for money	Inexpensive restaurant that has a children's menu
	Suitable accommodation and facilities	Cots, small beds, highchairs, en suite toilet, shower and bath
	Activities	Outdoor/indoor play area, games, swimming pool

	**Business customers**	Suitable accommodation for meetings	Meeting places/conference rooms
		Computer technology	Smart screens to show films and presentations, internet access throughout, video conferencing facilities, smartphone charging points
		Catering	Business lunches, refreshments available throughout the day
	**Travellers/ tourists**	Suitable, reasonably priced accommodation	Single/double rooms, dormitories (large room containing beds for numerous people); en suite toilet, shower and bath; space to store bicycles, walking boots, body boards, etc.; laundry services
		Activities	Arrange local tours, walks, theatre trips, etc.; swimming pool, gym, beauty therapy, spa
		Flexible availability of food	Packed breakfasts and lunches; hot food and drinks available out of set mealtimes; vending machines selling snacks and drinks
	**Millennials (people born from 1980 to 2000), who have a big influence on the hospitality and catering industry**	To eat 'on the go'	Packed breakfasts and lunches; hot food and drinks available out of set mealtimes; vending machines selling snacks and drinks
		To eat locally produced, healthy, fresh food	
		Use of all types of social media, digital and computer technologies	Internet access throughout; smartphone charging points
		Environmentally sustainable services and products	Minimal use of plastics; recycling bins, etc. in use; provide food that is mainly plant based and has been produced sustainably; use biodegradable products such as cleaning products and paper drinking straws
		High-quality and contemporary (modern) products and services, e.g. to book and use services through a mobile phone at their own convenience	Provide exciting, well-designed, user-friendly social spaces to meet with friends, with computer technology available throughout

Customer rights and equality

... know and understand

Customers are protected by various laws when they buy products or services. These include:

Trade Descriptions Act 1968

- Products and services must be described accurately and correctly

The Consumer Protection Act 1987

- It is against the law to sell unsafe products and services
- Health and safety information must be be given on products and services
- Correct prices must be charged for products and services

Consumer Rights Act 2015

Products must:
- Be good quality
- Work correctly
- Match the description given about them
- Be fitted properly

Services must be:
- Carried out with care
- Completed for a reasonable price
- Completed within a reasonable time

Equality Act 2010

- Protects the rights of individual people
- Protects people from unfair treatment
- Promotes equal opportunities for all people no matter what age, race, religion or gender they are or whether they have a disability

Business and corporate needs and wants
...know and understand

Large businesses (corporates) and small businesses use the hospitality and catering industry for many types of event that they run, to provide a range of products and services:

Local residents
...know and understand

If a hospitality and catering business is located in or near an area where people live, it should try to make sure that it meets the needs and expectations of local residents by:

- Employing local people
- Keeping noise from customers, music and cars to a low level, especially late in the evening
- Providing parking for customers to prevent traffic problems in local streets
- Employing security officers to maintain order and using CCTV cameras to monitor the local area
- Offering reasonable prices for hosting local events such as fetes, school proms and festivals.

PLEASE LEAVE QUIETLY THIS IS A RESIDENTIAL AREA

Knowledge check – can you remember...?

1. The three levels for what customers need, want and expect, with an example for each in a restaurant or hotel?

2. Two good quality points for the environment of a hospitality and catering business?

3. Two good quality points for the ingredients and materials used in a hospitality and catering business?

4. Four benefits of good customer service?

5. Two trends in the ways in which customers choose and use products and services?

6. Three essential requirements that customers expect hospitality and catering businesses to provide with their products and services.

7. Two laws that protect customers when they buy products and services?

8. Three types of events that businesses and corporates run?

9. Three products and services that the hospitality and catering industry can provide for business events?

10. Two ways in which a hospitality and catering business can meet the needs and expectations of local residents?

11. Two needs and wants for *each* of the following groups of people who are customers of a hospitality and catering business?
    a) Families with young children
    b) Business customers
    c) Travellers and tourists
    d) Couples or small groups of people

Practice exam questions

Short-answer questions

1. Customers have different needs, wants and expectations when they use a hospitality and catering business.

   List three essential needs that customers using a sports and leisure centre café would have.
   [1 mark each]

2. List three essential needs for restaurant customers who have physical disabilities. *[1 mark each]*

Graduated lead-in questions

3. A new bar and restaurant has opened in a small town, and is situated in a residential area where there are lots of homes occupied by families with young children. The bar/restaurant will open seven days a week, from 2 p.m. until 11 p.m., except on Sundays when it will open from 4 p.m. until 10 p.m.
   a) Suggest two ways in which the managers of the bar/restaurant can prevent local residents from being disturbed at night and when customers leave. *[2 marks]*
   b) Describe two ways in which the managers of the bar/restaurant could encourage local residents to become customers. *[2 marks]*

4. The local town council in the town of Ashburness is going to host a ceremony at the Town Hall for local people who have each received an award for their work with local charities. The event will be sponsored by several large businesses, and there will be guests from a range of organisations invited to attend the ceremony.

   Suggest two products/services that a hospitality and catering business could provide at the event. *[2 marks]*

Stretch and challenge questions

An organisation based in a large inner city is opening an after school and school holiday club for children aged 4 to 14 years old.

The club will provide activities for children to do and will employ a catering manager to run the catering kitchen and provide meals for the children and staff throughout the day.

1. Write about three things the catering manager will have to consider and do to make sure that the dietary and food safety needs and requirements of all the children and staff are met. Give reasons for your answers. *[6 marks]*

2. Suggest and describe two activities that the catering manager and club leaders could organise and run for children in the catering kitchen to help them learn about food. *[4 marks]*

Topic 1.3 Health and safety in hospitality and catering

Health and safety in hospitality and catering provision

Key learning

In the UK, every year, many employees have accidents or injuries while at work.

The main causes of accidents and injuries are:

- Slips, trips and falls
- Lifting/handling heavy or awkward objects
- Being hit by an object
- Being injured by a machine.

The Health and Safety Executive (HSE) is a government department that enforces health and safety rules and laws in the workplace.

The employers and all employees in hospitality and catering businesses are all responsible for personal safety in the workplace.

Hospitality and catering businesses must make sure that they minimise the health and safety risks for their employees and customers.

 Remember!
An *employer* is someone who owns a business and pays an *employee* to work there.

Laws about personal safety

…be aware of

Health and Safety at Work Act (HASAWA)

What an employer must do by law	What an employee must do to follow the law and stay safe
<ul><li>Protect the health, safety and welfare of their employees and other people (e.g. customers, people making deliveries)</li><li>Minimise the risks that could cause injury or health problems in the workplace</li><li>Give information to employees about risks in the workplace and how they are protected</li><li>Give health and safety training to all employees</li></ul>	<ul><li>Take care of other employees they work with who might be affected by what they do or do not do</li><li>Always follow the health and safety instructions their employer gives</li><li>Go to health and safety training sessions</li><li>Use all equipment properly</li><li>Report any safety or health hazards and problems with equipment, etc. to their employer</li></ul>

Reporting of Injuries, Diseases and Dangerous Occurrences Regulations (RIDDOR)

What an employer must do by law	What an employee must do to follow the law and stay safe
<ul><li>Report any serious workplace accidents, diseases and certain dangerous incidents (near misses) to the HSE</li></ul>	<ul><li>If an employee sees or is worried about a health and safety problem, first tell the person in charge, the employer or a union representative</li><li>If nothing is done about it, the employee can report their worries to the HSE</li></ul>

Control of Substances Hazardous to Health Regulations (COSHH)

What an employer must do by law

- Make sure that employees are not exposed (without protection) to items and substances that are unsafe and/or harmful (hazardous) to their health
- These items and substances include:
  - Cleaning chemicals
  - Fumes, e.g. from machinery, cooking processes or vehicles
  - Dusts and powders, e.g. icing sugar, flour, ground nuts
  - Vapours, e.g. from cleaning chemicals, machinery, pest control chemicals
  - Gases, e.g. from cookers
  - Biological agents, e.g. pests and their waste products, moulds, bacteria
- Some of these substances can cause short- or long-term illnesses such as cancer, asthma, skin problems, liver damage

What an employee must do to follow the law and stay safe

- Go to training sessions
- Carefully follow the instructions for using hazardous substances
- Always wear safety equipment, e.g. gloves, masks, goggles, etc., that the employer provides
- Make sure they learn the international symbols for different types of substances and how they can harm people:

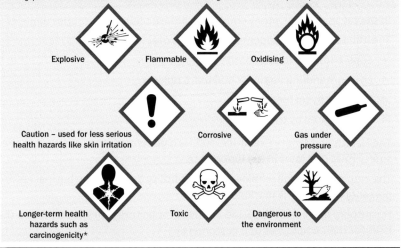

Explosive   Flammable   Oxidising

Caution – used for less serious health hazards like skin irritation   Corrosive   Gas under pressure

Longer-term health hazards such as carcinogenicity*   Toxic   Dangerous to the environment

Manual Handling Operations Regulations (MHOR)

What an employer must do by law

- Avoid risky manual handling operations if at all possible

  > **Manual handling** means moving or supporting a load by lifting, putting down, pushing, carrying or moving it by hand or with the force of the body.

- Assess any manual handling operations that cannot be avoided
- Reduce the risk of injury as far as possible, e.g. by using mechanical handling equipment such as fork-lift trucks
- Store heavy equipment, e.g. a food mixer, so that it is easy to take out and use, e.g. on a worktop or on a low shelf in a cupboard or storeroom

What an employee must do to follow the law and stay safe

- Go to training sessions on how to lift and handle loads
- Be aware of their own physical strength and any weaknesses/limitations
- 'Think before you lift'
- Do not take unnecessary risks
- Ask for help if needed
- Check the load before an attempt to lift or move it – is it hot, cold, sharp, hard to grip, heavy, likely to be become unbalanced if it is moved?
- Check the area in which they are working – is there enough space to lift something properly? Is the flooring uneven, slippery, unstable? Are there steps or obstructions?
- Follow the advice on lifting heavy and large objects:
  - Squat down with feet either side of the load to begin picking it up
  - Keep back straight while moving to a standing position
  - Keep the load close to the body when walking with it
  - Make sure you can see where you are going
  - Be very careful when lifting down heavy objects from high shelves. Use a purpose-built, sturdy set of step ladders or a step stool to stand on so that the object can be reached properly

wrong   right

Personal Protective Equipment (PPE) at Work Regulations (PPER)

What an employer must do by law

- Give employees PPE where it is needed
- Train employees so that they understand the importance of PPE
- Put up signs to remind employees to wear PPE
- Make sure that employees wear the PPE at all times when they are working in an area with health and safety risks
- Make sure PPE is good quality and is maintained properly

PPE protects different areas of the body, including:

- **Masks** to prevent breathing contaminated air into the lungs
- **Hard hats** and **reinforced shoes** to protect the head and feet from falling objects

- **Goggles/eye shields** to prevent the eyes being splashed with chemicals or injured by particles in the air
- **Thick/protective clothing** to prevent skin contact with heat, extreme cold or corrosive chemicals that burn the skin

What an employee must do to follow the law and stay safe

- Go to training sessions on the importance of and how to wear PPE
- Wear PPE as instructed by the employer, e.g.:
  - Chef's/cook's uniform to protect the body/arms from heat

  - Gloves and protective clothing when working in a freezer or handling frozen/chilled foods

  - Mask to protect the lungs when working with, e.g. flour, icing sugar, powdered nuts

  - Protective gloves for when using cleaning chemicals

  - Chain mail (metal) gloves or gauntlets (gloves with extensions that cover the arm up to the elbow) when using large sharp knives in butchery, e.g. boning and jointing a meat carcase

  - Reinforced and closed kitchen clogs or shoes to protect the feet from being injured by falling heavy objects or hot liquid spillage

Knowledge check – can you remember...?

1. Three main causes of accidents/injuries in the workplace?
2. Two things an *employer* must do under the Health and Safety at Work Act?
3. Two things an *employee* must do under the Health and Safety at Work Act?
4. Two things an *employer* must do under the Control of Substances Hazardous to Health Regulations?
5. Two things an *employee* must do under the Control of Substances Hazardous to Health Regulations?
6. Two things an *employer* must do under the Manual Handling Operations Regulations?
7. Two things an *employee* must do under the Manual Handling Operations Regulations?
8. Three types of Personal Protective Equipment used in the hospitality and catering industry?
9. Two things an *employer* must do under the Personal Protective Equipment at Work Regulations?
10. Two things an *employee* must do under the Personal Protective Equipment at Work Regulations?

Activity: Safety symbols for harmful substances

Match the safety symbols used in the COSHH regulations to the correct type of harmful substance:

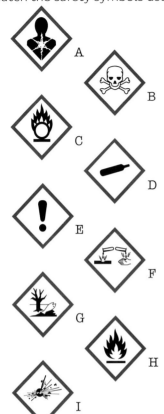

1	A substance that is dangerous for the environment
2	A gas under pressure that could explode
3	A substance that is corrosive (seriously damages the skin)
4	A substance that is toxic (poisonous)
5	A substance that causes long-term harm, e.g. cancer
6	A substance that is flammable (can catch fire)
7	A substance that can explode
8	A substance that should be used with caution
9	A substance that combines with oxygen in a chemical reaction

Activity: Which Personal Protective Equipment is worn in a catering kitchen?

Match each of the following items of Personal Protective Equipment that should be worn with the correct activity that would take place in a catering kitchen:

Placing an item in the oven	1
Removing items from the freezer	2
Using cleaning chemicals	3
Cutting joints of meat	4
Working with icing sugar, flour or powdered nuts	5
Preparing food and walking to different places in the kitchen	6
Using oven cleaner spray	7

Practice exam question

Short-answer question

1. Every year in the UK, many employees have accidents or injuries while at work.
   a) State two main causes of accidents and injuries in the workplace. *[2 marks]*
   b) Identify the government department that enforces health and safety rules in the workplace. *[1 mark]*
   c) List two additional types of accident/injury that could happen to a food handler working in a kitchen. *[2 marks]*

Risks and control measures

...*know*

Key learning

A **hazard** is something that could damage someone's health or cause an accident that would physically hurt (injure) them.

Here are two examples:

1. A health hazard – fine particles of flour dust that are produced when flour is sieved

2. A physical hazard – some food, water or oil spilt on the floor of a catering kitchen

A **personal safety risk** is how likely it is that someone's health will be damaged or they will be hurt by a hazard.

The personal safety risks for the two examples above are:

1. The flour dust particles that a baker breathes in when making bread every day for several years may gradually damage their lungs, and eventually the baker may not be able to breathe properly.

2. Food, water or oil spilt on the floor may cause a kitchen worker to slip, fall over and be physically hurt (injured).

Something that is **high risk** is more likely to damage someone's health or hurt them than something that is **low risk**.

Key terms you should try to include in your answers

Control measure – an action or object used to reduce the risk of a hazard damaging a person's health or physically hurting them

Hazard – something that could damage a person's health or cause an accident that would physically hurt them

Personal safety risk – how likely it is that someone's health will be damaged or they will be hurt by a hazard

Risk assessment – a way of showing how much risk is involved in an activity, a situation or when using an object

Remember!
A personal safety risk is different from a food safety risk.

What is a personal safety risk?
While working in or visiting a hospitality and catering business, a person could ...

- Be electrocuted
- Get trapped under or inside something
- Slip or trip and fall over
- Damage their lungs by breathing in something
- Fall off something
- Damage their hearing by loud noise
- Be hit by something
- Become unwell because of too much heat
- Be cut by something
- Get frostbite by working in a very cold place
- Be burned by something
- Injure themselves by picking up or moving something heavy

What is a food safety risk?
A person could become ill because they have eaten food that has ...

- Not been stored properly
- Become unsafe to eat because it is contaminated with microbes and/or poisons
- Not been cooked properly
- Not been chilled quickly enough after cooking
- Passed its use-by date
- Been left out in a warm place for too long
- Been prepared with equipment that is contaminated with microbes
- Been prepared by someone who does not have clean hands

A **personal risk assessment** is used to show how much risk is involved in:

- An activity, e.g. carrying a heavy pan of hot food
- A situation, e.g. getting out of a building in an emergency
- Using an object, e.g. using a large slicing machine in the kitchen.

A **control measure** is an action or object that is used to prevent or reduce the risk of a hazard damaging someone's health or hurting them.
The control measures for the two examples on page 59 are:

Example 1.

a) The baker should wear a mask to prevent breathing in the flour dust

b) Extractor fans should be used in the kitchen to remove dust particles from the air

Example 2.

a) Kitchen workers should wipe up spilt food, water or oil from the floor as soon as possible

b) Warning signs should be placed in an area where the floor is wet or slippery

The following charts give information about possible hazards and risks to the health, safety and security of people who work in or visit a hospitality and catering business, and the control measures used to control the risks:

 Remember!
An *employer* is someone who owns a business and pays an *employee* to work there.

Front-of-house employees:
Reception staff; security staff; waiting staff; bar staff

Possible health hazards and risks	Control measures
• Muscle strain and back problems from lifting and carrying heavy items, moving tables and chairs, etc. Level of risk: medium to high	**Employers should:** • Give training on how to lift and carry heavy objects properly • Provide equipment, e.g. trolleys, to assist moving equipment and materials • Design customer service areas to limit the amount of twisting, reaching up, bending down and carrying that employees have to do
• Tiredness due to long working hours, leading to increased risk of injury Level of risk: medium to high	**Employers should:** • Limit the amount of repetitive work and standing for long periods of time that employees have to do • Provide employees with sit-stand stools and anti-fatigue mats to stand on 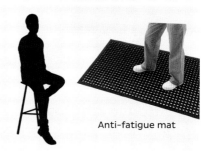 Anti-fatigue mat
• Stress: leading to high blood pressure, headaches, poor eating habits, days off sick from work, etc. (often caused by workload and problems between employees, e.g. bullying) Level of risk: medium to high	**Employers should:** • Encourage good relationships between employees in the workplace • Encourage employees to report work problems, and make changes where needed • Deal with workplace bullying and harassment when it is reported • Use counselling and support services for employees who are stressed

Possible safety risks	Control measures
• Slips, trip, falls • Burns and scalds from coffee machines, etc. • Electric shocks • Fire or other emergency Level of risk: medium to high 	**Employers should make sure that:** • All work areas are well lit and free from obstructions, and floors are in good condition • Equipment, e.g. a ladder, is provided so employees can get items safely from high shelves, cupboards, etc. • Employees are trained to use all equipment correctly • Electrical wiring and equipment is safe to use and regularly tested • There are enough electrical safety switches and sockets so the wiring is not overloaded • Electrical equipment is kept away from water and wet areas • There are plenty of warning and safety signs to remind employees about safety • All emergency exits are working properly and do not have any obstructions that would stop people being able to get out in an emergency

Employees should:

- Wear non-slip shoes
- Wipe up any spills when they happen
- Make sure items are put away and drawers and doors are closed
- Avoid blocking passageways with boxes, equipment, etc.

Possible security risks	Control measures
<ul><li>Physically and verbally aggressive customers</li><li>Intruders coming into the building</li><li>Personal belongings being stolen</li></ul> 	**Employers should:** <ul><li>Employ security staff and enable other staff to contact them quickly from any part of the building</li><li>Install closed-circuit television cameras (CCTV)</li><li>Install security lighting outside the building, e.g. where bins are located near the back entrance to the kitchen</li><li>Provide staff with security passes to go into the building and secure places to store their personal belongings when they are working</li></ul>**Employees should:** <ul><li>Make sure they lock up their personal belongings in a secure place when working</li><li>Report potential intruders to security staff</li></ul>

Back-of-house employees:
Chefs and cooks; stock controller; kitchen workers; pot wash staff; cleaners

Possible health hazards and risks	Control measures
Having contact with: <ul><li>Cleaning chemicals</li><li>Extremes of heat and cold</li><li>Diseases from pests</li></ul>Possibly developing: <ul><li>Muscle and back strain from lifting, carrying and storing heavy items</li><li>Muscle and back strain from:<ul><li>bending awkwardly, e.g. cleaning the insides of large pots and ovens</li><li>reaching into a deep chest freezer</li><li>lifting heavy equipment or containers of ingredients</li><li>standing for a long time</li></ul></li><li>Repetitive strain injury, e.g. in the wrists and hands, from repeated chopping, kneading and mixing</li></ul>Level of risk: medium to high	**Employers should make sure that:** <ul><li>Employees are given and wear protective equipment, e.g. rubber gloves, eye protection and masks; insulated gloves and clothing to work in cold areas</li><li>Employees are trained to store and use chemicals safely and follow COSHH guidelines (see page 56)</li><li>The kitchen is well ventilated and has air conditioning</li><li>Employees always have water to drink when they are working</li><li>The kitchen layout is designed so work stations are away from sources of heat</li><li>Employees take plenty of rest breaks in a cool place</li><li>Employees are trained how to lift and carry heavy objects correctly</li><li>There is equipment, e.g. trolleys, plate dispensers, conveyors, etc., to help move heavy items and materials</li><li>Staff can use machines, e.g. for mixing, kneading, cutting, slicing and peeling, to reduce strains to the hands and wrists</li></ul>

- Workers have foot rails so they can move their bodyweight and reduce the stress to their back and legs
- If possible, workbenches of different heights are provided for food preparation, to avoid back strain when bending or reaching
- The kitchen and storerooms are regularly inspected and pest controlled

Possible safety risks	Control measures
<ul><li>Slips, trip, falls</li><li>Burns and scalds</li><li>Cuts and scrapes</li><li>Electric shocks</li><li>Fire or other emergency</li></ul> Level of risk: medium to high 	**Employers should make sure that:** <ul><li>All work areas are well lit, free from obstructions, and floors are in good condition</li><li>Equipment, e.g. a ladder, is provided so employees can get items safely from high shelves, cupboards, etc.</li><li>All machinery has safety guards fitted</li><li>Splatter guards are fitted around deep fat fryers to stop hot oil burns</li><li>Guards are fitted around hot surfaces</li><li>Hot liquids can be drained from large pans rather than being tipped out by hand</li><li>Gas ovens, grills and hobs are regularly tested, e.g. for gas leaks and correct burning of the gas</li><li>Electrical wiring and equipment is safe to use and regularly tested</li><li>There are enough electrical safety switches and sockets so the wiring is not overloaded</li><li>Electrical equipment is kept away from water and wet areas</li><li>There are plenty of warning and safety signs to remind employees about safety</li><li>Employees are trained to use all equipment correctly</li><li>Employees are trained to give first aid in case of an injury</li><li>All emergency exits are working properly and do not have any obstructions that would stop people being able to get out in an emergency</li></ul> **Employees should:** <ul><li>Wear non-slip shoes</li><li>Wear PPE and protective clothing</li><li>Wipe up any spills when they happen</li><li>Remove any food that has fallen on the floor</li><li>Make sure equipment is put away properly and drawers and doors are closed</li><li>Avoid blocking passageways with boxes, equipment, etc.</li><li>Carry and use knives safely</li><li>Handle electrical equipment with dry hands</li><li>Use oven cloths to handle hot baking trays and pan handles</li><li>Report any safety problems to the manager/employer</li></ul>

Customers

Allergen List
1 Celery
2 Cereals containing gluten
3 Crustaceans
4 Eggs
5 Fish
6 Lupin
7 Milk
8 Molluscs
9 Mustard
10 Nuts
11 Peanuts
12 Sesame seeds
13 Soya
14 Sulphur Dioxide (Sulphites)

Possible health hazards and risks	Control measures
• Food poisoning • Illness due to food allergies and intolerances Level of risk: low to medium	• Hazard Analysis of Critical Control Points (HACCP) – see pages 69–72 • Give customers information about ingredients in dishes on menus, so they can make safe choices

Possible safety risks	Control measures
• Trips, slips, falls • Fire or other emergency Level of risk: low to medium	**The managers of the business should make sure that:** • All customer areas are well lit and free from obstructions, floors are in good condition and steps/stairs are clearly marked and have handrails • All emergency exits are working properly and do not have any obstructions that would stop people being able to get out in an emergency

Possible security risks	Control measures
• Credit card fraud • Theft of personal belongings Level of risk: low to medium	**The managers of the business should make sure that:** • All customer payments are processed in front of the customer • Customers are provided with secure places to leave their belongings, e.g. a secure cloakroom, a digital safe in hotel bedrooms

Suppliers (who deliver to hospitality and catering businesses)

Possible health hazards and risks	Control measures
• Muscle strain and back problems from lifting, carrying and storing heavy items Level of risk: medium to high	**The managers of the business should make sure that:** • Equipment, e.g. trolleys, provided to help suppliers move equipment and materials safely

Possible safety risks	Control measures
• Trips, slips, falls • Fire or other emergency Level of risk: medium	**The managers of the business should make sure that:** • All areas are well lit and free from obstructions, floors are in good condition and steps/stairs are clearly marked and have handrails • All emergency exits are working properly and do not have any obstructions that would stop people being able to get out in an emergency

Possible security risks	Control measures
• Attempted theft of property Level of risk: low	**The employees of the business should make sure that:** • They check the identity of callers to the business, e.g. suppliers • They lock away their personal belongings in a secure place

Activity: Safety and security equipment used in the front and back of house

Every job has hazards and risks which need to be controlled. For each of the following groups of people who work in the hospitality and catering industry, find out, explain and describe why and how each piece of equipment is provided to help prevent damage to health, accidents and injuries at work, and risks to people's personal security.

Front-of-house employees: reception staff; security staff; waiting staff; bar staff

Equipment used to control health hazards and risks

Why and how do these pieces of equipment help to prevent health problems and accidents/injuries?

Trolley

Anti-fatigue mat

Sit-stand stool

Equipment or processes used to control personal safety hazards and risks

Why and how do these help to prevent accidents and injuries, and control emergencies?

Step ladder

Emergency escape route sign

PAT (Portable Appliance Testing) testing of electrical equipment

RCD (Residual Current Device) electrical safety unit in kitchen

Equipment or processes used to control personal security hazards and risks

Why and how do these help to prevent accidents and injuries, and control emergencies?

Security card to enter building

Staff lockers in rest room

CCTV camera in restaurant

Back of house employees: chefs and cooks; stock controller; kitchen workers; pot wash staff; cleaners

Equipment/clothing used to control health hazards and risks

Why and how does this equipment/clothing help prevent health problems and accidents/injuries?

Working in the freezer warehouse of a food factory or stockroom

Extractor fans above a cooking range in a catering kitchen

Chilled water dispenser

Air conditioning unit outside on the roof of a catering kitchen

Large electric mixer

Equipment or processes used to control personal safety hazards and risks

Why and how do these help to prevent accidents and injuries, and control emergencies?

Blade guard

Slicing Machine
Switch off/disconnect power supply at mains before cleaning. The guard provided must be in the correct position before operating the machine. Always return the slicing thickness indicator to the zero position when work is finished to avoid injury to hand.

First aid kit

Temperature control and thermostat

Deep fat frying machine

Mopping up spilt liquid

Knife wallet

Clean up all spillages immediately

Warning signs

Activity: Personal safety risks and control measures

Match each personal safety risk to the correct control measure used to prevent the health of someone being damaged or a person being hurt in a hospitality and catering business:

Personal safety risk

Carrying heavy boxes of wine from the delivery lorry to the bar	**A**
Lifting a heavy food mixer from a high cupboard	**B**
Using electrical equipment in the kitchen	**C**
Storing and organising food in a walk-in freezer storeroom in a large hotel kitchen	**D**
Sieving large amounts of icing sugar every day for decorating cakes in a bakery	**E**
Using a knife to cut whole fresh chickens into separate pieces in a large hotel kitchen	**F**
Removing hot baking trays from the oven	**G**
Working in a very hot kitchen for 8 hours	**H**
Using a deep fat fryer to fry fish and chips	**I**
Reaching up for items of equipment and ingredients from high shelves	**J**

Which control measure?

1 Wear insulated clothes, gloves and shoes

2 Ventilate the kitchen and drink plenty of water

3 Safety test all electrical equipment

4 Use a sack barrow

5 Place a fire extinguisher and fire blanket near the frying area

6 Use a stepladder

7 Keep knives sharp so they work properly and safely

8 Move heavy items to a worktop or low cupboard

9 Use oven gloves

10 Wear a mask

Knowledge check – can you remember...?

1. What a hazard is?
2. What a personal safety risk is?
3. What a risk assessment is?
4. What a control measure is?
5. Two things an employer should do to prevent health hazards and risks in the front of house?
6. Two things an employee should do to prevent safety risks in the front of house?
7. Two things an employer should do to prevent security risks in the front of house?
8. Four things an employer should do to prevent health hazards and risks in the back of house?
9. Three things an employer should do to prevent safety risks in the back of house?
10. Four things an employee should do to prevent safety risks in the back of house?
11. Two things the managers of a business should do to prevent security risks for customers?
12. Two things employees should do to prevent security risks when suppliers deliver goods to the back of house?

Practice exam questions

Short-answer questions

1. There are numerous personal safety risks that employees, employers, customers and suppliers may face in the hospitality and catering industry. List three personal safety risks. *[3 marks]*

2. A hazard is something that could damage a person's health or cause an accident that would physically hurt them. List three hazards that might be found in a catering kitchen. *[3 marks]*

Graduated lead-in question

3. In recent weeks, several front-of-house bar staff in a busy city bar and restaurant have been unable to work due to a number of health issues, including muscle strain and back problems, excessive tiredness and stress. The managers of the business are concerned and decide to investigate what control measures they can take to protect the health of their staff and enable all the staff to work without these health risks.

   a) Identify one possible reason for each of the following problems that have been reported by bar staff: *[3 marks]*
      - Muscle strain and back problems
      - Excessive tiredness
      - Stress

   b) Suggest two control measures that the management could introduce to prevent each of these problems from happening in future: *[6 marks]*
      - Muscle strain and back problems
      - Excessive tiredness
      - Stress

   c) Explain why it is important for the success of a hospitality and catering business to carry out risk assessments and put control measures in place for the personal safety and security of their front-of-house employees. *[3 marks]*

All laws are complicated. You are not expected to know all the details of food safety laws, but you need to understand the basic **rules** and the **responsibilities** of people who work in a hospitality and catering business to make sure the laws are followed. These are set out on the following pages.

The Food Safety Act 1990 ...be aware of

All food businesses must make sure that all the food they produce for sale or give away is:

1. Safe to eat
2. What people expect it to be
3. Not labelled, advertised or presented in a way that is confusing or not true.

Food Safety (Food Hygiene) Regulations 2006 (updated to The Food Safety and Hygiene (England) Regulations in 2013) ...be aware of

Anyone who owns, manages or works in a food business, whatever its size, must:

1. Make sure food is handled, supplied and sold in a hygienic way
2. Identify possible **food safety hazards** in all the operations and activities of the food business
3. Know which stages in their food-handling activities are critical for food safety: i.e. the stages at which things could go wrong – the **critical control points**
4. Decide what **controls** can be put in place to prevent risks to food safety
5. Make sure that food safety controls are in place, are always followed by everyone and are regularly maintained and reviewed.

The food hygiene regulations cover:

HACCP ...know and understand

All food businesses must:

- Protect the health of their customers
- Show **due diligence** in the operation and activities of their business: this means they have carried out reasonable actions to avoid a food safety risk.

To make sure all the things that the Food Hygiene Regulations (rules) require are done properly, a food safety management system called **Hazard Analysis of Critical Control Points (HACCP)** is used.

> ### HACCP – Hazard Analysis of Critical Control Points

What are the **critical control points**? Each stage of food production	*Analysis* What are the **hazards** at each stage?	*Analysis* How are these hazards **controlled**?	*Analysis* How are the controls **checked**?

The word 'analysis' means that the operation of the food business is separated into stages. Each stage is looked at in detail to identify possible hazards and to explain how these are controlled to prevent a food safety risk.

Key terms you should try to include in your answers

Critical control points – stages in a food-production operation where food safety could go wrong

Due diligence – being able to prove that reasonable actions have been taken to avoid a health risk

Hazard Analysis of Critical Control Points (HACCP) – a food safety management system to identify possible hazards to food safety

A food business should produce evidence that they have carried out a HACCP, so that an Environmental Health Officer (see pages 91–93) can check it when they carry out an inspection.

To help you understand what HACCP means, the table below is a detailed example of a HACCP document for a café that sells hot and cold lunches, as well as hot and cold drinks. The critical control points, hazards, controls and correct temperatures used to prevent food safety risks are all clearly set out.

Stage of food production: Critical control points	Possible hazards	Controls and checks used to prevent a food safety risk	What are the correct temperatures?
Buying the ingredients	• Chilled or frozen foods delivered to cafés might not be cold enough, so bacteria could multiply	• Food suppliers are visited regularly to check what HACCP controls they have in place • Temperature (and cleanliness) of chilled delivery van/lorry is checked at each delivery, before accepting the foods	The temperature of the food delivered in a van/lorry must be: **0°C to 5°C for chilled foods** **minus 18°C to minus 22°C for frozen foods**
Storing the ingredients	• Bacteria may grow and multiply in chilled and frozen foods if they are not stored at the correct temperatures	• Refrigerator and freezer temperatures are checked every day and recorded in a log book • Refrigerator and freezer motors and door seals are regularly checked and serviced to make sure they work properly • Alarms that make a warning noise if the inside temperature goes up too much are fitted to refrigerators and freezers to warn kitchen staff • The dates on all stored foods are regularly checked and older foods are used up first (FIFO – first in, first out)	Refrigerators: **0°C to 5°C** in England, **0°C to 8°C** in Wales and Scotland Freezers: **minus 18°C to minus 22°C**
	• Dry foods will go mouldy if they become damp	• Dry foods are stored in a ventilated room, on shelves in airtight containers	
	• Bacteria could spread from one food to another	• Raw and cooked foods are kept separate in the refrigerators to prevent cross-contamination	
	• Pests can contaminate food and make it unsafe to eat	• Pest traps are placed inside the storage area • Regular pest-control inspections are carried out • Loose foods are stored in pest-proof containers	

Preparing the food	• Bacteria could spread from one food to another	• Colour-coded chopping boards and knives are used for different foods • Raw foods are prepared in a separate area from cooked foods • Frozen high-risk foods (meat, poultry, fish, cream) are defrosted on a tray in the refrigerator	Defrost foods at: **0°C to 5°C**
	• Bacteria from the soil could contaminate food • Food handlers could contaminate food with bacteria from their hands, body or clothes	• All vegetables and fruits are washed before storage and preparation • All staff have passed their Food Safety and Hygiene training and have up-to-date certificates • All staff wear clean uniform each day	
Cooking the food	• High-risk foods such as meat, poultry, fish and seafood may not be cooked all the way through, so harmful bacteria could still be alive	• Food probes are used to measure the temperature at the core (centre) of the cooked food before serving to customers	Core temperature: **minimum 70°C for 2 minutes**
Cooling cooked food for storage	• Bacteria could multiply in cooked food if it is not cooled quickly enough before being stored in the refrigerator or freezer	• Cooked rice is rapidly cooled in cold water and then refrigerated • Other cooked dishes are covered and cooled in a ventilated room away from the kitchen before being refrigerated or frozen	Cooked foods should reach: **5°C or lower within 1½ hours**
Reheating cooked and chilled foods	• Bacteria can multiply in reheated foods if they are not heated all the way through	• Food probes are used to measure the temperature at the core of the reheated food before serving to customers • Foods are reheated only once	Minimum core temperature: **70°C for 2 minutes** in England, Wales and Northern Ireland. In Scotland, the core temperature must be: **minimum of 82°C**
Keeping the food hot or cold before serving to customers	• Bacteria may multiply inside cooked meat, poultry or fish and seafood dishes if they are not kept hot enough before serving	• Food probes are used to measure the temperature at the core of the hot food before serving to customers	Core temperature: **minimum 63°C**

	• Bacteria can multiply in chilled foods, e.g. salads, cooked cold meats, pâtés, cold desserts containing eggs and cream, if they are not kept cold enough	• All high-risk cold desserts, salads, cooked cold meats, pâtés, cream, etc. are refrigerated until served to customers	Refrigerate at **0°C to 5°C**
Washing up and cleaning	• Bacteria will multiply on pieces of food if they are left on equipment, plates, dishes and cutlery	• All equipment, plates, dishes, cups, glasses and cutlery are either hand washed or washed in a dishwasher and air dried in an area away from contamination	Hand washing: **55°C** with washing up liquid Rinse in very hot water: **82°C** Dishwashers: **82°C to 89°C**
Getting rid of food waste and rubbish	• Bacteria and moulds will multiply in food waste and rubbish • Microbes will live and multiply on the lids and inside of waste bins	• Waste bins are located outside the kitchen • Waste bins are foot operated so staff do not need to touch the lids • Waste bins are collected and emptied regularly • Staff are trained to wash their hands after handling food waste and rubbish	
Cleaning the kitchen	• Microbes will multiply on all surfaces, in corners, on ceilings, under kitchen units, etc. • Sink units and drains are ideal places for bacteria to grow and multiply	• The kitchen surfaces, walls, floors and sinks are washed and dried at the end of every working day using cleaning chemicals • Twice a week, the refrigerator shelves are cleared and cleaned • Twice a year, the extractor hoods in the kitchen are taken down and cleaned • Twice a year, the kitchen has a deep clean	

We recommend that you also read pages 73–79 for more information on food safety.

Knowledge check – can you remember ... ?

1. What HACCP is?

2. Three examples of critical control points in a food business?

Practice exam question

Short-answer question

1. Food hygiene regulations require food businesses to use a food safety management system called HACCP.

    a) What does HACCP stand for? *[1 mark]*

    b) Explain what is meant by critical control points. *[1 mark]*

    c) Who will check that a food business is obeying food safety laws? *[1 mark]*

Food-related causes of ill health
(including Symptoms and signs of food-induced ill health)

1.4.1
1.4.2

Key learning

There are three main causes of food-related ill health (sometimes called food-induced ill health):

1. Microbes
2. Chemicals, metals and poisonous plants
3. Food allergies and intolerances

Key terms you should try to include in your answers

Bacteria – tiny living things, some of which cause food poisoning

Contaminate – make a food unsafe to eat by infecting it with microbes that will grow and multiply in it

Cross-contamination – how microbes are spread from one place onto some food

Microbes – tiny plants and animals that you can only see under a microscope (also called micro-organisms)

Moulds tiny plants, similar to mushrooms

Pathogenic – something that makes people ill

Toxins – another name for poisons; if something is toxic, it is poisonous

---

Microbes

... know and understand

You need to be able to explain	What you need to know about microbes
What microbes are	They are: • Tiny plants and animals • Often called micro-organisms • So small, you can only see them clearly under a microscope.
What microbes are called	There are three groups: • **Bacteria** • **Moulds** • Yeasts There are many different types of each.
Where microbes come from	• They are found in many places: air, water, soil, dust, dirt, sewage, food, food packaging, clothes, rubbish, surfaces, equipment, people, insects, animals, birds. • They are so small that it is usually impossible to know they are there.
What microbes do to food	• They live on or in food, where they grow and multiply. • They make the food unsafe to eat, and often smell, taste and look bad. • If food is stored, handled, prepared and cooked properly, it is possible to slow down or prevent microbes from growing and multiplying in it.
What makes microbes grow and multiply	• The right temperature • Water (moisture) • Food to eat • Time to grow • The correct level of acid or alkali (pH) In the correct conditions, bacteria can multiply every 15 minutes.

Why microbes make food unsafe and unfit to eat	• They put **waste products** and **toxins** (poisins) into the food.
	• If people eat these, they become ill with **food poisoning**.
	• Large numbers of microbes in a food can make people ill because they irritate the digestive system.
	• Not all microbes make people ill.
	• Some microbes are needed for food production, e.g.:
	  – some types of bacteria are used to make yogurt
	  – yeast is used to make bread
	  – some moulds are used to make cheeses, e.g. Brie, blue Stilton.
	• Microbes that do make people ill are called **pathogenic** (harmful) **microbes**.

What food handlers can do to stop microbes making food unsafe	• **Prevent cross-contamination** by:
	  – **washing hands** before handling food; after handling raw meat, poultry, fish and eggs; after visiting the toilet; after putting food waste in the bin; after sneezing into a tissue
	  – **keeping raw and cooked foods separate** during storage and using separate equipment to prepare them
	  – **using colour-coded boards and knives** to prepare different types of food.
	• **Cook** food to a high temperature (at least 70 °C) which will kill many microbes.
	• **Cool** food to a low temperature (0–5 °C in a refrigerator). Microbes will still grow and multiply, but only very slowly.
	• **Freeze** food (minus 18 °C to minus 22 °C in a freezer). Microbes will become inactive (dormant) **but will still be alive**.
	• **Dry** food by taking out moisture, which will kill many microbes.
	• **Cover** food and store it correctly to stop microbes getting into it.
	• **Preserve** food by killing microbes:
	  – in acid (e.g. vinegar in pickles)
	  – in salt (e.g. dried salted fish)
	  – in sugar (e.g. jam).

Food poisoning

... know and understand

What is food poisoning?

- A common and nasty illness that can lead to serious health problems
- Harmful (pathogenic) bacteria are the main cause of food poisoning

What are the signs (symptoms) that someone has food poisoning?

Signs you cannot see

Headache

Weakness

Feeling cold and shivery

Bad stomach ache

Feeling sick

Not wanting to eat food

Aching muscles

Signs you can see

Diarrhoea

High body temperature

Being sick (vomiting)

Dizziness

Notes

- A person with food poisoning is not likely to have all these signs
- Different types of bacteria cause different symptoms
- A person can start to feel ill after a few hours to several days after they have eaten **contaminated** food
- They may feel ill for several days
- Food poisoning is very dangerous for:
  – young children
  – pregnant women
  – elderly people
  – people who have been ill
  – people who have a weak immune system

Bacteria

...know

This chart will help you remember the most common food-poisoning bacteria:

Bacteria name	Usually found in:	Signs of food poisoning	How long it takes for this bacteria to make someone ill
Bacillus cereus	fresh custard/cream pastries fresh herbs cooked rice		1–16 hours
Campylobacter	Not heat treated Dirty water		48–60 hours
E. coli (Escherichia coli)	Not heat treated Dirty water	+ kidney damage	12–24 hours
Salmonella			12–36 hours
Listeria	Made from untreated milk Unwashed salad Pâté	Feels like having the flu Can cause miscarriage of unborn baby	1–70 days
S. aureus (Staphylococcus aureus)	Not heat treated Hands Runny nose Wound/cut		1–6 hours
Clostridium perfringens			12–18 hours

What happens to bacteria at different temperatures?

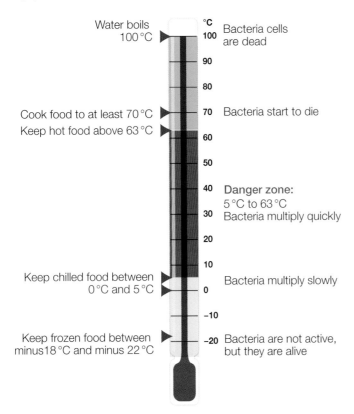

Water boils 100°C — 100 — Bacteria cells are dead

90

80

Cook food to at least 70°C — 70 — Bacteria start to die
Keep hot food above 63°C — 60

50

40 — Danger zone: 5°C to 63°C
30 — Bacteria multiply quickly

20

10

Keep chilled food between 0°C and 5°C — 0 — Bacteria multiply slowly

−10

Keep frozen food between minus 18°C and minus 22°C — −20 — Bacteria are not active, but they are alive

Activity: Which food-poisoning bacteria are found in which foods and liquids?

Look at the pictures of different foods and liquids.

Match which types of food-poisoning bacteria are found in the different foods and liquids.

Remember that more than one type of bacteria may be found in a food or liquid.

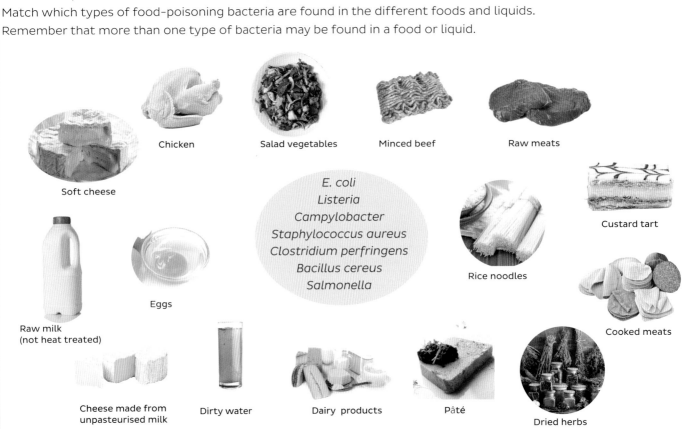

Chicken

Salad vegetables

Minced beef

Raw meats

Soft cheese

Custard tart

E. coli
Listeria
Campylobacter
Staphylococcus aureus
Clostridium perfringens
Bacillus cereus
Salmonella

Rice noodles

Eggs

Cooked meats

Raw milk (not heat treated)

Cheese made from unpasteurised milk

Dirty water

Dairy products

Pâté

Dried herbs

Activity: Storing foods

Look at the images of the foods in the table below.

For each food, choose the best way of storing it from column A, and the reason why you would store it this way from column B (the first one has been done for you as an example):

A How would you store it?	B Why would you store it this way?
1 In a refrigerator	A It is a low-risk food that does not need to be chilled
2 In a well-ventilated cupboard or room (not in a kitchen)	B It is a high-risk food so must be chilled to slow microbial growth
3 In a kitchen cupboard	C It is a high-risk food because it has been opened and must be chilled
4 In an airtight container	D It is likely to go stale and soft because it will pick up moisture from the air
5 In a dark, cool place	E It may be contaminated by insects if it is left uncovered
6 Uncovered in a kitchen or other room	F It is likely to react to light and become a health risk
	G It needs time to ripen
	H It will lose water and wilt if left in a warm place

Food		How would you store it?	Why?
	A raw chicken	1	B
	1. A can of baked beans		
	2. An opened carton of long-life milk		
	3. An opened packet of flour		
	4. Shortbread		
	5. Raw potatoes		
	6. A hard mango		
	7. A lettuce		
	8. A pack of fresh minced beef		
	9. Left-over meat curry		
	10. An iced fruit birthday cake		

Moulds

...know

- Moulds make food unsafe and unfit to eat by sending out tiny spores ('seeds') which land on the surface of food
- The spores **germinate** (start to grow) and send down roots into the food if conditions are right
- Moulds can be seen growing on foods
- Moulds make food taste and smell very unpleasant
- The waste products produced by the mould go into the food through the roots
- The waste products contain poisons (toxins) that can make people ill
- The waste products can stay in the food even if the mould you can see is cut off

Yeasts

...know

- Yeasts are found in the air. They make food unsafe and unfit to eat by settling on food and breaking down (**fermenting**) any sugars it contains into **CO_2 gas** and alcohol
- Yeasts growing on foods can be seen as they produce small brown spots on the surface
- Foods such as fruit yogurts, dried fruit and fruit juices can be spoiled by yeasts
- Wild yeasts are used to make sourdough bread, which is safe to eat

Apple with yeasts growing on the skin

Chemicals

...know

Sometimes food becomes contaminated with chemicals that are poisonous and will make people ill very soon after they have entered their body. Some other chemicals gradually build up in the body over many months or years, and may eventually cause illnesses such as cancer or liver and kidney failure. Chemicals may get into food because of **environmental pollution**, e.g. from factories that let chemicals get into rivers and the sea or soil.

To avoid food being contaminated with chemicals in the food industry:

- Food handlers **must not**:
  - Accidentally add too much of a food additive, e.g. food colourings or preservatives, to food products when they are being made
  - Use too much of a cleaning product when cleaning equipment in a food factory or catering kitchen
  - Store a chemical, e.g. bleach, in an unlabelled container, as it may be added by mistake to a food.
- Farmers **must not**:
  - Use too much of a chemical pesticide or fertiliser on plant foods that are being grown.

Did you know?

Poisonous plants

Some plants contain natural substances that are poisonous to humans, e.g.:

- Mouldy nuts and cereals, e.g. corn.

  The mould produces a poisonous substance.

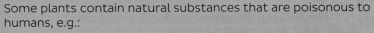

- Raw red kidney beans.

  These contain a poison and must be boiled for at least 15 minutes to destroy it. Canned red kidney beans have already been cooked and are safe to eat.

- Rhubarb leaves contain a poisonous acid.

  The stems are safe to eat.

- Poisonous wild mushrooms.
  Many wild mushrooms are poisonous. The picture shows the 'death cap' mushroom, which is one the most poisonous fungi known to exist. If eaten, the poison it contains quickly damages the liver and other organs in the body. It has caused many deaths.

Did you know?
Metals

Some metals are poisonous if they get into the body, e.g. aluminium, copper, lead, iron, tin, zinc. Some old cooking pans, which were made from aluminium, copper, zinc or iron would react with acids in foods such as lemons, rhubarb, tomatoes and wine and the metal would get into the food. Pans made from stainless steel do not react with acids.

Knowledge check – can you remember...?

1. What a microbe is?
2. Two types of microbes?
3. Four places where microbes are found?
4. Three things that microbes need to grow and multiply?
5. Why microbes make food unsafe and unfit to eat?
6. Two ways that food handlers can prevent the cross-contamination of microbes into food?
7. What happens to microbes when food is frozen?
8. What happens to microbes when food is stored in a refrigerator?
9. Three signs (symptoms) of food poisoning that cannot be seen?
10. Two signs (symptoms) of food poisoning that can be seen?
11. Two groups of people for whom food poisoning is very dangerous?
12. The names of two bacteria that cause food poisoning?
13. Two foods where salmonella is often found?
14. How moulds start to grow on foods?
15. What bacteria do in the temperature danger zone?
16. Why stainless-steel pans are used in food preparation?
17. Why food should be cooked to at least 70°C?
18. Why cleaning chemicals must not be stored near foods in unlabelled containers?

Practice exam questions

Short-answer questions

1. List two main causes of food-related illness. *[2 marks]*
2. State two reasons why microbes make food unfit to eat. *[2 marks]*
3. Suggest three ways in which food handlers can stop microbes making food unsafe. *[3 marks]*
4. Explain why the following practices are important:
   a) Keeping hot chicken curry above 63°C in serving dishes at a buffet. *[1 mark]*
   b) Keeping fresh cream cakes at 0°C to 5°C in a bakery shop. *[1 mark]*

Key terms you should try to include in your answers

Allergen – something that causes an allergy

Anaphylaxis – a very severe and life-threatening allergic reaction that affects breathing, the heart, the digestive system and the skin

Food allergy – a condition where the body's immune system reacts to certain foods, which causes a range of symptoms

Food intolerance – a long-term health condition where certain foods make someone unwell

Key learning

Food handlers need to know about what causes people to have a **food allergy** or **intolerance** so they can:

- Avoid contaminating foods with food **allergens** (ingredients that people are allergic to) when preparing food
- Tell customers about the ingredients in the food they are selling or serving them
- Make sure that menus show all the ingredients they contain, so that customers avoid buying foods they know they cannot eat
- Recognise and know what to do if a customer becomes ill with a food allergy.

Food allergies

... know and understand

What is a food allergy?	What are the signs (symptoms) that someone has a food allergy?		Notes
• A food allergy is a serious and possibly life-threatening reaction to certain foods • It is caused by the body reacting to something in the food (an allergen) • A severe allergic reaction is called **anaphylaxis**, which can cause death – the person must have medical treatment immediately • Someone who is allergic to foods must: – avoid eating them – read food labels carefully to see if those foods are in the ingredients list (food allergens are shown in bold lettering on food labels).	*Signs that happen inside the body and that may not be seen* • The mouth, tongue and throat swell • The person cannot breathe, speak or swallow properly • Wheezing • Stomach pain • Feeling sick – may be sick • Blood pressure drops • Person may collapse and become unconscious.	*Signs that can be seen* • Skin becomes red • A raised, red/pink itchy rash shows on the skin (called hives) 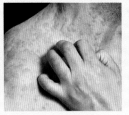 • The skin swells – often on the face • The nose and eyes itch • The lips and eyelids swell. 	An allergic reaction can happen within a few seconds, minutes or hours after eating the food. If someone has an allergic reaction: • Stay calm and call 999 for an ambulance • Make the patient comfortable • If they have an EpiPen, use it (it will control their symptoms while they are going to hospital). People who work for a hospitality and catering business should be trained to use an EpiPen. An EpiPen 

The most common foods that cause allergies are:

Eggs

Milk and dairy foods

Fish, shellfish and crustaceans

Peanuts

Soya

Other nuts, e.g. almonds, hazelnuts, walnuts, etc.

Seeds

Citrus fruits (oranges, lemons, limes, grapefruit)

Strawberries

Kiwi fruit

Mustard

Lupin beans/flour, found in a variety of foods including baked goods, pasta, noodles, sauces, burgers and sausages

Celeriac

Celery

Some preservatives, e.g. sulphur dioxide and sulphites

Food intolerance

Food intolerance happens when something in certain foods makes a person feel unwell most of the time but is not as life-threatening as a food allergy can be. People with a food intolerance may have a range of symptoms:

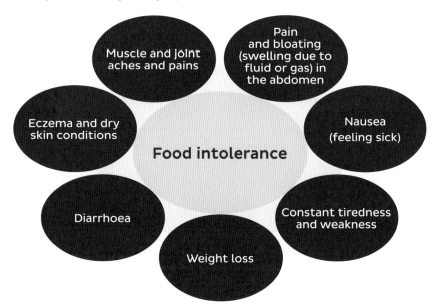

Muscle and joint aches and pains

Pain and bloating (swelling due to fluid or gas) in the abdomen

Eczema and dry skin conditions

Food intolerance

Nausea (feeling sick)

Diarrhoea

Constant tiredness and weakness

Weight loss

Lactose-/dairy-free food products

Lactose intolerance

...know and understand

Lactose is the natural sugar found in dairy milk (from cows, goats, sheep, etc.). People who have lactose intolerance cannot digest (break down and absorb) lactose in their body, so the bacteria in their large intestine break it down instead. This produces a lot of gas and causes bloating (swelling) of the abdomen (belly/tummy), flatulence (wind/gas), abdominal pain, diarrhoea and nausea (feeling sick). People with lactose intolerance must not eat dairy foods or foods that contain them.

Which foods contain lactose?

All dairy foods (milk, cheese, yogurt, cream, butter, crème fraiche, sour cream, cream cheese, whey and milk powder), and any foods that contain them (e.g. cakes, biscuits, desserts, some snack foods and sweets, some ready meals, sauces, custard, chocolate, some vegetable fat spreads, ice cream, etc.) contain lactose.

⚠️ *Remember!*
Eggs are not a dairy food and do not contain lactose.

It is possible to buy lactose-free or dairy-free food products such as milks and yogurts.

The small intestine

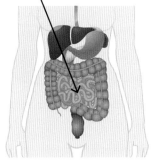

Coeliac disease

...know and understand

Coeliac disease is a condition that involves the body's immune system, but it is not an allergy.

The small intestine in the body is lined with thousands of tiny finger-like projections called villi. Normally, the villi allow lots of nutrients from the food we eat to be absorbed and then sent into the bloodstream to go round the body.

Coeliac disease is caused by the immune system not tolerating gluten, which is found in wheat, barley, oats and rye and food products that contain them. This causes the villi in the small intestine to become damaged, so they cannot absorb enough nutrients into the body:

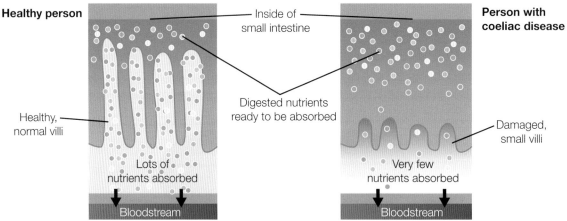

Healthy person — Inside of small intestine — **Person with coeliac disease**

Healthy, normal villi — Digested nutrients ready to be absorbed — Damaged, small villi

Lots of nutrients absorbed — Very few nutrients absorbed

Bloodstream — Bloodstream

If someone has coeliac disease:
- They will not have enough nutrients going into their body
- They will not have enough energy and will be tired much of the time
- They can lose weight and become ill
- Children with coeliac disease might not grow properly.

Someone with coeliac disease must not eat any food containing gluten. This will allow the villi in their small intestine to gradually get better and work properly.

Which foods contain gluten?

Gluten is found in wheat, barley, oats and rye and food products that contain them, e.g. pasta, bread, pizza, cakes, pies, pastries, buns, croissants, biscuits, snack bars, crackers, seasonings and spice mixes, breakfast cereals, sausages, burgers and other processed meats, couscous, semolina, soy sauce, noodles, malt vinegar, some beers and ales.

It is possible to buy gluten-free food products in most supermarkets.

They often show a gluten free symbol, like this one:

Aspartame and PKU

... know and understand

Aspartame is an artificial food sweetener that is used in many food products (e.g. 'diet' soft drinks, confectionery, sugar-free chewing gum, desserts, vitamin supplements, milk drinks, etc.). It contains a substance that must be avoided by people who have a health condition called PKU, as it can cause brain damage, especially in babies and young children.

Monosodium glutamate (MSG)

... know and understand

MSG is a salt that is found naturally in many foods, e.g. broccoli, peas, cheese, tomatoes, mushrooms and soy sauce.

It is also sold as a white powder that is used in the food industry to make the flavour of savoury foods taste stronger.

Eating a lot of foods containing MSG may lead to symptoms of food intolerance in some people, such as reddening of the skin, headache, drowsiness, numbness and tingling sensations in the back, arms and face.

Activity: Adapting menus for people with food intolerances

Look at the lunch menu choices below for patients in a hospital:

Getwell Hospital

Lunch menu

Choose 1 item from each group:

A.

Cream of chicken soup with bread roll

Mixed leaf and avocado salad with olive oil dressing

Vegan lentil pâté with wheat crackers

*

B.

Roasted vegetables and pasta in cheese sauce

Baked chicken breast, stuffed with mozzarella cheese and herbs, served with seasonal vegetables

Vegan chickpea and coconut curry

*

C.

Fresh fruit salad

Chocolate mousse, served with a shortbread biscuit

Traditional apple crumble and custard

*

1. Describe and explain how the chefs could change the ingredients in some of the menu choices to suit a patient who has lactose intolerance.

2. Describe and explain how the chefs could change the ingredients in some of the menu choices to suit a patient who has coeliac disease.

Knowledge check – can you remember...?

1. What a food allergy is?

2. What food intolerance is?

3. Two things that a food handler should do to help people who have food allergies or intolerances?

4. Three visible signs (symptoms) that someone is having an allergic reaction to food?

5. Five of the most common foods that cause allergies?

6. Three visible or non-visible signs (symptoms) that someone has a food intolerance?

7. Two signs (symptoms) that someone has lactose intolerance?

8. Two foods someone with lactose intolerance should not eat?

9. Two foods that someone with coeliac disease should not eat?

10. Two visible or non-visible signs (symptoms) that someone has coeliac disease?

Practice exam questions

Short-answer questions

1. Suggest one way in which a waiter in a restaurant can help a customer who has food allergies to choose from the menu. *[1 mark]*

2. How are food allergens shown on a food label? *[1 mark]*

3. List three foods that someone who has lactose intolerance cannot eat. *[3 marks]*

4. List three foods that a person with coeliac disease cannot eat. *[3 marks]*

Stretch and challenge question

A catering company has been asked to prepare a cold buffet lunch for a group of twenty people on a training course. Four of the people have coeliac disease.

Plan a menu for:
- Four savoury main course dishes, plus three side dishes/accompaniments
- Two desserts, plus two accompaniments.

The menu must include some dishes that people with coeliac disease will be able to eat.

Explain which dishes are suitable for people with coeliac disease and why.

Explain how the catering company will enable people to identify and choose the dishes that are suitable for them to eat.

Key learning

Many people are affected by food poisoning each year.

Food poisoning can be prevented.

Food safety laws make sure that food is safe to eat.

Food safety laws

...be aware of

Food safety laws protect:

Consumers	Food businesses
• To stop them getting food poisoning	• To make sure all food handlers are trained in food safety
• To make sure all food businesses have high food safety standards	• To make sure working conditions are good so food handlers can obey the law
• To take action if a food business breaks the law	• To prevent consumers making false claims about being ill after eating food

All parts of the food industry are covered by food safety laws, including:

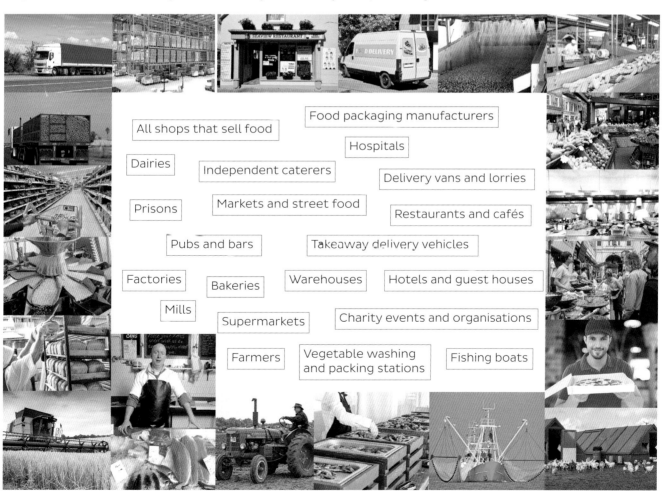

All shops that sell food

Food packaging manufacturers

Hospitals

Dairies

Independent caterers

Delivery vans and lorries

Prisons

Markets and street food

Restaurants and cafés

Pubs and bars

Takeaway delivery vehicles

Factories

Bakeries

Warehouses

Hotels and guest houses

Mills

Supermarkets

Charity events and organisations

Farmers

Vegetable washing and packing stations

Fishing boats

Food premises (buildings, kitchens, storerooms, washrooms, etc.) where food is prepared

...know and understand

These premises:

Must be:

Clean and well maintained

Hygienic

Easy to keep clean

Free from pests

Well lit

Well ventilated

Must have:

A supply of safe drinking water

Enough space for people to work in

Good drainage to get rid of dirty water

Good, hygienic staff washing and toilet facilities

A good waste disposal system

Responsibilities of food handlers

...know and understand

Food handlers must have good personal hygiene:

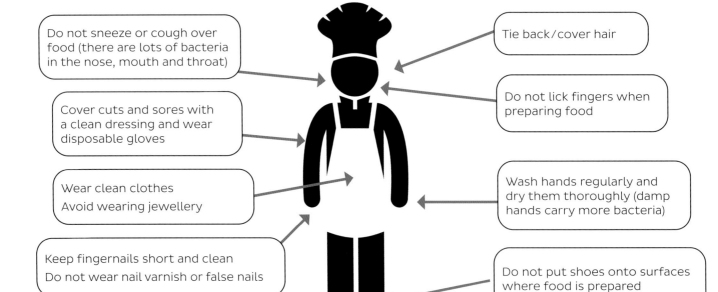

Do not sneeze or cough over food (there are lots of bacteria in the nose, mouth and throat)

Cover cuts and sores with a clean dressing and wear disposable gloves

Wear clean clothes
Avoid wearing jewellery

Keep fingernails short and clean
Do not wear nail varnish or false nails

Tie back/cover hair

Do not lick fingers when preparing food

Wash hands regularly and dry them thoroughly (damp hands carry more bacteria)

Do not put shoes onto surfaces where food is prepared

Always wash your hands:
Before: handling food
After: using the toilet; coughing, sneezing, blowing your nose; touching money; handling rubbish and bins; touching animals/insects; coming in from outside; handling raw foods.

Food handlers must **prevent cross-contamination** of bacteria:

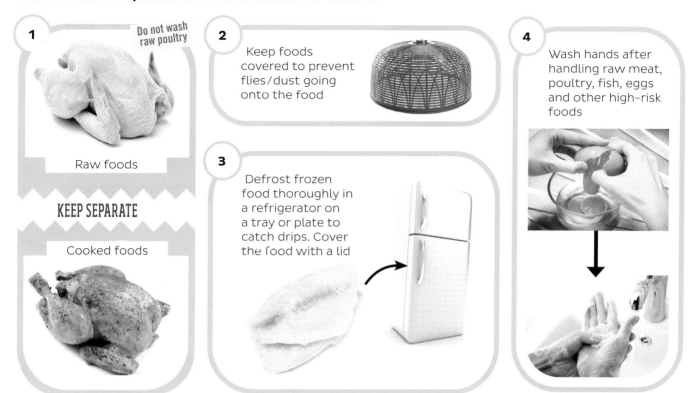

1 Do not wash raw poultry

Raw foods

KEEP SEPARATE

Cooked foods

2 Keep foods covered to prevent flies/dust going onto the food

3 Defrost frozen food thoroughly in a refrigerator on a tray or plate to catch drips. Cover the food with a lid

4 Wash hands after handling raw meat, poultry, fish, eggs and other high-risk foods

Food handlers must store, cook, cool and serve food properly:

Storing food   ...know and understand

1. Store food correctly as soon as possible after buying it.

2. Do not leave high-risk foods for any length of time in a warm place such as a car boot on a sunny day.

3. Check use-by and best-before dates regularly. Use up older foods first. This is called stock rotation.

4. Refrigerators and freezers:
   - Check internal temperatures regularly (0 °C to 5 °C refrigerators, minus 18 °C to minus 22 °C freezers)
   - Check door seals are working
   - Defrost regularly to keep them working properly
   - Place away from the cooker or boiler in a kitchen so they can work normally
   - Do not leave refrigerator doors open for any length of time.

Cooking, cooling down and serving food

- Cook food thoroughly. Check core temperature is at **70 °C or hotter** for at least 2 minutes, using a food probe
- Hot cooked food must be kept at **63 °C or above**
- Left-over hot cooked food should be cooled to **5 °C or cooler** within **1½ hours**
- Left-over cooked food must only be reheated **once** to a minimum core temperature of **70 °C** for at least 2 minutes
- Use **different utensils** to serve different foods to prevent cross-contamination.

Using a food probe

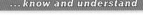

1. Reset to zero
2. Sterilise/use antibacterial wipe to clean probe
3. Insert metal probe into core of food
4. Do not touch hot pan with probe
5. Allow temperature to stabilise (**70 °C or hotter for 2 minutes)**
6. Sterilise/use antibacterial wipe after use.

Activity: Hygiene in the kitchen

Scenario: Read the story below about a chef working in the kitchen of a busy café.

Find ten things to do with kitchen and personal hygiene that the chef did wrong when he was preparing food.

Sam arrived late at the café, so quickly got ready to start work. He forgot to bring a clean uniform to work, so he put on the dirty one he had worn the day before, which he had rolled up and put in his locker after work instead of taking it home because he was going out for the evening. Sam used the toilet and went straight to the kitchen without washing his hands as he didn't want to be told off for being late. He was not feeling particularly well as he had a sore throat and runny nose and kept sneezing.

Sam's first job was to prepare some raw chicken. He could not find the red chopping board, so used a yellow one instead. He sneezed three times and wiped his nose on the same tissue, which he put down on the worktop and did not wash his hands afterwards.

After preparing the chicken, Sam wiped his hands on a wet dishcloth, which he then used to wipe the worktop and the chopping board. He left the chicken in an uncovered tray on the worktop.

His next job was to prepare 36 raw eggs that would be used later to make omelettes. Sam cracked the eggs into a bowl, whisked them and wiped his hands on his apron. He left the whisked eggs in a bowl next to the chicken he had prepared. He then went straight on to his next job, which was to make some salad.

Sam took the salad ingredients from the boxes in the storeroom and prepared them on a green chopping board. Some of the lettuce had soil on the leaves, which Sam brushed off with his fingers.

Sam then had a coffee break and as it was a warm, sunny day, he went outside and sat on the rubbish bins in the yard behind the café. After his break, he returned to the kitchen and noticed a few flies round the uncovered chicken, so brushed them off with his hands and put the chicken in the refrigerator.

Food labelling regulations

...be aware of

Food labels tell (inform) people about the food they are choosing to buy.

In the UK, food labelling is controlled by law by:
- **Department of Health and Social Care** – nutritional labelling
- **Food Standards Agency** – food safety labelling.

Food labels must be:
- Clear and easy to read
- Easy to understand
- Easy to see
- Truthful about the food inside.

By law, the following information must be shown on a food label:

1	Nutritional information
2	Ingredients that are known food allergens
3	List of ingredients (in descending order of amount)
4	The quantity of certain ingredients
5	The name of the food product
6	A description of the food product if it is not obvious to the consumer from the name what the food product actually is
7	Indication of how long the food is safe to eat (the shelf-life of the food product) by 'use-by' or 'best-before' date
8	The weight/quantity of the food product
9	Place of origin (provenance) of the food product or a specific ingredient
10	Cooking or usage instructions
11	Storage conditions and instructions
12	Contact details of food product manufacturer, distributor or retailer

5 Savoury quiche

Egg and cheese flan with broccoli and red pepper in a shortcrust pastry case

2 Allergy Information: Contains milk, egg, gluten (wheat flour)

1 Nutritional Information:

Nutrient	Per 100g	Per serving (90g)
Energy	1038kJ/248kcal	934kJ/223 kcal
Fat of which:	15g	13.5g
Saturates	6g	5g
Monounsaturates	5g	4.6g
Polyunsaturates	2.7g	2.4g
Carbohydrate of which:	21g	19g
Sugars	1.8g	1.6g
Starch	18.2g	16.5g
Fibre	1g	0.7g
Protein	8g	7g
Salt	0.5g	0.4g

Serves 6

7 Use by 15 March

8 Net weight 540g

9 Made with British grown broccoli

6 Ingredients: wheat flour, vegetable fat spread, whole milk, eggs, cheddar cheese, broccoli (15%), red pepper (10%), seasoning, flavourings.

10 Cooking instructions:
Oven: remove outer packaging and place on an oven tray. Heat for 20 minutes at Gas 4/180°C.
Can be eaten cold.

11 Storage instructions:
Keep refrigerated between 0°C and below 5°C.
Consume by the use-by date.
Can be frozen. Follow star ratings on your freezer.

12 Contact information:
Made in the UK by Freshly Foods, London.
www.freshlyfoods.uk

freshlyfoods

9 781908 682789

Knowledge check – can you remember...?

1. One way that food safety laws protect consumers?

2. One way that food safety laws protect food businesses?

3. Two things that all food businesses must do under the Food Safety Act?

4. Two things that all food businesses must do under the Food Hygiene Regulations?

5. Three things that food premises must be?

6. Three personal hygiene rules that food handlers must follow?

7. Two rules about cooking food safely?

8. Two rules about food labels?

Practice exam questions

Short-answer questions

1. List five responsibilities of food handlers to make sure that food is safe to eat. *(5 marks)*

2. Food storage is a critical control point in food production. It is very important that food is stored correctly to keep it safe to eat.
   a) What will happen to bacteria in chilled foods if the foods are not stored at the correct temperature (i.e. too warm)? *[1 mark]*
   b) State three controls and checks that a food business should use to prevent a food safety risk in frozen and refrigerated foods. *[3 marks]*

Stretch and challenge question

The temperature of food during cooking, serving, chilling and storage is a critical control point. Food probes are often used in a kitchen to check the temperature of foods.

a) Justify why a food probe should be used to check the temperature of food. *[1 mark]*

b) Explain how to use a food probe to check the temperature of some oven-baked chicken legs. *[5 marks]*

c) Describe how you should safely cool, store and reuse left-over cooked meat curry. *[4 marks]*

Key learning

In the UK, Environmental Health Officers (EHOs) are employed by local authorities.

EHOs carry out inspections in businesses where food is sold to the public.

EHOs investigate complaints from members of the public about food businesses.

EHOs also investigate complaints from members of the public and employees about non-food problems in hospitality and catering businesses.

The Food Standards Agency sets out what EHOs have to do during inspections to make sure that food businesses follow food safety laws.

Why are food businesses inspected by EHOs?   ...know and understand

Inspections of food businesses are carried out to make sure that:

Food is stored, handled and cooked hygienically and safely

Pests cannot contaminate the food

Food is safe to eat

The food business's building is in good condition and regularly cleaned

Food handlers are trained in food safety

Food handlers have good personal hygiene

The food business is using HACCP

What does an EHO do during an inspection?   ...know and understand

By law, an EHO can:

Enter a food business without an appointment for an on-the-spot inspection

Look at all the records the business keeps, e.g. staff training, refrigerator temperatures, etc.

Check the use-by and best-before dates on foods being stored in the business

Take food away if it is unsafe to eat

Take food samples away to test for bacteria

Tell the business to make hygiene improvements by a certain date

Watch how the food is handled during storage, preparation, cooking and serving

Close the business immediately if it is dangerous to the health of customers

Take photographs / videos of what is seen during an inspection

EHOs also investigate:

- Complaints about a food business
- Outbreaks of food poisoning and infectious disease
- Complaints about poor standards of health and safety in hospitality and catering businesses.

Their other duties include:

- Giving evidence to a judge if a business is taken to court for breaking the law
- Granting licences to food businesses
- Deciding the hygiene rating for a food business
- Giving talks at public enquiries, meetings and exhibitions
- Educating and training people about food safety and environmental health.

Activity: What would the EHO do?

For each scenario below, choose one or more of the actions (listed on the right) that the EHO could carry out to deal with the situation.

Scenario 1

A member of the public has contacted the EHO to complain that they have been ill with food poisoning after eating a meat pie from a takeaway shop three days ago.

Scenario 2

A member of the public reports seeing several rats on and near some rubbish bins that belong to a restaurant. The bins are reported to be overflowing with food waste.

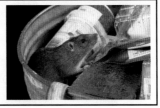

Scenario 3

During an on-the-spot inspection of a restaurant kitchen, the EHO finds the following:

- Cooked rice being kept on the kitchen floor in a bucket covered with a dirty cloth
- Mouse droppings in food preparation bowls and on the shelves
- Several staff wearing very dirty kitchen uniform
- Uncovered raw chicken being stored next to (and touching) cooked meat pies in a refrigerator that has an internal temperature of 11 °C.

Raw chicken

Scenario 4

A small bed and breakfast business is reported to the EHO by a customer who has stayed the night there. The customer was concerned about:

- A leak of sewage at the back of the toilet onto the floor in the bathroom he used
- Patches of black mould on the walls and ceiling of the bedroom he stayed in
- Being bitten by bed bugs during the night
- Being served his cooked breakfast on a cracked plate and being given a fork that had dried food stuck between the prongs.

Black mould on a wall

Bed bug (not actual size!)

Actions that an EHO could carry out:

1. Visit the business without an appointment to carry out an inspection

2. Ask for evidence of illness (e.g. a letter from a doctor) from the person who has made a complaint against a food business

3. Take food samples away to test for bacteria

4. Take samples of water, pests, faeces, etc. away to identify and test, and use as evidence

5. Check that the business is using pest-control equipment, e.g. traps, wire meshes, fly killers

6. Take photographs / videos of what is seen during an inspection

7. Look at all the records the business keeps, e.g. staff training, refrigerator temperatures, maintenance of equipment and plumbing, etc.

8. Remove (seize / confiscate) food being sold by the business because it is unsafe to eat

9. Tell the business to make hygiene, food safety and / or other improvements by a certain date

10. Close the business immediately because it is unsafe for customers to buy food or stay there.

Knowledge check – can you remember…?

1. Four reasons why food businesses are inspected by EHOs?
2. Four things that EHOs can do by law when they inspect a food business?
3. What an EHO can do if the food business is dangerous to the health of customers?
4. What an EHO can do if there are a few things that need improving in a hospitality and catering business?

Practice exam questions

Short-answer questions

1. State three reasons why Environmental Health Officers inspect food businesses. [3 marks]

2. State three things that an Environmental Health Officer is allowed to do by law during the inspection of a food business. [3 marks]

3. Apart from inspecting food businesses, Environmental Health Officers have other duties. State two other duties that they have. [2 marks]

Remember!

Always read a question carefully and several times before you start to answer it.

Make sure you understand what the question is asking you to do.

Highlight any key words in the question so you do not miss out anything in your answer.

Key learning

The Unit 1 Assessment is a **written examination (exam)** that you will sit when you have completed the whole Technical Award course. The exam lasts for **1 hour and 20 minutes**. It is worth **80 marks**, which is **40%** of the Technical Award qualification.

You must answer **all** of the exam questions.

This section of the book has been designed to help you understand the terminology (words/sentences) that is used for the Assessment in Unit 1. It includes information, advice and tips to help guide you to success in this written assessment.

You will learn about several important aspects of the assessment:
- How it is structured
- The different types and styles of question that could appear in the assessment
- What you may be assessed on
- Useful hints and tips to help you through the assessment.

This is how the exam will be arranged:

Time allowed: 1 hour and 20 minutes
All questions must be answered
Maximum total mark = 80 marks

Study tip
Be prepared and ready!

This chapter will help you get ready for your written exam.

The written exam is worth 40% of your final grade, so it is important to be well prepared for it so that you do your best.

If you are well prepared, you will be:

- More relaxed and less nervous

- More confident about answering questions

- More likely to be successful and to achieve your potential.

Study tip
During the course

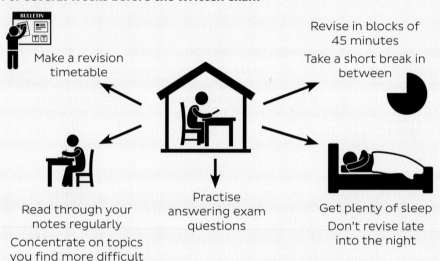

Read your notes after each lesson to check your understanding

If you are unsure about a topic, ask for help

Make revision notes/mind maps/revision cards

Organise your notes and keep them together

Learn each section as you go through the course

Study tip
For several weeks before the written exam

Make a revision timetable

Revise in blocks of 45 minutes
Take a short break in between

Read through your notes regularly
Concentrate on topics you find more difficult

Practise answering exam questions

Get plenty of sleep
Don't revise late into the night

Study and revision tips

To help you remember a topic more effectively:

- 'Teach' a topic to a friend or adult and then test each other
- Get someone to ask you questions about a topic
- Cut down the topic into small pieces of information
- Make a mind map of a topic using key words/colours/pictures
- Make notes with key points/ words highlighted
- Make some revision flash cards with key words/definitions on them
- Read the information several times in the weeks before your assessment
- Test yourself with practice questions and quizzes on different topics
- Produce a glossary of key words and terms with their meanings.

Study tip
On the day of the examination

Important advice you must follow **before** you start answering the questions in this assessment:

Read the instructions on the front page of the examination paper carefully.

These instructions tell you what you must do to make sure you give your name, school centre number and examination number correctly, and also how to fill in the examination paper with your answers. **MAKE SURE YOU FOLLOW ALL THE INSTRUCTIONS!**

Write clearly (and not too small), so that the examiner can read your answers – if they cannot read your answers, they cannot give you any marks.

Read each question at least twice before you start to answer it, to make sure you are absolutely clear about what the question is asking you to do.

What will you be assessed on?

The written exam will ask you questions about Unit 1: The Hospitality and Catering Industry, which covers a range of topics in the following sections:

1.1: Hospitality and catering provision

1.2: How hospitality and catering providers operate

1.3: Health and safety in hospitality and catering

1.4: Food safety in hospitality and catering.

You will have seen, throughout the book, that topics are labelled as follows, according to the way in which you should develop your knowledge, understanding and skills in each, i.e.:

- Learners should know
- Learners should know and understand
- Learners should be aware of
- Learners should be able to.

These labels are called **specification stems** (see pages 96–98) and, for the Unit 1 written exam, these stems mean that questions on certain topics will need to be answered in a particular way:

Learners should know – in exam questions for these topics, you will need to recall facts in either a *short answer question* or *a stimulus question* (see page 109), or *a list* or *category*.

Learners should know and understand – in exam questions for these topics, you will need to show your understanding by recalling facts and either explain/justify/analyse/describe/review/identify/suggest or recommend them in a *graduated lead-in question* (see pages 110–111), a *data response question* (see page 111) or a *free response question* (see page 112).

Learners should be aware of – you will not be asked for details of these topics in written exam questions, but you will need to show the examiner that you are aware of them in your answers, e.g. awareness of laws about food safety.

Learners should be able to – in these exam questions you need to apply what you know to a **specific situation (scenario)**. This will be set out in part of a question and you will be asked questions about it and to suggest or recommend an answer that is suitable, in either a *data response question* or a *free response question*.

The chart below shows how each topic in each section of Unit 1 is labelled:

Topics	Specification stems			
	You should know	You should know and understand	You should be aware of	You should be able to
1.1 Hospitality and Catering provision				
1.1.1 Hospitality and catering providers		1. Commercial and non-commercial hospitality and catering provision 2. Types of service in commercial and non-commercial provision: • Food service • Residential service 3. Standards and ratings for hotels, guest houses and restaurants		
1.1.2 Working in the hospitality and catering industry		1. Employment roles and responsibilities of: • Front-of-house staff • Kitchen brigade • Management • Housekeeping staff 2. Specific personal attributes, qualifications and experience an employer would look for		

1.1.3 Working conditions in the hospitality and catering industry		1. Employment contracts and working hours • Permanent • Temporary/seasonal • Casual • Full-time • Part-time • Zero hours contract	1. Remuneration and benefits: • A salary • A wage • Holiday entitlement • Pension • Sickness pay • Rates of pay • Tips, bonuses and rewards 2. Need for staff in the industry: • Supply and demand • Staff needs during peak times or large events • Seasonal staff
1.1.4 Contributing factors to the success of hospitality and catering provision		1. Basic costs of running a hospitality and catering business 2. Calculating gross profit and net profit 3. How new technology impacts the hospitality and catering industry in a positive way 4. Positive and negative effects of media types on hospitality and catering businesses	1. How the economy can affect the hospitality and catering industry • strength of the economy • Value added tax (vat) • Value of the pound and exchange rate. 2. Environmental impact of the hospitality and catering industry • Seasonality • Sustainability: reduce, reuse, recycle

1.2 How hospitality and catering provisions operate

	You should know	You should know and understand	You should be aware of	You should be able to
1.2.1 The operation of the front and back of house		1. Documentation required in a catering kitchen, e.g. stock control, ordering, invoices, delivery notes, food safety and health and safety documentation.	1. The workflow of the front and back of house 2. Equipment and materials needed and used in catering provision/kitchens 3. Dress code requirements for front- and back-of-house staff	
1.2.2 Customer requirements in hospitality and catering		1. How hospitality and catering provision meets the requirements of: • Customer needs, customer rights and inclusion (disability) • Equality		
1.2.3 Hospitality and catering provision to meet specific requirements		1. Hospitality and catering provision for the ever-changing customer climate: • Customer requirements • Customer expectations • Customer demographics (age, location, income, etc.)		

97

1.3 Health and safety in hospitality and catering

	You should know	You should know and understand	You should be aware of	You should be able to
1.3.1 Health and safety in hospitality and catering	1. The importance of being able to complete accident forms and risk assessments 2. That employers are responsible for the health and safety training of all their staff		1. Responsibilities of employers and employees for personal safety in the workplace 2. Laws relating to health and safety in the workplace	1. Complete an accident form and a risk assessment.
1.3.2 Food safety		1. The importance and principles of HACCP		1. Identify critical control points, and reduce and solve risks 2. Decide on what actions to take if something goes wrong 3. Complete a HACCP document 4. Complete records to show procedures are working

1.4 Food safety in hospitality and catering

	You should know	You should know and understand	You should be aware of	You should be able to
1.4.1 Food-related causes of ill health	1. That illness is caused by bacteria, allergies, chemicals, food intolerance 2. The following bacteria that cause food poisoning: • *Bacillus cereus* • *Campylobacter* • *Clostridium perfringens* • *e-coli* • *Listeria* • *Salmonella* • *Staphylococcus aureus*	The following food-related causes of ill health: 1. Food allergies: • celery/celeriac • crustaceans • dairy products • eggs • fish • kiwi fruit, citrus fruit and strawberries • lupin • molluscs • mustard • nuts • peanuts • sesame and other seeds • soya 2. Food intolerance: • gluten • lactose • aspartame • MSG	1. Food labelling regulations 2. Food hygiene regulations 2006 3. Food Safety Act 1990	
1.4.2 Symptoms and signs of food-induced ill health		1. Visible symptoms of food-induced ill health 2. Non-visible symptoms of food-induced ill health		
1.4.3 Preventative control measures of food-induced ill health		1. Control measures to prevent food-induced ill health		
1.4.4 The Environmental Health Officer (EHO)		1. The role and responsibilities of the Environmental Health Officer		

Key learning

Part of one of the questions in the Unit 1 written exam may give you a scenario to read.

A scenario describes the specific needs of different groups of people who are in a particular place (location) for a particular reason (occasion).

To answer the question, you will need to be able to do the following:

1. Write out clearly the types of hospitality and catering choices that you think would be most suitable for the needs of the people described in the scenario

2. Give good reasons for (justify) your choices.

 Remember!

Always read a question carefully several times before you start to answer it.

Make sure you understand what the question is asking you to do.

Highlight any key words in the question so you do not miss out anything in your answer.

Here is a list of hospitality and catering choices:

Hospitality choices

- Hotels: budget (low cost), five-star, spa, luxury, hotel resort, boutique (small, in tourist areas), business, eco-friendly
- Bed and breakfast businesses
- Hostels
- Caravan and campsites, family cabins
- Clubs and casinos
- Sports stadiums
- Concert/gig venues
- Visitor and tourist attractions, e.g. theme parks, museums, historical buildings, spas, aquariums, safari parks, gardens and parks
- Holiday camps

Catering choices

- Cafés, tearooms and coffee shops (self-service or waited at table)
- Takeaway and fast food outlets
- Restaurants and bistros
- Canteens and dining rooms
- Pubs and bars
- Mobile/roadside food vans; street food stalls; pop-up restaurants
- Self-catering facilities
- Play/activity centres with cafés
- Set meal, carvery meal, salad bar, buffet, picnic hamper, self-service café, takeaway, barbeque, packed lunch

 Remember!

These are the types of **residential** hospitality places (where people stay overnight) :

Hotels, guest houses, bed and breakfast, inns, pubs, farmhouses, holiday camps and parks, family cabins, luxury camping (glamping), cruise ships, long-distance trains, motorway services, hostels.

These are the types of **catering** places:

Restaurants, bistros, dining rooms, canteens, cafés, tearooms, coffee shops, takeaway and fast food outlets, pubs, bars, clubs, casinos, street food stalls, pop-up restaurants, mobile/roadside food vans, motorway services, visitor and tourist attractions (theme parks, museums, zoos, etc.), sports stadiums, concert/gig venues.

Customer needs and wants   ...know and understand

It is important to consider the needs and wants of customers.

You have to choose and write down what hospitality and catering provision would be most suitable for the situation/scenario you have been given in the exam question.

You may have to justify (give reasons) for your choices.

The chart below lists examples of hospitality and catering provision options that customers might need and want from a venue. You could use some of these (and others) to suit the situation/scenario in the exam question, and then justify your choices:

Feature of the hospitality and catering venue	Options (choices) available to customers
Opening hours	• 24 hours for late booking in • Accessible opening hours
Atmosphere	• Relaxed and welcoming atmosphere • Family friendly • Good inclusion policy for all people • Children's play area near to where adults can sit and relax • No dress code • No time limit on staying • Older and younger adult clientele catered for • Venue is in a pleasant setting
Meals	• Children's meal options • Eat in or take away • Table service/buffet/family-style/cafeteria • Good selection of dishes on the menu • Selection of hot and cold meals available • Light snacks/small-sized meals available • Food from different cultures in menu • People can choose to eat a meal or just have a drink • Special dietary choices (e.g. vegan), dietary restrictions/allergies catered for (e.g. gluten free, allergy warnings on menu) • Seasonal dishes and local foods available • Room service available • Special chef's dishes available • Set menu offers (budget-friendly) • Special offers available, e.g. curry night, two meals for the price of one, children eat for free • Baby chairs available
Other features	• WiFi available throughout the venue • Celebrations and special events catered for • Assistance dogs allowed into all places inside • Baby-changing facilities • Good value for money

Example scenario and question

A new eco theme park is being planned. It will have an environmentally friendly theme.

As well as entertainment and rides, the theme park will include an education centre and residential accommodation. Residential courses will be offered all year round to schools, youth groups, college students, families with young children and adult tourist groups.

Suggest and justify one type of hospitality and one type of catering place (establishment) that are suitable to meet the needs of the following groups who want to stay at the eco theme park:

a) Families on holiday with young children

b) School and college students on a residential course.

The examples, a) and b), below are suggestions for how you could answer the scenario question. The following are highlighted in the colours shown:

1. Write out clearly the hospitality and catering choices that you think would be most suitable for the needs of the people described in the scenario.
2. Give good reasons for (**justify**) your choices.

a) For families on holiday with young children, I suggest small family cabins that have a living room, self-catering kitchen, bathroom and two or three bedrooms, with a small outside area for the children to play in. These would be suitable places to stay because the parents can look after the children in a separate building, without having to worry about disturbing other people. They can cater for themselves if they want to, which would be cheaper than eating out all the time and easier with very young children, who may not eat very much in one meal.

If they decide to eat out, I suggest that a family-friendly restaurant, which sells reasonably priced adult- and child-sized meals in a buffet-style food service system, throughout the day and evening, would be suitable. The restaurant could be divided into separate dining areas, to make eating out together more family-centred and cosy. This would enable families to afford to eat out and give the parents a break from preparing meals. The restaurant could include an indoor play area for children, to allow the adults to relax a little while enjoying their meal, as well as baby-changing rooms and highchairs to make the care of their children more convenient.

b) For school and college students on a residential course, I suggest that hostel accommodation (either in one building or in separate purpose-built buildings) would be suitable. This would have bedrooms for four people to sleep, each with an en suite bathroom. This would enable staff who are in charge to keep a check on a small number of children/students in each room, rather than having them all in one large room. There would be a common room/sitting room, and a dining room/meeting room with a small kitchen facility for groups to prepare simple breakfasts, drinks and snacks. This would allow the children/students to meet together, relax, have whole group meetings and complete any work they have to do for the course.

For their lunches and evening meals, I suggest that the hostel accommodation area includes a separate dining room suitable for large groups. The meals could be served in a cafeteria food service system, which would allow for different needs and food choices. There would be a pre-order packed lunch service available. This would be a convenient way to give the groups a lunch if they are out all day on their courses.

The question might also ask you to give some other information about the scenario and your hospitality and catering choices, e.g.:

Information that might be asked for	Examples of information that you could give for families with young children for the example scenario of an eco-theme park
1. What are its unique selling points (USPs)? What features of your hospitality and catering choices will stand out and be attractive to families with young children?	• The accommodation will have everything that is needed for a family (it will be self contained), including adults and children with disabilities • There are suitable activities for children of different ages • There are suitable places to eat that are reasonably priced • The theme park will help people to understand the importance of environmental sustainability • A social media group will be set up to promote special events and offers to existing customers who subscribe to it
2. How does it fit in with current trends in the hospitality and catering industry? What are the current consumer trends and how will your hospitality and catering choices meet these?	• In all its accommodation, restaurants, education centre, etc. the eco theme park will aim to: – Use mainly renewable energy – Use as little plastic as possible – Recycle water and materials – Keep food waste to a minimum – Cater for customers with disabilities and those with special dietary needs
3. How will it be promoted? How will customers be attracted?	• An advertising plan – local newspaper; postal drop of leaflets; posters sent to schools, colleges, nurseries and play groups, tourist information centres • Interactive website featuring information about the theme park, accommodation, food, how it aims to be environmentally friendly, etc. • Promotional deals – e.g. discounts (cheaper prices) for group bookings and reduced prices for children under three years old
4. How will the theme park operate? What staff will be needed and how will the business meet the requirements of the law?	• Staff will need to be employed for jobs such as cleaning and preparing the accommodation; working in the family-friendly restaurant; maintenance of the theme park; providing entertainment for families and children • Documents and certificates will need to be kept up to date for health and safety, food safety, licences, insurance, fire, gas and electricity safety and water quality

Activity: Choosing hospitality and catering for different scenarios

For each scenario below, write brief notes about:

- The hospitality and catering choices that you think would be most suitable for the needs of the people described in the scenario
- Reasons (justification) for how your choices meet the needs of the people in the scenarios.

Scenario 1

A golden (50 years) wedding anniversary celebration for a couple and their family of three children and eight grandchildren and great-grandchildren (aged 2 years to 18 years)

Scenario 2

An event to raise money for sports facilities for children and young people with disabilities, in a town that has a Premier League football team with its own large stadium

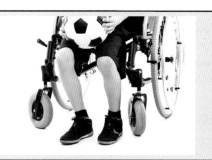

Scenario 3

A charity that supports elderly people has approached the local council with a proposal to open a lunch club in the town centre, in which local elderly residents could meet other people socially and be able to buy inexpensive meals and drinks

Scenario 4

A youth organisation has applied for permission to open and run a youth club for teenagers in an area of a large city where there are few facilities for that age group

The written exam

There are several ways in which exam questions are set out. In this section, examples of different types of question are given, to help you understand how to answer them.

Achieving your best marks in the exam

Your exam paper will be marked by an outside examiner. The examiner has to decide how many marks to give you, using the **mark scheme** and **mark bands**, which are set by the exam board.

The examiner will also want to see how well you use a **range of skills** to answer the questions. These skills are set out in three **assessment objectives (AOs)**:

AO1: What you **know** and **understand** about the different topics, including knowing and using the correct terminology.

AO2: That you can use and apply your **skills**, **knowledge** and **understanding** to answer questions about **different topics** and **situations**.

AO3: That you can **analyse** (break information into different parts to explain it) the topic that the question is about and **evaluate** (make judgements and conclusions about it).

So, to achieve your best marks when you answer the questions in the exam paper, you need to:

- Show the examiner in your answers that you **know** and **understand** what the questions are asking you to write about
- **Apply (use) your skills** (including your practical skills), **knowledge** and **understanding** to answer questions about a variety of situations
- **Analyse** (examine in detail) and **evaluate** (judge) information that the question is asking you about.

What are command words and what do they mean?

Each question in the written exam will have a command word to tell you what you should do to answer it.

The following chart shows you the command words that are often used, what they mean and what they require you to do.

Some command words are found in short answer questions and only need a one-word answer, a list or a short sentence. These are shown in the green-shaded areas of the chart.

Other command words are for questions that need a longer answer, where you have to give more information, details and explanations. These are shown in the yellow-shaded areas of the chart.

The chart includes some sample questions with the command words highlighted and example answers to give you an idea of what you would be expected to do.

SHORT-ANSWER QUESTIONS

Command word	What it means and what you should do	Example question and answer
Categorise	Put into a category (group/type)	Q **Categorise** the following food service systems into the following: Counter service Table service Personal service *[4]* a) buffet b) family style c) cafeteria d) online food delivery A a) *counter service* b) *table service* c) *counter service* d) *personal service*

Identify	To show that you know and understand something by being able to write down its main features and characteristics.	Q **Identify** two ways in which a restaurant can make sure that the customer rights of disabled people are met. *[2]* A i) *Allow assistance dogs inside the restaurant, so that they can continue to help their owner.* ii) *Provide a ramp and automatically opening doors so that wheelchair users can get in and out of the restaurant without assistance.*
List	Write the information in a list rather than full sentences.	Q **List** three foods that are high risk for being contaminated with food-poisoning bacteria. *[3]* A i) *Raw meat* ii) *Fresh fish* iii) *Raw poultry*
Name	Give the name of something (e.g. a piece of kitchen equipment) or someone (e.g. a job title such as restaurant manager).	Q **Name** the job title for the person who has to perform these roles in a hospitality and catering business: • Order ingredients and materials • Store all foods correctly • Keep stock tidy, clean and well organised • Keep a detailed list of all stock *[1]* A *Stock controller*
Recommend	Write down your idea of what would be suitable for a particular occasion or situation.	Q A new café has opened in the centre of a town that is visited by many tourists each year during the summer holiday season. **Recommend** three ways in which the management of the restaurant can continue to attract customers throughout the rest of the year in order to keep the business in profit. *[3]* A i) *Offer a loyalty scheme for regular customers, such as a card that is stamped each time the customer orders a lunch, and once they have ten stamps on their card, they get one free main lunch course* ii) *Offer a menu that is served only on one day each week at a discounted price, e.g. curries, pies or a chef's special* iii) *Offer regular discounts to certain target groups, e.g. children under five years old, pensioners, students*
State	Write down a short, clear and accurate list.	Q **State** three personal qualities that a barista in a coffee shop would need in order to make the business a success. *[3]* A i) *Someone who welcomes customers with a smile and is cheerful* ii) *Someone who knows a lot about what the coffee shop sells so they can help customers make a choice* ii) *Someone who works hard as a team member to make sure all the jobs in the coffee shop are completed and carried out well*
Suggest	Give your ideas/plans to be considered by other people. Give reasons to support your suggestions.	Q **Suggest** two types of food provision that would suit a university campus food hall for students. *[2]* A i) *A self-service cafeteria, so students can choose what they want and pay at a till* ii) *A multi-point counter service offering different types of food to suit a wide range of student needs, e.g. vegetarian, gluten free, 'grab and go' pre-packed foods, religious dietary rules*

LONGER-ANSWER QUESTIONS

Command word	What it means and what you should do	Example question and answer
Describe	Write down the features and details about something or someone. You do not need to explain them.	Q **Describe** the importance of filling out an accident form correctly in a hospitality and catering business. [4] A *Accidents can happen in any department of a hospitality and catering business. All staff need to be trained to fill out an accident form correctly, because they might be the victim of the accident, or witness an accident and be asked to make a statement, so that the accident can be investigated.* *They need to make sure that they include everything that they did or saw in their statement, giving details of, for example, where the accident victim was when the accident happened, at what time it happened, what they were doing, what equipment/tools/chemicals /temperatures, etc. they were using or exposed to. This information will help to make sure that the victim is correctly treated by a first aider and that they are taken to hospital for further treatment if necessary.* *It also will help the investigators to decide, for example, whether the victim, another person, a faulty piece of equipment or incorrect use of chemicals, caused the accident and whether or not the hospitality and catering business has to pay the victim any compensation. It may also show the business that they need to improve their staff training to help avoid more accidents.*
Evaluate	Write about and assess the importance, quality or value of something.	Q **Evaluate** the importance of highlighting foods on a menu that can cause allergies or intolerances for some people. [3] A *People who have food allergies and intolerances need to be able to choose dishes from a menu that are safe for them to eat, especially as food allergies can make someone dangerously ill very quickly after eating a food they are allergic to. The menu should make it clear what ingredients each dish contains, and the waiters need to be trained to know, too, so that they can help the customer choose safe dishes. For example, foods that can cause allergies or intolerances in some people can be an ingredient in a dish but may not be obvious by just reading the name of the dish, e.g. Thai chicken soup, may contain fish sauce, but the name of the dish does not mention fish. Therefore, a description of the dish should be given with the ingredients listed.* *The menu could also use symbols to show which dishes contain certain foods, e.g. wheat, eggs, fish, peanuts, milk.*
Review	Explain and evaluate the importance, quality or value of something.	Q **Review** the importance of a workflow in the operation of the kitchen. [4] A *Workflow means the order in which food passes through the kitchen from delivery to the customer.* *A good workflow helps the operations in the kitchen to run smoothly, because everything that is needed (e.g. ingredients, equipment, serving dishes, etc.) is in the right place and in the right order for the kitchen staff to use. This means that they do not waste time and energy looking for and collecting what they need for their part of the operations.* *A good workflow also means that food is prepared, cooked and served efficiently, on time and to the correct standards to make sure it is safe to eat, is appetising and has good flavour and texture. It also helps prevent accidents, because the workers do not have to keep walking about the kitchen in order to collect items to be able to complete their tasks.*

Analyse	Look at something carefully, thoroughly and in detail so that you can write about it.	Q **Analyse** why the use of information and computer technology (ICT) is important for the success of hospitality and catering businesses. [6] A *Computer technology includes social media, digital technology, mobile smartphones and smart devices that are linked to them (e.g. smart watches), satellite navigation and the internet. Research shows that many customers want and expect hospitality and catering businesses to provide high-quality and modern products and services, and they want to use environmentally and sustainable services and products. Hospitality and catering businesses can send information about their services directly to customers using ICT, so they can easily find the type of food/accommodation they want, which saves them time and effort. Customers can also make online bookings and orders for food and drink, etc. This helps businesses to know how many customers to cater for, which helps to prevent wastage of food, etc. Satellite navigation helps customers to easily find places to eat or stay in an area and can direct them to the ones they choose. Social media enables customers to instantly review their experiences of a hospitality and catering business, which can help increase customer numbers if the reviews are good.* *Reviews also help hospitality and catering businesses to improve their customer services. Comparison websites on the internet enable customers to compare prices, facilities and services of different hospitality and catering businesses, which can help increase customer numbers.*
Justify	Write down the reasons why you think something is better than something else. Give examples/ evidence to back up your reasons.	Q The managers of a city-based youth group for teenagers are organising a one-week outdoor activity holiday in a rural area. Suggest two types of accommodation they could use and **justify** which one you think is the most suitable to meet the needs of the staff and teenagers. [8] A *The youth group could go to:* a) *A bed and breakfast hotel that could offer packed lunches and evening meals each day for an extra cost* *Or* b) *A youth hostel that offers bed and breakfast and the use of a self-catering kitchen and dining room.* *Having all meals provided by a hotel would save time and effort, but it is likely that the youth group will have a limited amount of money to spend on accommodation and food, so the youth hostel will probably be better value, because they can save money on meals by self-catering. They could arrange a rota so that every teenager is involved in preparing meals and clearing away, which will teach them some cooking and organisation skills, as well as working together as a team.* *Self-catering also means that it will be easier to cater for teenagers and staff who may have special dietary needs, such as religious or cultural needs, food allergies or intolerances. The youth hostel will also have special facilities for washing and drying clothes and shoes that are used in the outdoor activities, which might not be the case in a hotel. The dining room in the youth hostel can also be used to hold meetings during the activities holiday. In a B&B, there may be other guests staying at the same time, so it may be difficult to find a suitable space for such meetings.*

| **Explain** | Write about something very clearly, giving examples to illustrate your answer, to show that you understand what you are writing about. |

Q **Explain** the role and importance of Environmental Health Officers in the prevention of food poisoning. [8]

A *Environmental Health Officers are employed by local authorities to enforce food safety laws by inspecting businesses where food is sold to the public, e.g. restaurants, cafés, hotels, guest houses, pubs, etc.*

The purpose of an inspection is to make sure that customers who eat food that they buy do not become ill and also to protect the business from customers who make a false claim for food poisoning against it. The Environmental Health Officer will do this by making sure that, for example:

- *Food is being stored, handled and cooked hygienically and safely*
- *Food is not being contaminated by harmful bacteria and is safe to eat*
- *Food handlers have been trained in food hygiene and safety*
- *Food handlers know the importance of personal hygiene (washing hands, clean clothing, etc.)*
- *There are control measures in place to prevent pests such as flies and mice from contaminating food*
- *The place where the food is produced is in good condition and regularly cleaned.*

Environmental Health Officers will also:

- *Check to make sure that food safety hazards and risks have been identified and are being controlled by using a food safety management system, such as HACCP*
- *Offer advice to the owners of a food business about staff training and improving food hygiene and safety in the business.*

If the Environmental Health Officer finds a problem in a food business, they can:

- *Remove food that they think is a food safety hazard (e.g. because it has been stored in a refrigerator that is too warm or has passed its use-by date) from the business, so that it cannot be sold to customers*
- *Tell the owners of the business to make hygiene and food safety improvements within a set time, and come back to make sure that they have done this*
- *Close the business and stop them selling food if there is a high risk of food poisoning, e.g. because the kitchen is very dirty, there is evidence of rats/mice in the kitchen, or high-risk food is being stored incorrectly*
- *Give evidence in a law court if the owners of the business are prosecuted for breaking the law.*

What types and styles of questions are used in the written exam?

There are various types of questions that are used in the exam:

- Some questions are designed to test your **memory** (recall) of information
- Some questions want you to **apply** what you know and understand to a particular situation
- Some questions want you to write about some **data** that you are given.
- Some questions will begin with a **sentence** or **statement** so that you know what the topic of the question is.

Command words are **highlighted** in each question.

Activity: Answering questions

The assessment will be a mixture of different styles of question, and examples of these are set out below. Have a go at answering them.

Short-answer questions

These questions ask you to remember/recall information that you have learned.
They often use the following command words:

Identify   **List**   **Name**   **Recommend**   **State**   **Suggest**

Q1   **List** two job roles for each of the following staff in a hospitality and catering business:
    a) Executive Head Chef *[2]*
    b) Housekeeper *[2]*
    c) Maintenance Manager. *[2]*

Q2   **Identify** three factors that affect the success of a hospitality and catering business. *[3]*

Q3   **List** four things that affect the profit made by a hospitality and catering business. *[4]*

Q4   **State** four things that make good customer service in a hospitality and catering business. *[4]*

Q5   **List** four foods that are known to cause an allergic reaction in some people. *[4]*

Q6   **Name** three types of residential, commercial hospitality and catering venues (places). *[3]*

Q7   **List** three residential, non-commercial hospitality and catering establishments (places). *[3]*

Q8   **State** three responsibilities of food handlers. *[3]*

> ⚠️ *Remember!*
> Check how many marks each question is worth, by looking at the number of marks in brackets by each question. This will give you an indication of how much you should write. The higher the number, the more you should write.

Stimulus questions

These questions give you either an image or some words that you have to match to the box you have chosen as the correct answer, e.g.:

Q1   Food safety rules require food handlers to make sure that food is stored, cooked and served at the correct temperature, so that bacteria cannot cause food poisoning.

    a) Look at the thermometer and **identify** the correct temperature for each of the following, by **matching** them to the correct letter: *[4]*

       i) The correct temperatures to store chilled food between ☐

      ii) The correct temperature to keep cooked food hot above ☐

     iii) The correct temperature to store frozen food ☐

     iv) The correct temperature to cook food to at least ☐

    b) **State** what happens to bacteria at the following temperatures: *[4]*

       i) 100 °C

      ii) 5 °C to 63 °C

     iii) −18 °C to −22 °C

     iv) 0 °C to 5 °C

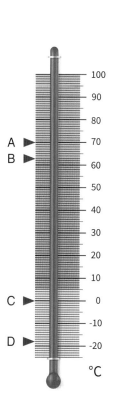

Q2 Safety signs are used in hospitality and catering businesses to make customers and employees aware of personal safety hazards and risks.

Match the signs to the correct description box: *[4]*

i) Safe to drink	
ii) Emergency exit	
iii) Toxic	
iv) Slippery surface	

Graduated lead-in questions

Graduated lead-in questions give a statement at the beginning and then follow on with questions about the statement.

Command words often used:

State   Describe   Explain.

The first questions normally need short answers and then gradually increase to longer-answer questions with higher marks.

Q1 A large hotel is advertising for a new front-of-house receptionist.

(a) **State** two personal attributes that a receptionist would need to work successfully in the hotel. *[2]*

(b) **Describe** two of the duties of a hotel receptionist and **explain** why they are important for the success of the business. *[4]*

Q2 Food safety regulations require all food handlers to know about foods that can cause allergic reactions in some people and how to recognise if someone is having an allergic reaction.

a) **Describe** four signs which indicate that someone is having an allergic reaction to a food. *[4]*

b) **Suggest** and give reasons for two things that a hospitality and catering business can do to reassure customers who have food allergies that they can eat safely in their restaurant. *[4]*

Q3 Developments in smartphone technology have given customers a range of options and information for using hospitality and catering businesses.

Explain how smartphones can be used by customers for the following activities:

a) Going for a meal in a restaurant [3]

b) Going to stay in a hotel or guest house. [3]

Data response questions

These give you some information (data), which you need to use to answer the questions that follow after it.

Q1 A motorway services company has produced this data about visitors in a year to one of its service locations that has overnight accommodation, parking spaces for cars and lorries, restaurants, shops, toilet facilities and a fuel station.

a) **Describe** two types of non-food hospitality services that the company could provide to meet the needs of each of the following visitors who use the motorway services:

i) Long distance lorry drivers

ii) Business people. [4]

b) **Suggest** three food service options that the company could offer to suit families and overseas visitors. [3]

c) **Review** your suggestions for food service options and **justify** why each would be suitable for the needs of families and overseas visitors. [6]

Q2 Hazard Analysis of Critical Control Points (HACCP) is a food management safety system that all catering businesses must use to identify and control possible food safety risks.

A small café serves hot and cold drinks, light lunches (soups, sandwiches, salads, omelettes, warmed paninis, etc.).

The chart shows part of the HACCP for the café, which has to be completed by the manager.

Identify one control for each of the possible hazards listed in the HACCP to prevent a food safety risk, with a reason for each. [10]

Stage of production: Critical Control Points	Possible hazards	Control used to prevent a food safety risk
Storing the food	Chilled foods may be stored above the safe temperature	
	Dry foods may be infested by pests	
	Bacteria could spread from one food to another	
Preparing the food	Bacteria can spread from one food to another	
Cooking the food	High-risk foods may not be cooked all the way through, so harmful bacteria can stay alive	

Free-response questions

These questions are about a topic or scenario, and are often worth quite a few marks. You can choose how to answer them, but you must remember to include details, examples and explanations and try not to repeat what you have already written.

Q   A new bar and restaurant is opening in a busy town centre. It is in part of an old, disused department store that has been restored and modernised. The restaurant kitchen and customer toilet facilities will be in the basement of the building and there will be a drinks bar and customer tables on the ground floor and first floor.

   Describe the safety features that will need to be included in the building to make sure that customers and staff are safe at all times, and how the food will be delivered from the basement kitchen to the customers on the ground floor and first floor in the most efficient way. *[9]*

Activity: Getting good marks for your answers

In this activity, the same question has been answered by two different students.

When you have read through their answers, say how many marks you would give them if you were the examiner, and explain why.

Here are some guidelines to help you.

Has the student:

- Given a clear or a muddled answer?
- Followed what the command word asked them to do?
- Covered the needs of the stated group of people?
- Given details and examples in their explanation?
- Given enough information or only a little?
- Given information that is correct or incorrect?

Q   A charity is setting up a lunch club for elderly adults in a small town, many of whom live alone and find it difficult to cook for themselves. The lunch club will provide a two-course lunch followed by tea or coffee, and will operate three times a week from a community centre, which has a well-equipped catering kitchen and hall.

   a) **Suggest** two types of food provision that the club could provide to meet the needs of the elderly people. *[2]*

   b) **Review** your suggestions and **justify** which one you think is the most suitable. *[8]*

   c) **Suggest** and **justify** two non-food ideas that the charity could provide to make the club an enjoyable social occasion for the elderly people. *[4]*

Student 1 answer

a) Suggest two types of food provision that the club could provide to meet the needs of the elderly people. *[2]*

   i) *Sandwiches and cakes that people choose from a cafeteria*

   ii) *Ready meals that the people choose and are heated up for them*

b) Review your suggestions and justify which one you think is the most suitable. *[8]*

People like sandwiches and cakes and the elderly people can choose the ones they want, but sandwiches are cold, so they might prefer to have a hot ready meal. The ready meals can be bought in by the lunch club and stored in the freezer, which will save them time as they won't have to cook anything. So the ready meals would be best as they are easy to prepare and the elderly people can choose what they want.

c) Suggest and justify two non-food ideas that the club could provide to make the club an enjoyable social occasion for the elderly people. *[4]*

   i) *They could play some games, e.g. bingo*

   ii) *They could watch a film*

Student 2 answer

a) Suggest two types of food provision that the club could provide to meet the needs of the elderly people. *[2]*

    i) *A choice of two cooked meals made in the kitchen and served to the elderly people at their tables (table service system)*

    ii) *A choice of two cooked meals served to the elderly people at the counter (cafeteria system)*

b) Review your suggestions and justify which one you think is the most suitable. *[8]*

It is important to offer people a choice of meal, e.g. a vegetarian and non-vegetarian meal so that everyone is catered for. However, the charity will have to be careful not to spend too much money on ingredients or to waste food, so maybe the elderly people can choose what they want from the menu a few days before, either at the previous lunch club, or a charity volunteer could contact them by telephone. The charity would keep a record of what they choose in case they have forgotten on the day of the lunch club. This will help the charity to plan how much food they need to order and cook in advance.

As many of the elderly people have difficulty cooking for themselves, having a hot meal that is cooked at the club and eating it with other people will be very comforting and sociable for them and will give them greater variety in their diet. It will also be like being at a restaurant, which makes the experience very enjoyable.

I think the most suitable option is to have the meal served to the elderly people at the table, because if they have problems standing and walking, they would find it very difficult to queue up at a counter and carry their tray of food back to their table. This could also be dangerous if one of them slipped and fell.

c) Suggest and justify two non-food ideas that the club could provide to make the club an enjoyable social occasion for the elderly people. *[4]*

    i) *If there is a piano in the community hall, the charity could ask someone to play background music during the meal (or they could use a sound system instead), and maybe have a popular song singing session at the end of the meal, using songs that the people knew when they were young. Singing is a good activity to help keep elderly people's brains active, as well as being fun.*

    ii) *After the meal, the charity could perhaps set up some tables with board/card games for people to play in groups or for them to sit and chat, in order to extend the social aspect of the club, as this is very important for elderly people who live alone, and it is also another good way of keeping their brains active.*

Topic 2.1 The importance of nutrition

2.1.1 Understanding the importance of nutrition

Key terms you should try to include in your answers

Balanced diet – a diet that provides a person with the right amount of nutrients for their needs

Diet – the food people eat every day

Good nutrition – eating a wide variety of foods (mainly plant foods), that are mostly unprocessed (whole foods) and drinking plenty of water

Nutrients – natural chemical substances in foods that are essential for body growth, function and health

Nutrition – the study of what people eat and how all the nutrients in foods work together in the body

Key learning

- **Nutrients** are natural substances that are essential for our bodies to grow, work properly and stay healthy.
- Water is not a nutrient, but we cannot live without it.
- **Nutrition** is the study of what people eat and how all the natural substances (including nutrients) in foods work together in the body so it can grow, stay healthy and work properly.
- **Good nutrition** means eating lots of different fresh fruits, fresh vegetables and other plant foods such as wholegrain cereals (wheat, oats, barley, rice, rye), and smaller amounts of fish, meat, poultry, dairy foods and eggs, and drinking plenty of water.
- The food people eat every day is called their **diet**.
- A **balanced diet** gives a person the right amount of nutrients for their needs. There are also special diets, e.g. a low-salt diet or a high-fibre diet.
- All foods contain different amounts and types of nutrients.
- **Whole foods**, such as wholegrain cereals, beans and whole milk are **nutrient dense** because they contain the most nutrients. They have not had any nutrients removed by processing.
- **Nutrient-rich** foods contain a lot of a particular nutrient; e.g. fresh orange, kiwi fruit and broccoli are rich sources of vitamin C.

Why the body needs water and nutrients from food

... *know and understand*

Nutrient: Protein		
Why it is needed (Function)	- **Growth** of the body - **Repair** of the body when it is injured - Gives the body **energy**	**Which foods contain it (Sources)** **Plant foods:** Beans, peas, lentils, cereals (rice, wheat, oats, barley, rye) and cereal products (bread, pasta, etc.), nuts, seeds, soya beans, quinoa, tofu, textured vegetable protein (TVP), Quorn. **Animal foods:** Meat, poultry, fish, eggs, milk, cheese, yogurt, quark, gelatine.
What happens to it when food is prepared and cooked	- The appearance and texture of protein is changed (it is **denatured** and **coagulated**) by heat and acids (e.g. lemon juice) - It can be over-cooked, which makes it difficult to digest in the body	

Nutrient: Carbohydrate

Why it is needed (Function)	• Main source of **energy** for the body • **Dietary fibre** helps the body get rid of solid waste products (faeces)	**Which foods contain it (Sources)** There are two groups of carbohydrates: **Group 1 – sugars:** **Glucose:** ripe fruits and vegetables (e.g. apples, onions, beetroot, parsnips, sweet potato). **Fructose:** fruits, vegetables and honey. (**High fructose corn syrup** – HFCS — is used as a sweetener in many processed foods and fizzy soft drinks.) **Galactose:** milk from mammals. **Maltose:** barley, a syrup (malt extract) added to breakfast cereals, biscuits, hot drink powders, confectionery (sweets). **Sucrose:** 'sugar' from sugar cane and sugar beet, used in cooking and many processed foods, drinks and confectionery. **Lactose:** milk and milk products.
What happens to it when food is prepared and cooked	• Starch (carbohydrate) is **gelatinised** when cooked in a liquid, which makes it easier for the body to use • Sugars melt and dissolve in water. As they are heated, they boil and turn into a syrup, which **caramelises**. Over-heating causes sugars to burn	**Group 2 – complex carbohydrates:** **Starch:** cereals (e.g. wheat, rice, oats, barley, maize [corn]), cereal products (e.g. breakfast cereals, pasta, bread, cakes, pastry, biscuits); starchy vegetables (e.g. potatoes, yams, sweet potatoes, parsnips, pumpkin, butternut squash, peas, beans, lentils); seeds, quinoa. **Pectin:** some fruits, e.g. oranges, lemons, limes, apples, apricots, plums, greengages and some root vegetables, e.g. carrots. **Dextrin:** formed when starchy foods (e.g. bread, cakes, biscuits) are baked or toasted. **Dietary fibre / non-starch polysaccharide (NSP):** wholegrain (wholemeal) cereals and cereal products, e.g. breakfast cereals, bread, pasta, flour; fruits and vegetables, especially with skins left on (e.g. peas, beans, lentils); seeds, nuts.

Nutrient: Fat

Why it is needed (Function)	• Gives the body **energy** which is stored in the body under the skin and elsewhere • **Insulates** the body from cold temperatures • **Protects** the bones and kidneys from physical damage • Gives the body **'fat-soluble' vitamins A, D, E, K**	**Which foods contain it (Sources)** **Plant foods:** Plant oils, e.g. olive, rapeseed, palm, coconut, sunflower and corn; and also oily fish, avocados, nuts, seeds and some vegetable fat spreads. **Animal foods:** Oily fish, eggs, fresh meat, poultry, milk, butter, cream, cheese, lard, suet, ghee, the fat in meat, and chocolate. **Visible fats and oils:** Fats/oils in a food that you can easily see, e.g. fat in meat, oil in tuna, butter, lard, suet, block vegetable fat, ghee, plant oils such as olive, palm, sunflower oil.
What happens to it when food is prepared and cooked	• Fats and oils are damaged by repeatedly being heated to fry foods • They can break down into substances that are harmful to the body	**Invisible fats and oils:** Fats/oils in a food that you cannot easily see, e.g. in cakes, pastries, potato crisps, chips, biscuits, chocolate, nuts, cheese, fried foods, meat products, etc.

Activity: Make a poster

Choose **one** of the following nutrients and design and draw a poster to explain clearly why the body needs it and which foods it is found in. Make the poster colourful and clearly set out so that it attracts people to read it.

Protein   Fat   Carbohydrate   Vitamin C   Vitamin D   Iron   Calcium

Nutrient: Vitamins	Why it is needed (Function)	Which foods contain it (Sources)	What happens to it when food is prepared and cooked
Vitamin A	• For **healthy skin** • To see in **dim light** • To help children **grow** • To keep mucus membranes in the body **moist** and **prevent infections** • **Antioxidant** which helps prevent heart disease and cancers	**Animal foods (retinol):** Milk; cheese; butter; eggs; liver, kidney; oily fish, vegetable fat spreads (added by law) **Plant foods (beta carotene):** Cabbage, spinach, kale, lettuce; peas; orange/yellow/red vegetables and fruits (e.g. carrots, apricots, mango, papaya, peppers, tomatoes)	Not affected
Vitamin D	• Helps the body **absorb calcium** • Helps calcium add **strength** to bones and teeth	Sunlight on skin; oily fish, meat, eggs, butter, vegetable fat spreads (added by law), fortified breakfast cereals	Not affected
Vitamin E	**Antioxidant** which helps prevent heart disease and cancers	Soya, corn oil, olive oil, nuts, seeds, whole wheat, vegetable fat spreads	Not affected
Vitamin K	Helps blood **clot** after injury	Green leafy vegetables, liver, cheese, green tea	Not affected
Vitamin B₁	Allows **energy** to be released from carbohydrates	Meat, especially pork; milk, cheese, eggs, vegetables, fresh and dried fruit, wholemeal bread, fortified breakfast cereals, flour	Damaged by heat and dissolves in water
Vitamin B₂	Allows **energy** to be released from carbohydrates, fats and proteins	Milk and milk products, eggs, fortified breakfast rice, mushrooms	Damaged by heat and dissolves in water
Vitamin B₃	Allows **energy** to be released from carbohydrates, fats and proteins	Beef, pork, wheat flour, maize flour, eggs, milk	Damaged by heat and dissolves in water
Folate (Vitamin B₉)	• Makes healthy **red blood cells** • Helps prevent **spinal cord problems** in unborn babies	Green leafy vegetables, yeast extract (e.g. Marmite), peas, chickpeas, asparagus; wholegrain rice, fruits, added to some breads and breakfast cereals	May be damaged by high heat
Vitamin B₁₂	• Makes healthy **red blood cells** • Makes healthy **nerve cells**	Liver, meat, fish, cheese, fortified breakfast cereals, yeast	May be damaged by high heat
Vitamin C	• Helps the body **absorb iron** • Maintains **connective tissue** to bind body cells together • **Antioxidant** which helps prevent heart disease and cancers	Fruits and vegetables, especially citrus fruits (e.g. oranges, lemons, limes and grapefruit), blackcurrants, kiwi fruit, guavas, Brussels sprouts, cabbage, broccoli, new potatoes, milk, liver	Damaged by heat and dissolves in water Damaged when exposed to the air

Activity: Which vitamin?

Look at the boxes below and work out which vitamin each set of pictures is about. Explain how you worked out the answers from the picture clues.

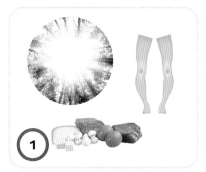

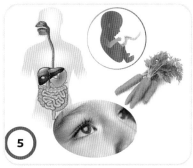

Nutrient: Minerals	Why it is needed (Function)	Which foods contain it (Sources)	What happens to it when food is prepared and cooked
Calcium	• To make strong **bones and teeth** • Makes **nerves and muscles** work • Helps **blood clot** after injury	Milk, cheese, yogurt; green leafy vegetables; canned fish; some nuts; enriched soya drinks; flour	Not affected
Iron	Makes **haemoglobin** in **red blood cells** to carry **oxygen** to all body cells and produce **energy**	Red meat, kidney, liver; wholemeal bread, added to wheat flour (except wholemeal); green leafy vegetables (e.g. watercress, spinach, cabbage); egg yolk; dried apricots; lentils; cocoa, plain dark chocolate; curry powder; fortified breakfast cereals	Not affected
Sodium	• Controls **water** in body • Makes **nerves and muscles** work properly	Salt (**sodium** chloride); salted foods; cheese, yeast extract, stock cubes, gravies and seasonings, snack foods (e.g. crisps), canned fish, bacon, ham, dried fish, soy sauce, salted butter, fast foods and many ready meals; baking powder (cakes, biscuits, baked desserts); takeaway foods	Not affected
Magnesium	• Makes all **body cells** work properly • Helps release of **energy** in the body • Helps **enzymes** work in the body	Green leafy plants, e.g. kale, spinach, cabbage, broccoli, Brussels sprouts	Not affected
Potassium	Makes all **body cells** work properly, especially **nerve cells** in the **heart**	Wide range of foods including bananas, broccoli, potatoes, spinach, salmon, mushrooms and courgettes	Not affected

Activity: Which mineral?

Look at the boxes below and work out which mineral each set of pictures is about. Explain how you worked out the answers from the picture clues.

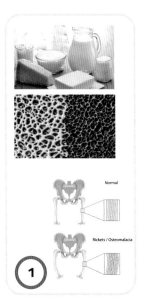   

1   2   3   4

Water

What it does in the body (Function)	Which foods contain it (Sources)
• Controls **body temperature** • Needed for **chemical reactions** in the body • Removes **waste products** from the body • Keeps **mucous membranes** moist and healthy • Keeps **skin** moist and healthy • Needed for all **body fluids** • Found in all **body cells**	• Drinking water (tap and bottled water), other drinks • Naturally found in many foods – milk, milk products, fruit, vegetables, meat, fish, eggs • Added to many foods – soup, sauces, pastries, breads, boiled rice, pasta, beans, pulses, etc.

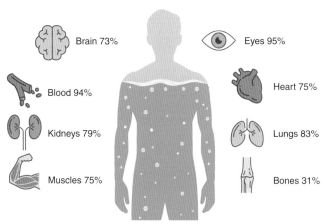

Brain 73%   Eyes 95%

Blood 94%   Heart 75%

Kidneys 79%   Lungs 83%

Muscles 75%   Bones 31%

The approximate amounts of water in some of the parts of the body

What are the dietary guidelines? ...know and understand

Key learning

Dietary guidelines are **recommendations** (from a government organisation called Public Health England) about what to eat in order to be healthy.

There are eight recommendations:

1. Base your meals on starchy foods
2. Eat lots of fruit and vegetables
3. Eat more fish – including a portion of oily fish each week
4. Eat less saturated fat and sugar
5. Eat less salt – no more than 6g (1 level teaspoon) a day for adults
6. Get active and be a healthy weight
7. Don't get thirsty – drink plenty of water
8. Don't skip breakfast.

They are shown in an illustration called the Eatwell Guide:

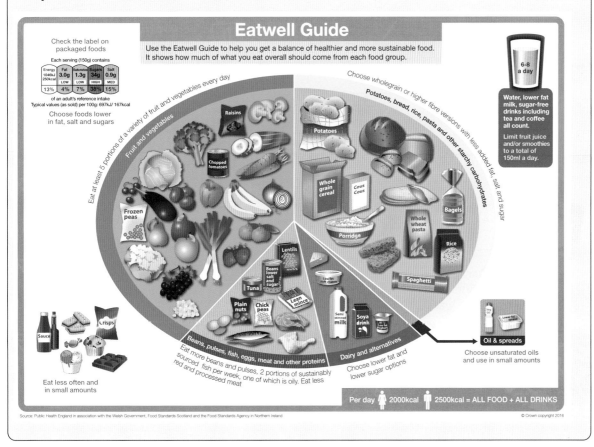

Activity: Why are dietary guidelines recommended?

Using your knowledge of nutrients in foods, match the dietary guidelines with the correct reason why each is recommended:

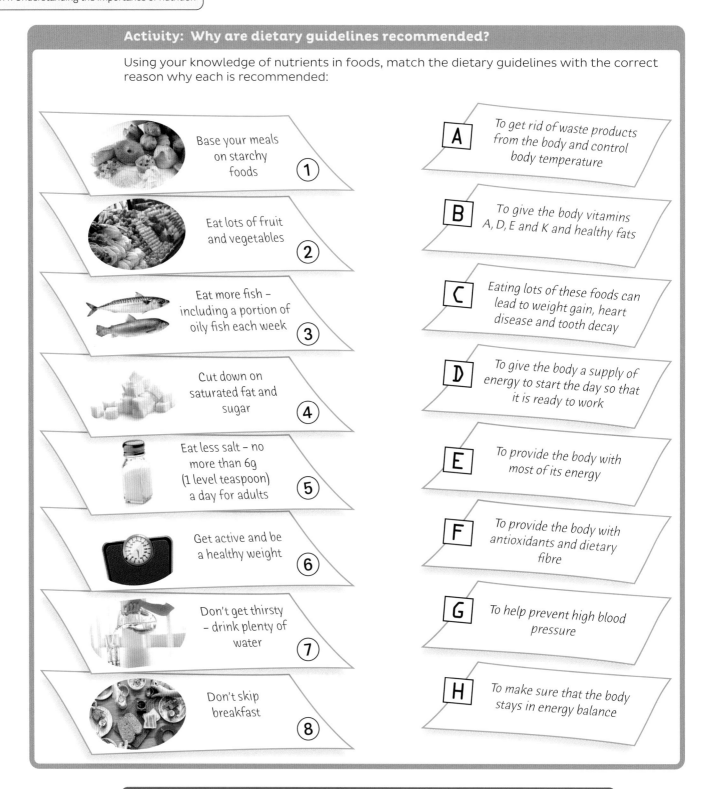

Base your meals on starchy foods **1**

Eat lots of fruit and vegetables **2**

Eat more fish – including a portion of oily fish each week **3**

Cut down on saturated fat and sugar **4**

Eat less salt – no more than 6g (1 level teaspoon) a day for adults **5**

Get active and be a healthy weight **6**

Don't get thirsty – drink plenty of water **7**

Don't skip breakfast **8**

A To get rid of waste products from the body and control body temperature

B To give the body vitamins A, D, E and K and healthy fats

C Eating lots of these foods can lead to weight gain, heart disease and tooth decay

D To give the body a supply of energy to start the day so that it is ready to work

E To provide the body with most of its energy

F To provide the body with antioxidants and dietary fibre

G To help prevent high blood pressure

H To make sure that the body stays in energy balance

Key terms you should try to include in your answers

Life stages – stages of development that people go through during their life: i.e. infancy (babyhood), childhood, adolescence (teenagers), adulthood and later adulthood (elderly people)

Free sugars – sugars, honeys, syrups and fruit juices/fruit concentrates that are added to foods and drinks by manufacturers, cooks/chefs and consumers to sweeten them during preparation, processing, cooking and serving

Peak bone mass – when bones and teeth have the maximum amount of minerals and are at their strongest and most dense

What are the nutritional needs of people at different life stages?

...be able to

Life stage	Which nutrients / foods are especially important?
Babies 0–1 year • Fast body growth and development • Energy needs increase as baby becomes more active	• All nutrients, especially protein, vitamins and minerals • All nutrients come from human breast milk or baby formula milk for first 6 months • Other foods gradually introduced during weaning • Avoid adding sugar and salt in foods and drinks
Pre-school children 1–4 years • Fast body growth and development • A lot of energy is used in physical activity	• All nutrients, especially protein, vitamins and minerals • Limit the amount of **free sugars** and salt in foods and drinks
Children 5–12 years • Growth continues in 'spurts' • Children should be physically active most of the time to prevent them becoming overweight or obese	• All nutrients, especially protein, vitamins and minerals • Limit the amount of free sugars and salt in foods and drinks
Adolescents (teenagers) • Fast body growth and development from a child into an adult • Minerals are put into the bones and teeth, so the skeleton reaches **peak bone mass** when they are adults	• Protein, vitamins A, B group, C, D, E, carbohydrate (starch and fibre; limit free sugars) • Fats – especially essential fatty acids • Minerals – all • Calcium and vitamin D
• Girls start to have periods, which means they may become anaemic	• Iron and vitamin C
• Not enough sleep and pressures of school may lead to lack of energy, poor concentration and tiredness	• Vitamin B group, iron and vitamin C
Adults • The body stops growing around 21 years of age • The body needs to be looked after to prevent disease, and be strong and active • Can gain weight if the diet is unbalanced and they are not physically active	• Protein, vitamins A, B group, C, D, E, carbohydrate (starch and fibre; limit free sugars), fats – especially essential fatty acids, minerals – all
• Peak bone mass is reached at around 30 years of age	• Calcium and vitamin D
• Women continue to have periods until the menopause (approximately late 40s to early 50s), which may mean they become anaemic	• Iron and vitamin C
Older adults • Body systems such as digestion, blood circulation, etc. start to slow down • Blood pressure may increase • The body needs to be looked after to prevent disease, and be strong and active • Can gain weight if the diet is unbalanced and they are not physically active • The appetite usually gets smaller • The senses of smell and taste may weaken	• Protein; vitamins A, B group, C, D, E; carbohydrate (starch and fibre; limit free sugars); fats – especially essential fatty acids; minerals – all • Iron and vitamin C (especially women) to avoid scurvy and anaemia
• Short- and long-term memory may become poor	• B group vitamins to help the body use energy and to help prevent memory loss
• The eyesight may weaken	• Vitamins A, C and E to help prevent age-related eye conditions
• Bones and teeth gradually start to lose minerals and become weak. This can develop into osteoporosis.	• Calcium and vitamin D

These graphs show how some nutrient needs change at different life stages, and why this happens:

Amount of protein (g) needed per day

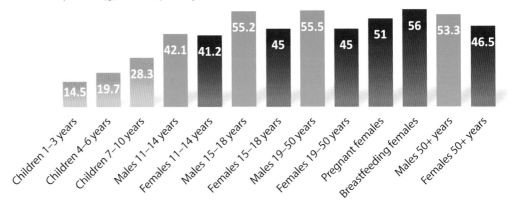

You can see that as children get older, they need more protein to allow them to grow. When they are teenagers, they have big growth spurts, so they need even more protein, but as they become adults and have finished growing, they need less. Pregnant and breastfeeding females need more protein to allow the baby to develop and grow.

Amount of iron (mg) needed per day

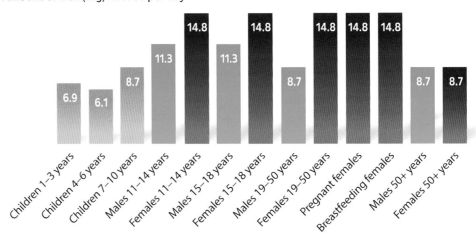

You can see that as children get older, they need more calcium (and vitamin D) to allow their bones and teeth to grow and become stronger. When they are teenagers, they have big growth spurts, so they need even more calcium, but as they become adults and have finished growing, they need less, but enough to allow them to reach peak bone mass so that their bones and teeth are really strong. Pregnant and breastfeeding females need more calcium to allow the baby's bones and teeth to develop and grow.

Amount of calcium (mg) needed per day

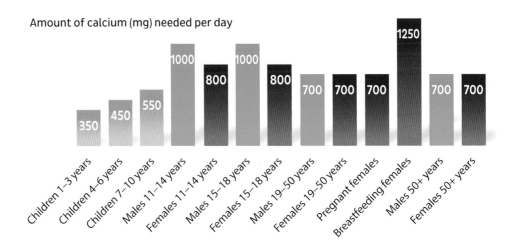

You can see that as children get older, they need more iron (and vitamin C) to produce enough red blood cells to take oxygen around the body and produce energy in all body cells. When they are teenagers, they have big growth spurts and many are physically active and need plenty of energy, so they need even more iron. Females need more iron than males because they lose blood when they have their periods and the iron that is lost must be replaced. As they become adults, females continue to need the same amount of iron because their periods continue, but males need less. Pregnant and breastfeeding females need more iron than males because they need enough to enable the baby to develop and grow and to make sure they have enough for themselves to prevent them from becoming anaemic. As males and females reach older adulthood, they need less iron (the same amount as each other) because women do not have periods after the menopause.

Amount of vitamin A (mcg) needed per day

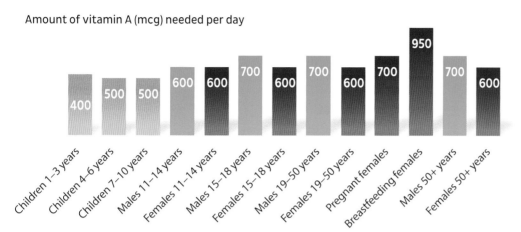

You can see that as children get older, they need more vitamin A to allow them to grow normally, fight disease, and keep their eyes, skin and mucous membranes healthy. When they are teenagers, their need increases and stays the same throughout their adult life. Breastfeeding females need more vitamin A to allow the normal development of their baby.

Special diets for different food choices and medical conditions

...be able to

 What they do eat   **Reason(s) for following this diet**   **What they do not eat**

milk and milk products

eggs

all types of plant foods

Lacto-ovo vegetarian diet
Health, religious, ethical (what people believe is the right thing to do) or other

meat

fish

shellfish

gelatine

milk and milk products

all types of plant foods

protein alternatives: tofu, tempeh, TVP

Lacto vegetarian diet
Health, religious, ethical or other

meat

fish

gelatine

shellfish

eggs

What they do eat	Reason(s) for following this diet	What they do not eat

all plant foods

fish and other seafood

milk and milk products

eggs

Pescatarian diet
Health, religious, ethical or other

meat, meat products

poultry and poultry products

all plant foods

protein alternatives: tofu, tempeh, TVP

Vegan diet
Health, religious, ethical, environmental or other

all animal foods

fish and shellfish

animal milk, milk products and eggs

rice, rice products, soya

maize (corn), cassava (tapioca)

linseeds, polenta, beans, peas

lentils, quinoa, sorghum, agar, nuts

Gluten-free diet
To prevent symptoms of coeliac disease

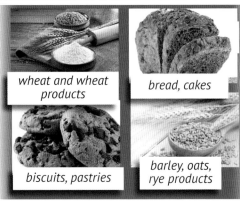

wheat and wheat products

bread, cakes

biscuits, pastries

barley, oats, rye products

specially produced lactose-free milk and milk foods

Lactose-free diet
To prevent symptoms of lactose intolerance

milk, milk products, and any food containing milk products

fruits, vegetables

wholegrains

rice, peas

beans, lentils

High-fibre diet
To prevent the development of diseases of the intestines, e.g. constipation, diverticular disease

white flour and products

white rice

smooth fruit juice

fresh fruits and vegetables

milk, unsweetened milk products

Low-sugar diet

To control the symptoms of types 1 and 2 diabetes; as part of a diet to lose weight

free sugars that have been added to cakes, biscuits, drinks, confectionery, desserts, sauces, ice cream, breakfast cereals, honey, syrup, jam, etc.

naturally low-fat foods, e.g. fruits vegetables, cereals, white fish, fat-reduced cheese, spreads, milk, etc.

Fat-reduced diet

To prevent the development of heart disease; as part of a diet to lose weight

full-fat milk and milk products, pastries, meats, crisps, chips, doughnuts, cakes, biscuits, fried foods, desserts, ice cream

fruits, vegetables, milk, eggs

Low-sodium (salt) diet

To prevent the development of heart disease, high blood pressure, kidney disease

yeast extract, cheese, dried fish, canned fish, soy sauce, ketchup, pickles, many ready meals and takeaways, snack foods, cakes, biscuits, scones

Iron-rich foods, e.g. red meat, liver, kidney, corned beef, dried apricots, nuts, seeds, cocoa, high cocoa solids, dark chocolate, dark green leafy vegetables, lentils, wholemeal bread, curry powder, fortified breakfast cereals; foods rich in vitamin C (helps iron to be absorbed in the body), e.g. fresh oranges, lemons, limes, grapefruit, kiwi fruit, peppers, strawberries, blackcurrants, broccoli, Brussels sprouts, guava, papaya, new potatoes

Iron deficiency

To prevent iron deficiency anaemia causing tiredness, weakness, and weak and split nails

> **Key terms you should try to include in your answers**
>
> **BMR** – basal metabolic rate is the amount of energy we need to keep our body alive
>
> **Energy balance** – the amount of energy we get from food each day is the same as the amount of energy we use each day
>
> **Energy dense** – a food that contains a lot of fat and/or carbohydrate (sugar, starch) and has a high energy value
>
> **PAL** – this means physical activity level, and is the amount of energy we use for movement and physical activity every day

Nutritional needs for different activity levels

▶ ...be able to

Energy is needed for different jobs in the body. Energy comes from food and is converted to **glucose** in the body to give us energy.

If a person is physically active they are less likely to develop diseases such as obesity and heart disease. Being physically active also improves the strength of the bones and muscles and keeps the brain active and alert.

Physically active people need enough food every day to give them sufficient energy for their **BMR** and their **PAL**.

People who are not very physically active (sedentary people), need to limit the amount of energy they have from food in order to prevent them putting on weight.

The mind map below will help you understand about the body and energy.

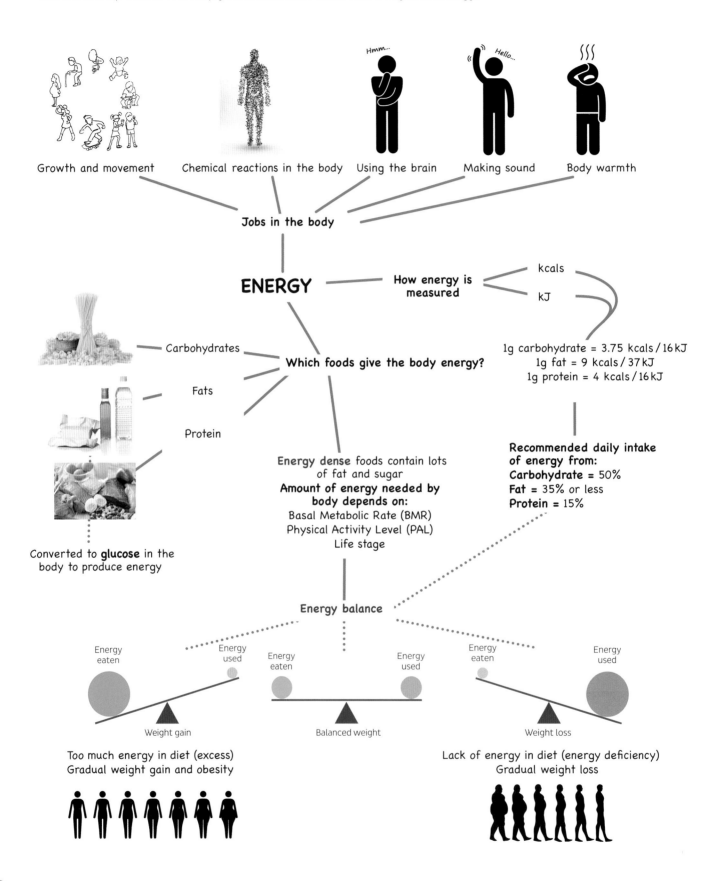

Growth and movement   Chemical reactions in the body   Using the brain   Making sound   Body warmth

Jobs in the body

ENERGY

How energy is measured

kcals

kJ

Carbohydrates

Fats

Protein

Which foods give the body energy?

1g carbohydrate = 3.75 kcals / 16 kJ
1g fat = 9 kcals / 37 kJ
1g protein = 4 kcals / 16 kJ

Energy dense foods contain lots of fat and sugar
Amount of energy needed by body depends on:
Basal Metabolic Rate (BMR)
Physical Activity Level (PAL)
Life stage

Recommended daily intake of energy from:
Carbohydrate = 50%
Fat = 35% or less
Protein = 15%

Converted to **glucose** in the body to produce energy

Energy balance

Energy eaten   Energy used   Energy eaten   Energy used   Energy eaten   Energy used

Weight gain   Balanced weight   Weight loss

Too much energy in diet (excess)
Gradual weight gain and obesity

Lack of energy in diet (energy deficiency)
Gradual weight loss

Activity: Which foods are energy dense?

Look at the pictures in the chart and work out which ones **are** energy dense or **are not** energy dense.
For each one you say **is** energy dense, explain why the ingredients it contains make it energy dense.
For each one you say **is not** energy dense, explain why it is not.

	Energy dense or not energy dense?	Explain why you have given this answer
cucumber and lettuce		
jam doughnut		
chocolate chip cookies		
low-fat strawberry yogurt		
pork pie		
lentil and vegetable soup		
chips, cheese and mayonnaise		
kebab and fries		
sausage roll made with puff pastry		
fresh fruit salad		

Key learning

- The different types of menu
- What a menu should tell customers about the food they are choosing
- What to think about when planning a menu
- Why careful menu planning is important
- Food and its effects on the environment
- How to plan menus for dishes (food items) that have the least effect on the environment when they are prepared and cooked.

Different types of menu

...be aware of

A menu is a list of dishes for customers to choose from.

Many catering businesses have different menus that are changed each day, week or month.

This adds variety for regular customers and is more interesting for the chefs.

Types of menu:

À la carte: a menu where the dishes are all listed and priced separately under different headings

Cyclic menu: a set of menus with limited choices that are changed every week, two weeks or month

Du jour menu: a menu that changes each day or is only served on a certain day of the week

Function menu: similar to table d'hôte, but with a more limited choice and used for functions such as weddings, parties and conferences

Meal menu: menu choices for specific meals: breakfast, brunch (late breakfast / early lunch), lunch, afternoon tea, dinner (evening meal). Often used in hotels and in some restaurants and cafés

Speciality menu: for target groups of people, e.g. children, pensioners, ethnic groups, special diets; used in fast food outlets, some restaurants and cafés

Table d'hôte: a set menu with limited choices, which has a set price for a meal (e.g. a two- or three-course meal)

Activity: Which type of menu?

Using the types of menu chart on page 128 to help you, match each type of menu to the correct image.

A À la carte **B** Cyclic menu **C** Du jour menu **D** Function menu

E Meal menu **F** Speciality menu **G** Table d'hôte

1

Spice up your day with our
CURRY CLUB
£4.49
Every Thursday all day
TUCK IN!
Your choice of curry and a drink from the selection on the menu

2

Small Businesses Conference 2022

Menu
Vegetable soup (v)
Seafood cocktail

Mains
Grilled chicken salad
Vegetable curry with rice (v)
Fish pie with seasonal vegetables

Desserts
Fresh fruit salad with cream
Apple pie with custard or cream
Salted caramel cheesecake
Selection of cheeses and crackers

3

	Week 1	Week 2
Monday	Margherita Pizza Vegetable Bolognaise Jacket Potato with Tuna Mayo Carrots & Garden Peas Fruit Crumble with Custard Yoghurt/Fresh Fruit Platter	Margherita Pizza Quorn & Vegetable Rice Jacket Potato with Tuna Mayo Roasted Peppers & Sweetcorn Berry & Apple Strudel & Custard Yoghurt & Fresh Fruit Salad
Tuesday	Spaghetti Bolognaise (made with Organic Mince Beef) Vegetable Pasta Bake Filled Baguette with Ham/Cheese/Tuna or Egg Sweetcorn & Broccoli Chocolate & Beetroot Brownie Yoghurt/Fresh Fruit Salad	Chicken Fajita with Jacket Wedges Macaroni Cheese Filled Baguette with Ham/Cheese/Tuna or Egg Peas & Coleslaw Lemon Drizzle Cake Yoghurt/Fresh Fruit Platter
Wednesday	Roast Gammon with Roast Potatoes & Gravy Quorn Roast with Roast Potatoes & Gravy Jacket Potato with Beans Seasonal Vegetables Cheese & Biscuits Jelly/Fresh Fruit Platter	Roast Pork with Roast Potatoes & Gravy Vegetable Pasty with Roast Potatoes Jacket Potato with Beans Seasonal Vegetables Cheese & Biscuits Oaty Cookie/Fresh Fruit Salad

4

- Kids' Corner -
For children 12 and under.

Funny Face
A big chocolate chip pancake with a whipped topping smile. Buttermilk version available upon request 2.79
Panqueque Cara Graciosa

★ **Silver Five**
Five silver dollar-sized buttermilk pancakes with an egg and bacon 2.99
Cinco de Plata

Egg Sandwich
One egg, one strip of bacon and cheese on a toasted English muffin. Served with hash browns 2.79
Sandwich de Huevo

★ **Rooty Jr.®**
Kid-sized version of our famous Rooty Tooty. One egg, one bacon strip, one pork sausage link and a fruit-topped buttermilk pancake 2.99

Cheese Omelette
With two buttermilk pancakes 1.99
Tortilla de Huevos con Queso

French Toast
Two triangles of French toast with two bacon strips 2.79
Torrija

Pigs in Blankets
Two pork sausage links rolled in buttermilk pancakes and served with hash browns 2.79
Salchichas Enrolladas en Panqueques

Chicken Strips
With French fries 3.99
Tiras de Pollo

Hamburger
Served with fries in a basket 2.99
With cheese 2.99
Hamburguesa

Grilled Cheese Sandwich
Served with French fries 2.99
Sandwich de Queso a la Plancha

Drinks
Soft Drinks, Milk, Chocolate Milk, Hot Chocolate .99
Bebidas

Dessert
Ice Cream Sundae 1.39
Postres

5

6

Menu
2 courses £21
3 courses £25

Starters
Soup of the day
Liver pâté with Melba toast
Avocado salad (v)
Prawn cocktail

Mains
Chicken curry with rice and seasonal vegetables
Vegetable quiche with salad and new potatoes (V)
Braised beef with creamed potatoes and seasonal vegetables
Grilled fillet of lemon sole, new potatoes, samphire and carrots

Desserts
Two scoops of local ice cream served with a wafer and fruit coulis
Gooseberry crumble with custard or cream
Vanilla cheesecake
Selection of cheeses and crackers

7

Special Lunch Time Menu
Monday to Friday 11am - 3pm
Traditional Scottish Fayre

	Single	Supper	Chips		Pizza			
Fish	3.50	4.00	Chips	1.60			Ham & Cheese	2.60
Chicken	3.50	4.00	Chips & Cheese	3.00	Pizza Slice & Can	3.00	Pasterami & Cheese	2.60
Sausage	2.60	3.00	Chips & Curry /Gravy	3.00	10" Pizza & Can	4.50	Salami & Cheese	2.60
Haggis	2.60	3.00	Chips, Cheese & Curry	3.40			Ham & Salami	2.60
Black Pudding	2.60	3.00	Deep Fried Mars Bar	2.00	Sandwiches			
King Rib	2.60	3.00	Cheese	2.30			Lasagne	3.50
Smoked Sausage	2.60	3.00	Ham & Cheese	2.60			Spaghetti Bolognese	3.20
Steak Pie	2.60	3.00	Tuna Mayo	2.60			Macaroni Cheese	3.00
Mince Pie	2.20	3.00	Salami & Cheese	2.60			Penne Picante	3.50
			Ham & Salami	2.95			Spaghetti Carbonara	3.50

What a menu should tell customers

...be aware of

A menu should:
- Be easy to read and understand
- Be clearly set out
- Have clear descriptions /images of the dishes.

A menu should also give customers the following information:

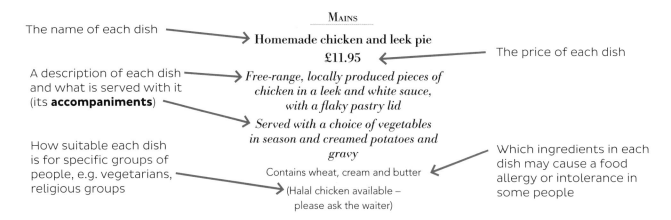

The name of each dish → **MAINS**
Homemade chicken and leek pie
£11.95 ← The price of each dish

A description of each dish and what is served with it (its **accompaniments**) → *Free-range, locally produced pieces of chicken in a leek and white sauce, with a flaky pastry lid*

Served with a choice of vegetables in season and creamed potatoes and gravy

How suitable each dish is for specific groups of people, e.g. vegetarians, religious groups

Contains wheat, cream and butter ← Which ingredients in each dish may cause a food allergy or intolerance in some people

(Halal chicken available – please ask the waiter)

Planning a menu

... *be aware of*

When planning a menu, a hospitality and catering business needs to think carefully about:

1. Customers

- What types of food do they need?
- What types of food do they want to eat?
- What is their age group?
- How much are they willing to pay for food?
- What are their cultural and religious food needs?
- What time of day will they be eating?

2. The business

- Will the menu make money (a profit)?
- Is there enough equipment available to make the menu?
- Will the menu attract new customers?
- How and where would the menu be served, e.g. in a restaurant; as room service; in a bar?

3. How the menu would be prepared

- Is there enough space to store, prepare and serve all the items on the menu?
- Are there enough skilled staff?
- Is there enough time to prepare the menu?
- How will food safety be guaranteed?
- How will the menu be prepared in a way that is environmentally sustainable?
- What size portions of food will be served (portion control)?

4. The dishes

- Is there a variety of colour, texture and flavour in the menu?
- Is there a variety of foods in the menu?
- Are the foods of a good quality?
- Are all the ingredients available to buy?
- How many of the dishes use locally grown, seasonal ingredients?
- Are the menu items nutritionally balanced?
- Do the menu items meet current nutritional advice?

The benefits of careful menu planning   ...be aware of

A carefully planned menu will benefit the different parts of a hospitality and catering business in the following ways:

The customers

- Interesting, balanced and varied menus can be offered
- Plenty of choices for people with special dietary needs and wants can be offered
- Healthy choices for different groups of people can be offered

The success of the business

- The budget can be planned accurately
- The menu will attract customers
- The business will keep up-to-date with current food trends
- The menu will help to increase profits

The menu

- Ingredients and materials can be ordered in good time
- Local and seasonal foods can be used
- The business will be prepared for busy times, e.g. annual festivals such as Christmas, Diwali and special occasions and seasons, e.g. Valentine's Day, summer weddings, the tourist season
- Having alternative menus ready in case there are problems, e.g. with buying ingredients

The preparation of the dishes on the menu

Being able to plan ahead for:

- How and in what order the menu will be cooked (make a production plan)
- Who will prepare each dish
- What equipment will be needed
- How the dishes will be presented and served
- Which dishes can be made in advance and reheated.

Menu planning and the environment

Food production has a major effect on the environment:

PRODUCTION

The production of meat and dairy foods produces the most greenhouse gases

Making and using lots of man-made fertiliser pollutes land, water and air

PROCESSING & MANUFACTURE OF FOOD PRODUCTS

Uses a lot of non-renewable energy and water

Keeping food cold in refrigerators and freezers uses a lot of non-renewable energy and produces greenhouse gases

FOOD PACKAGING

A lot of plastics and paper are used in food packaging

Many plastics do not break down (they are not biodegradable) so must be dumped in landfill sites or burnt, which causes pollution

Plastic production uses a lot of non-renewable materials and energy (oil) and produces greenhouse gases. Many plastics are not recycled and are causing serious harm to animals and plants in the oceans and on land

TRANSPORTING FOOD

Many foods and ingredients are transported very long distances (called **food miles**)

Air, sea and land transport use a lot of non-renewable energy (oil) and cause pollution

All use non-renewable energy (coal, oil) and produce **GREENHOUSE GASES**
e.g. CO_2, methane, nitrous oxide

Greenhouse gases trap heat and warm the planet

which causes **climate change**

Higher or lower than normal temperatures

Drought (lack of water)

Extreme storms

Flooding

The effects of climate change:
- Crops fail
- Livestock dies
- Soil and nutrients are blown or washed away
- Land and farm buildings are damaged
- Pollination of crops is affected
- Landslides and forest fires cause loss of land, crops and livestock
- Water, soil and land are polluted by sewage, rubbish, stones during flooding
- Temperature changes cause insects and moulds to grow in large numbers
- Some plant species die out with climate change

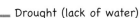

How to plan menus that have the least effect on the environment

...know and understand

Ingredients

Hospitality and catering businesses should try to:

- Use ingredients that have been grown locally and have only travelled a short distance
- Plan the menus so that the food can be delivered to the kitchen in as few journeys as possible, e.g. buy food in bulk; buy from one supplier
- Offer a range of vegan/vegetarian options
- Use foods that are in season in the UK, e.g. strawberries and green beans in the summer, so that they do not have to be imported from other countries
- Use (where possible) ingredients that have been grown organically or are 'free range' (where animals and birds are able to live outside).

Packaging

Hospitality and catering businesses should try to:

- Use ingredients that have as little packaging as possible
- Use ingredients such as spices, flavourings, sauces, etc. that come in refillable or recyclable catering-sized containers
- Avoid serving dishes with individually packaged portions of sauces, salad dressings, salt and pepper, butter and other spreads, jams, marmalade, etc.

Food storage and preparation

Hospitality and catering businesses should try to:

- Make sure refrigerators and freezers are placed in cool areas of the kitchen – if they are in hot areas, their motors have to work very hard, which uses more energy
- Make sure the refrigerator/freezer door seals are in good condition, so that warm air is kept out
- Avoid opening the door of the refrigerator or freezer too often or leaving it open
- Avoid putting hot food into a refrigerator or freezer – cool it down first
- Defrost refrigerators and freezers regularly to make sure they work efficiently.

Cooking food

Hospitality and catering businesses should try to:

- Make sure that oven door seals are in good condition, as they help prevent heat being lost from the oven
- Fill up the oven with items to cook to make full use of the energy used to heat it
- Cook more meals on the hob – make sure that the pans fit properly over the gas flame/electric ring to prevent heat escaping
- Keep pan lids on to cut down heat loss
- Use an electric induction hob, microwave oven or slow cooker where possible, which all use small amounts of electricity
- Use quick methods of cooking, e.g. stir frying and sautéing, to cut down on the amount of gas/electricity used
- When cooking several types of vegetables, place them in different sections of a tiered steamer, so only one hob ring is used to cook them.

Wonky veg

Food waste

Hospitality and catering businesses should try to:

- Avoid buying too much food by planning menus as accurately as possible
- Avoid serving very large food portions to cut down on food waste
- Store food correctly so it stays fresh
- Make use of oddly shaped fruits and vegetables that are often cheaper to buy and are just as nutritious and well flavoured
- Serve some fruits and vegetables with their skins left on to avoid unnecessary food waste
- Send food waste to be turned into compost so that it can be used to grow more plants
- Use left-over cooked and uncooked foods to make other dishes
- Send left-over food to charities who collect it for people in need.

Activity: Using left-over foods

Think of some dishes you could make using these left-over foods:

Left-over food	Your suggestions for dishes you could make
1. Cooked chicken breast	
2. Cooked carrots and potatoes	
3. Cooked beef Bolognese sauce	
4. Cold cooked pork sausages	
5. Fresh fruit salad	
6. Cooked pasta	
7. Uncooked mushrooms that are starting to go wrinkly	
8. Some fresh chopped tomatoes, half an onion, some slightly wilted basil leaves and two cloves of garlic	

Menus should meet customers' needs

... be aware of

Key learning

Menus should be **balanced**, which means they should have:

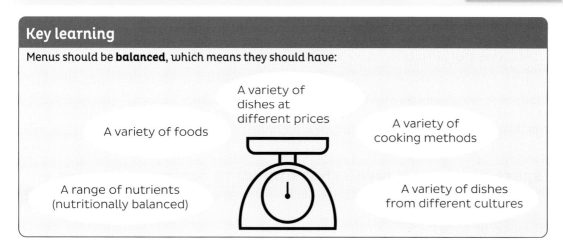

A variety of dishes at different prices

A variety of foods

A variety of cooking methods

A range of nutrients (nutritionally balanced)

A variety of dishes from different cultures

Nutritional needs

... be aware of

Many customers want healthy food for themselves and their children. Ideally, the menu should follow dietary guidelines (see page 119), by including a variety of dishes that use the recommended amounts of foods that people need to be healthy, i.e.:

Mostly:

Vegetables and fruit

Complex carbohydrates (rice, potatoes, pasta, bread)

Some:

Proteins (beans, peas, lentils, eggs, meat, poultry, fish)

Dairy foods (milk, cheese, yogurt, cream)

Only a small amount:

Fats and oils

Only sometimes:

Foods such as chocolate and savoury snacks

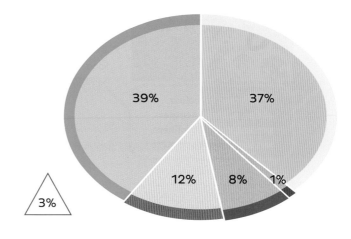

Special dietary needs

... be aware of

The menu should offer some dishes that suit people on special diets, e.g.:

- Dairy free
- Gluten free
- Nut free
- Low salt, low sugar, low fat
- High fibre
- Vegetarian/vegan
- Religious dietary laws, e.g. Jewish people do not eat pork or shellfish; Hindus do not eat beef.

Alternative foods could be offered for people on special diets, e.g.:

- Soy, oat or nut milk instead of cow's milk
- Gluten-free bread rolls
- Wholemeal bread instead of white bread
- A vegan version of a menu item
- Boiled or baked potatoes instead of fried chips.

Sensory needs

Eating food is one of life's pleasures and to enjoy it, all the body's senses (**sight, smell, taste, touch** and **sound**) need to work together.

Menu planning, food preparation, cooking and serving should be carried out really well so that the dishes that are produced are **appetising** (people want to eat them) and appeal to all the senses.

The following mind maps and text explain how the senses affect customer enjoyment of food, and how to plan menus to appeal to customer senses. There are also examples of words that describe foods, some of which are used in menus.

How to plan and prepare dishes on a menu that appeal to customers' senses

SIGHT (appearance of food)

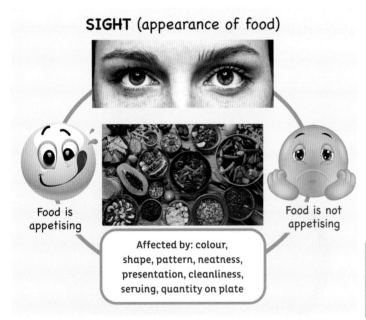

Food is appetising — Food is not appetising

Affected by: colour, shape, pattern, neatness, presentation, cleanliness, serving, quantity on plate

Present, decorate and garnish food neatly and creatively.

Make use of colours – natural food colours, serving dishes, table settings.

Cut and form food into decorative shapes and presentations.

Make sure plates and dishes are cleaned before serving the food, to remove drips and splashes.

Make sure the food fits neatly on the plate or dish.

Words to describe how food looks (appearance): appetising, neat, colourful, decorative, fresh, frothy, bite-sized, charred, comforting, glazed, glossy, healthy

SOUND (e.g. crispy, crunchy, fizzy)

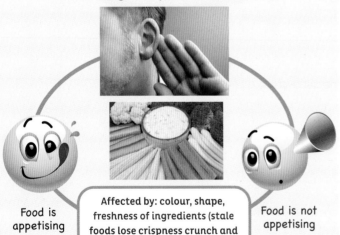

Food is appetising — Food is not appetising

Affected by: colour, shape, freshness of ingredients (stale foods lose crispness crunch and fizziness), storing food correctly

Plan menus to include a variety of textures.

Store food correctly so it stays fresh and keeps its texture and sound, e.g. salad foods should be stored in a cool place; dry foods, such as biscuits, should be kept in an airtight tin away from moisture so that they stay crisp.

Cook foods correctly to develop their texture and therefore their sounds.

Words to describe how food sounds: crispy, crunchy, crackling, fizzing, hissing, snap, bubbly, popping, sizzling

SMELL (aroma of food)

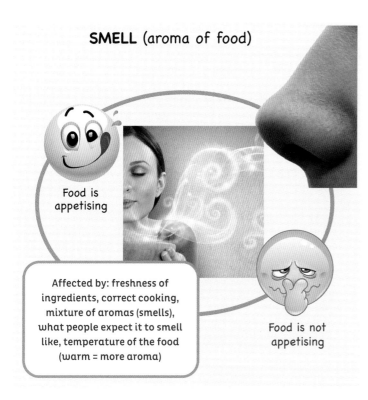

Food is appetising

Food is not appetising

Affected by: freshness of ingredients, correct cooking, mixture of aromas (smells), what people expect it to smell like, temperature of the food (warm = more aroma)

Use a mixture of foods to produce a variety of aromas (smells), but do not using too many, as the overall effect will be spoiled.

Make sure that food is cooked properly – aromas are released when food is heated, but they can easily be spoiled if the food is over-cooked.

Make sure that only fresh ingredients are used – stale foods do not produce good aromas.

Use natural foods that produce strong (robust) aromas, e.g. fresh and dried herbs and spices, garlic, orange, lemon and lime zest; and cooking methods that develop aromas, e.g. grilling, roasting, baking, sautéing, frying.

Words to describe how food smells (aromas): fresh, fragrant, savoury, sweet, pungent (a strong smell), rancid ('gone-off'), sour, aromatic (pleasant), fruity, fishy, citrusy (like lemons/oranges), earthy (like mushrooms), stale, piquant (strong, makes the nose tingle, e.g. vinegar)

TASTE (flavour of food)

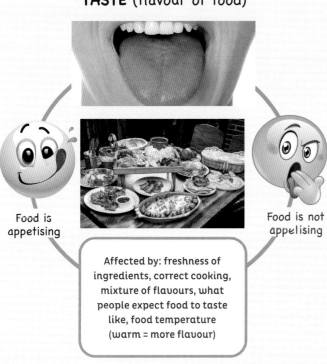

Food is appetising

Food is not appetising

Affected by: freshness of ingredients, correct cooking, mixture of flavours, what people expect food to taste like, food temperature (warm = more flavour)

Use fresh food – stale food loses its flavour.

Cook food carefully to avoid damaging flavours, e.g. over-cooking can make some flavours bitter, such as those in spices, butter and green vegetables.

Use cooking methods that 'bring out' (develop) flavours, e.g.:

- Sautéing vegetables in butter or oil
- Making stock from meat, poultry or fish bones plus vegetables, herbs, peppercorns and other spices
- Roasting root vegetables (e.g. carrots, beetroot, onions, garlic, parsnips), which makes flavours stronger (concentrates/intensifies the flavour) by allowing water to escape from them (evaporate) and caramelises the natural sugars they contain
- Reducing a sauce (allowing water to evaporate by heating it) so that its flavours become stronger.

Use natural flavours, e.g. citrus fruit zest, fresh herbs and spices, e.g. rosemary, sage, basil, ginger and lemongrass.

Do not add too much of strongly flavoured ingredients such as chilli, fish sauce and soy sauce, as they can easily overpower other flavours and make the food unpleasant to eat.

Do not add too many other flavours to delicately flavoured foods such as fish.

Try mixing a few different flavours, but be careful: too many flavours together may not work.

⚠️ **Remember!**
Always taste food before you serve it so you can check the flavour and change it a little if needed.

⚠️ **Remember! FOOD HYGIENE!**
Do not taste the food and put the spoon you have licked back into the food without washing it first!

Words to describe how food tastes (flavours): salty, umami (savoury/meaty), sweet, sour, bitter, bland (very little flavour), spicy, herby, peppery, nutty, smoky, tangy, yeasty, acidic

TOUCH (texture and mouthfeel of food)

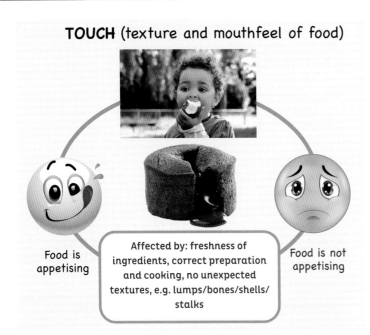

Food is appetising

Affected by: freshness of ingredients, correct preparation and cooking, no unexpected textures, e.g. lumps/bones/shells/stalks

Food is not appetising

Plan menus that include a variety of textures.

Use fresh foods – stale foods lose their texture quite quickly, e.g. vegetables, fruits, fish.

Prepare food carefully and remove parts that cannot be eaten, e.g. shells, bones, stalks, tough skins, fruit stones and seeds, small stones and grit.

Cook food well to avoid unexpected textures, e.g. lumps in a sauce, under-cooked egg white, under-cooked cake mixture, over-cooked and tough meat.

Cook food at the correct temperature and for enough time to allow textures to develop, e.g. when melting chocolate, baking a cake or bread, frying doughnuts.

Words to describe how food feels (textures):
chewy, creamy, crispy, crumbly, crunchy, crusty, doughy, melt-in-the-mouth, flaky, puffy, fluffy, juicy, moist, succulent, sticky, gooey, smooth, tender, oily/greasy, mushy, frothy, spongy

Activity: Planning menus to meet customers' sensory needs

Look at the three-course dinner menu below. Identify and describe which parts of the dishes particularly appeal to the different senses – an example is given to show you.

Menu/Dish	Sight	Smell	Taste	Touch	Sound
Starter: Lentil and tomato soup	Red/orange colour of the soup Green parsley and cream garnish		Fresh tomatoes, garlic, sautéed onion and celery add flavour	Cooked lentils thicken the soup Smooth texture produced by liquidising the soup Croutons add crunchy texture	
Served with baked garlic croutons *(made from bread, melted butter, crushed garlic, salt and pepper)*					
Main course: Thai chicken curry Sticky rice Steamed green beans					
Dessert: Molten chocolate surprise puddings *(sponge pudding with hidden chocolate that melts during cooking and pours out when opened by a spoon)* Served with vanilla ice cream and fresh raspberries					

Activity: How would you make these dishes look more appetising?

Suggest some ways that you could make the following dishes look more appetising and creative:

| Tomato soup |  | |

| Cauliflower with cheese sauce (cauliflower au gratin) | 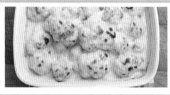 | |

| Spaghetti Bolognese |  | |

| Grilled chicken |  | |

| Plain sponge cake |  | |

| Plain crème caramel |  | |

| Plain panna cotta |  | |

Planning a menu to meet customer needs

Include a variety of dishes to cater for different likes and dislikes

Do the dishes on the menu appeal to customers' senses – sight, smell, taste, touch and sound?

Offer some dishes that would suit different health conditions

Offer suitable portion sizes for different needs, e.g. children, older adults, active people

Show customers which dishes may not be suitable for them if they have food allergies or food intolerances

Things to take into account when planning menus to meet customer needs

Offer some dishes to suit different customer lifestyles, e.g. active / inactive / a busy family / an office worker, etc.

Offer some dishes that would suit a range of religious or cultural dietary rules

Are the prices of dishes on the menu affordable for the target customers?

Think about the type of meal to be eaten – everyday or special occasion, packed meal, etc.

Seasonal/local foods – are these available? What do they cost?

Do the dishes in the menu meet dietary guidelines?

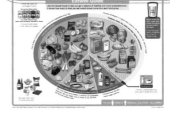

Key learning   ◀ ...be aware of

Good planning and organisation are the most important factors for the production of dishes to a high standard for a menu.

Bad planning and poor organisation lead to:

- A badly run kitchen
- Stress and wasted energy for the people who work in the kitchen and the front-of-house staff
- An unsuccessful business.

This is the order for the production of dishes for a menu, which is shown in detail on the following pages of this book: ◀ ...be aware of

1. Planning the dishes on the menu

2. Producing the dishes on the menu

3. Serving the dishes on the menu

4. Preventing and dealing with waste from the menu

◀ ...be able to

Sequencing/dovetailing. This means fitting together the different stages of a production plan into a logical order, which you will need to do when you write a time plan for making two or more dishes. You need to:

1. Print a copy of each of the recipes you are going to use.

2. In the method section of each recipe, highlight every activity you will need to do, e.g. make a dough, whisk eggs and sugar together, cut some vegetables, etc. Use a different colour highlight for each recipe to make it easier to follow.

3. Work out and show on your time plan which activity for which recipe you will do first – usually something that needs the longest time to be completed, e.g. setting a cold mousse in the refrigerator, leaving a bread dough to rise, making some pastry and letting it rest, or cooking something for a long time.

4. Show which activity from another dish you will do next while you are waiting for the first recipe to be ready to move on to the next stage and so on, until every activity has been included.

5. When you are dovetailing the activities, remember to allow enough time for, e.g. water to boil when cooking vegetables, meat to tenderise when you are making a stew or enough time to chop up some ingredients.

6. Remember to show when you would expect to take something out of the oven and how you would check to see that it is ready.

Key terms you should try to include in your answers

Contingency – a backup plan to deal with either an emergency situation (e.g. the cooker breaks down or a special ingredient is not available) so that customer service can be restored as soon as possible; or a seasonal peak in business (e.g. Christmas) so that extra staff and equipment can be hired to cope with the increase in customers

Sequencing – also known as 'dovetailing'. This means fitting together the different stages of a production plan into a logical order

Order of food production for a menu

Plan the menu
Recipes, ingredients, preparation and cooking method for chosen dishes
Number of portions of each dish to be made
How each dish will be served /presented /garnished /decorated

Who does it?
Head Chef and Assistant Chef
Who needs to know?
Stock Controller and every chef

Health and safety:
High-risk foods must be stored safely

Contingencies:
Plan alternative menus in case some ingredients are not available

Order
Ingredients and materials needed for the menu
Take in, check and store the delivery

Who does it?
Stock Controller and Kitchen Porter
Who needs to know?
Head Chef

Health and safety:
Check food delivery for quality and temperature

Contingencies:
Buy ingredients from more than one supplier, so if one does not have an ingredient, another may have

Store
Ingredients, materials, tools and equipment must be stored tidily so they can be found and used easily
Make sure tools and equipment are clean and working properly, e.g. knives are sharpened, food processor accessories are in place, etc.

Who does it?
Stock Controller and Kitchen Porter
Who needs to know?
All chefs and kitchen workers

Health and safety:
Food storage temperatures must be regularly checked
Oldest ingredients must be used first (first in, first out)

Contingencies:
Keep a list of companies who hire out emergency refrigerators and freezers in case one breaks down in the storeroom

Mise en place
Have everything (ingredients, tools and equipment) ready and in place before starting to cook
Read recipes carefully before cooking, to make sure that you know what you need to do to make a dish
Prepare ingredients, e.g. chop vegetables, prepare garnishes, weigh ingredients, cut poultry into joints

Who does it?
All chefs and their assistants

Health and safety:
Wash vegetables and fruits
Store prepared foods in suitable containers at the right temperatures until they are needed

Contingencies:
Have some extra ingredients ready in case there are more orders for a particular dish than originally planned

Sequencing
Prepare and cook dishes in a logical order
Dishes that take a long time to prepare and cook should be prepared first, e.g. bread dough needs time to rise; casseroles take a long time to cook; cold desserts need to set or freeze; stocks and sauces need time to reduce and develop flavour
Some ingredients/foods should be prepared/cooked last, e.g. green vegetables, baked soufflés, pan-fried fish

Who does it?
Head Chef and Assistant Chef

Health and safety:
Use temperature probes and correct storage to keep food safe to eat
Foods to be reheated for service must reach 70 °C for 2 minutes

Timing

The length of time it takes for different stages of a dish to be made, e.g. how long it takes to: peel and chop vegetables; fillet fish; prepare a piece of meat or poultry for cooking; boil a pan of potatoes; bake and cool down a sponge before it can be decorated as a gateau; set a cold cheesecake, etc.

Who does it?

Head Chef and Assistant Chef; all chefs

Health and safety:

If they are to be reheated later, cooked foods need to be cooled as quickly as possible to prevent the growth of micro-organisms

Contingencies:

It may save time and be cost-effective to use some ready-made ingredients (e.g. puff pastry, pasta sauces, partially baked bread rolls) and machinery such as an electric potato peeler and large mixing machine

Cooking

Food should be cooked correctly to produce a high-quality dish
Food should be cooked with high food safety standards
As little waste as possible should be produced

Who does it?

All chefs and supervisors

Health and safety:

'Clear as you go' throughout preparation and cooking
Use temperature probes to make sure food is cooked properly

Cooling / Hot holding

Food must be kept safe and nice to eat by cooling it within 1½ hours to 5 °C or below if it is to be used later
Use shallow trays or blast chillers to cool food quickly
Hot food must be kept at 63 °C or above

Who does it?

All chefs and supervisors

Health and safety:

Use temperature probes to make sure food is kept at the right temperature

Completion and serving

Finishing off dishes ready for service, e.g. garnishing, decorating, serving on plates, adding accompaniments such as salad and sauces

Who does it?

All chefs and assistants

Health and safety:

Use temperature probes to check core temperatures of high-risk foods

Use serving tongs, disposable gloves and other serving equipment to prevent cross-contamination

Keep cooked and raw foods away from each other

Contingencies:

Have some extra garnishes and accompaniments available in case there are more orders than originally planned

Waste from the menu

Should be kept to a minimum
Some left-over ingredients can be used for other dishes, e.g. raw or cooked vegetables could be used in a soup; cooked meats could be used in a pie; soft fruits could be used in a fruit sauce

Who does it?

All chefs and assistants

Health and safety:

Store left-over ingredients correctly to keep them safe to eat

Get rid of food waste properly in outside bins to prevent pest infestation

Label left-over foods with the date they were made and use up as soon as possible

Contingencies:

Make an agreement with a local charity that collects left-over foods, so that food is not wasted

Activity: Put the production of the menu into order

Look at the following menu carefully with one other person.

Decide the following between you:

1. The order (sequence) in which a professional catering kitchen would produce the dishes on the menu.
2. Which ingredients the chefs would prepare during mise en place and how they would store them until they were required.
3. How the chefs would garnish/decorate each dish.

Menu

Starters

Spring vegetable soup
Served with croutons and a homemade crusty bread roll and butter

Smoked mackerel pâté and toast
Served with a salad garnish

Prawn, melon and ginger cocktail

Main courses

Slow roasted shoulder of lamb
Roasted potatoes and parsnips
Seasonal vegetables

Locally produced pork sausages in a red wine gravy
Served with creamed potatoes and peas

Deep fried haddock in a crispy batter,
Served with chips and a salad garnish

Caramelised onion, tomato and basil quiche
Served with jacket potato or chips, green salad and homemade coleslaw

Desserts

Lemon mousse
Served with shortbread bites

Apple pie

Baked vanilla cheesecake
Served with fruit coulis

All desserts served with either homemade ice cream, custard or whipped cream

How to prepare and make dishes
(including 2.1.2 How cooking methods can impact on nutritional value)

2.3.1
2.1.2

Key learning

For the practical part of the Assessment in Unit 2, you will be asked to plan, prepare, cook and serve two dishes and accompaniments (see pages 169–171) that are:

- Suitable for a particular situation and customer needs
- Produced in a hygienic way so that the food is safe to eat
- Nutritionally balanced
- Appetising and creatively presented.

During the course, you will have had the opportunity to learn and develop a variety of skills, including:

- Menu planning
- Food preparation and cooking techniques
- Organisation and time management.

The practical part of the assessment is your opportunity to demonstrate these skills and produce and present a range of dishes that show what you are able to achieve.

 Remember!
When you plan your practical assessment, try to use a wide variety of food preparation techniques, cooking methods and food presentations to show the skills you have learned.

Study tip
In this section, a summary of the preparation and knife skills and techniques that you need to know about is given. You will find more information about each skill and technique in the student book (pages 166–223) and in your practical lessons during the course. There is also a more detailed section on cooking methods (skills), giving information on how the sensory qualities of food (flavour, aroma, texture) and nutrients are affected by the different cooking methods.

Skills and skill levels used for preparing and cooking food

...be able to

Preparation, knife and cooking skills are used to make food into dishes that are:

- Appetising (how they look and smell makes people want to eat them)
- Safe to eat (they will not make a person ill if they eat them)
- Good to eat (they have interesting and enjoyable flavours and textures).

Skills are also called techniques (meaning a way/method of doing something). The word 'skills' will be used throughout this section. These skills are divided into **three levels**:

Basic skills: These are simple skills, e.g. sieving, grating, chopping, boiling.

Medium skills: These are skills that are necessary to produce a well-completed dish, e.g. weighing and measuring ingredients properly; cooking ingredients at the correct temperature.

Complex skills: These are more difficult skills that must be thought about and carried out carefully, using knowledge about how ingredients work, so that they are completed well, e.g. piping whipped cream; whisking eggs and sugar to produce a sponge; caramelising sugar, filleting a fish.

 Remember!
If you use any ready-made/prepared factory-made /shop-bought ingredients (e.g. ready-made pastry, sponge flan case, cake mixes and sauces) for the preparation and cooking of dishes in your Unit 2 Assessment (see pages 180–200), they will all be classified as **basic skills**.

Preparation and knife skills

The following chart lists the basic, medium, and complex **preparation** and **knife skills** that you should be able to identify and demonstrate, to produce dishes in Unit 2. Methods of cooking food are covered in a separate section on pages 148–60.

A brief definition of what each skill means is given:

Preparation skills		
Basic preparation skill	**What does it mean?**	**Examples of foods/ingredients**
Beating	Thoroughly mixing ingredients together to trap air and make a smooth mixture	Cake mixtures; raw eggs
Blending	To mix one substance with another substance so that they become one	Blending cornflour with milk
Grating	To change hard, solid foods into small pieces by rubbing them through a grater	Cheese, chocolate, carrots
Hydrating	To soak dry foods in water/liquid	Dried beans, lentils, dried fruits, couscous, dried mushrooms
Juicing	To extract juice from a fruit or vegetable	Citrus fruits, apples, carrots, green leafy vegetables
Marinating	Leaving food in either a flavoured liquid, paste or dry rub (the marinade) for several hours, so that the food takes up the flavour	Meat, poultry, some vegetables
Mashing	Crushing a food (cooked or uncooked) to form a soft texture	Bananas, cooked carrots, swede, potatoes and sweet potatoes, avocados
Melting	Turning a solid food to a liquid over a low heat	Butter, vegetable fat, syrup, treacle, coconut oil, sugar
Proving (proofing)	Leaving a dough containing yeast to rise in a warm place	Bread and bun doughs, yeasted batters, e.g. blinis
Shredding	Cutting foods into long, thin strips	Vegetables, cheese
Sieving	Passing food through a fine net/mesh to: • trap air • spread out dry ingredients • separate large particles from small ones • make smooth	Flour, spices, icing sugar, cocoa, baking powder, cooked berries (to remove seeds), soups, sauces
Tenderising	To make meat easy to chew and eat by pounding it with a hammer, applying a marinade or using a meat tenderiser powder/paste	Meat and poultry
Zesting	Peeling the outer skin of citrus fruits very finely to use for flavour	Oranges, lemons, limes, tangerines and other citrus fruits
Medium preparation skill	**What does it mean?**	**Examples of foods/ingredients**
Creaming	Mixing (beating) fat and sugar together with a wooden spoon	Cake mixtures
Dehydrating	Removing water from food using heat	Thin slices of fruits and vegetables
Folding	Mixing a light ingredient or mixture with a heavier one, without losing much of the air it contains	Folding flour into a whisked egg and sugar mixture for a sponge
Kneading	Using the hands to make a dough smooth and/or stretchy	Bread and other yeast doughs, pastry and biscuit doughs
Mixing	Putting two or more ingredients together (wet and/or dry), and stirring them until they are thoroughly and evenly combined	Cake and biscuit mixtures, pâtés, stuffings, nut roasts

Puréeing	Passing foods through a strainer to make a smooth, thick pulp with an even texture	Raw or cooked fruits and vegetables
Rubbing-in	Using the fingertips to rub fat into flour to form a mixture that looks like breadcrumbs	Butter or vegetable fat and flour
Rolling	Flattening and spreading out a dough using a rolling pin	Bread, pastry, biscuit, and other doughs
Skinning	Removing the outer surface ('skin') of a food	Nut kernels, poultry birds, fish, fruits, vegetables
Toasting (nuts/seeds)	Heating in a dry pan without oil until the food changes to a golden-brown colour	Nuts, e.g. hazel, almond, Brazil, cashew; seeds, e.g. pumpkin, sesame, sunflower, pine nuts
Weighing and measuring	Providing the correct amount of ingredients for a recipe	Weighing: dry/solid ingredients such as flour, sugar, nuts, butter Measuring: liquids in a jug, ladle or spoon Measuring: dry ingredients such as spices in measuring spoons

Complex preparation skills	What does it mean?	Examples of foods/ingredients
Crimping	Giving a decorative edge to a dish made from pastry or biscuit dough	Pies, pasties, tarts, biscuits
Laminating (pastry)	Rolling and folding a raw flour and water dough with fat, to create separate layers	Puff and flaky pastry, Danish pastry and croissant dough
Melting using bain-marie	Melting foods in a bowl placed inside a larger pan of heated water	Chocolate, honey, butter, syrup
Moulding/unmoulding/shaping	Making ingredients into decorative shapes using the hands, moulds and tools	Fondant icing, chocolate, marzipan, jelly, mousse
Piping	Producing a wide range of decorative shapes and effects using a piping bag and variety of nozzles	Whipped cream, buttercream, chocolate ganache, icing, melted chocolate
Whisking (aeration)	Mixing ingredients at high speed to trap air and make them lighter	Egg white (meringue), eggs and sugar, cake mixtures

Knife skills

Basic knife skills	What does it mean?	Examples of foods/ingredients
Chopping	Using a sharp knife to cut foods into a range of shapes and sizes	Vegetables, fruits, meat, poultry, hard cheese
Peeling	Removing the outer skin of a food with a knife or peeler	Root vegetables, hard fruits, e.g. apples and pears, pineapples, root ginger
Trimming	Removing parts of a food that should not be eaten, e.g. fat, tough leaves, stems, stalks, fish heads, scales, roots	Whole fish, meat, outer leaves and stalk of cabbage, pineapple, apple cores, onion and leek roots

Medium knife skills	What does it mean?	Examples of foods/ingredients
Baton	Cutting a vegetable into sticks, about 1 cm thick	Carrots, potatoes, beetroot
Chiffonade	Cutting very thin slices	Basil, spinach, bok choy, chard
Dicing	Cutting food into same sized cubes	Meat, vegetables, cheese
Slicing	Using a sharp knife or a mandolin to produce slices of food the same thickness as each other	Bread, vegetables, salad ingredients, fruit, cheese
Deseeding	Removing seeds from fruits and vegetable fruits	Pomegranates, citrus fruits, peppers, squashes, courgettes, cucumbers, tomatoes
Spatchcock	Preparing a chicken by cutting and opening it out flat, so that it cooks more quickly	Raw chicken

147

Complex knife skills	What does it mean?	Examples of foods/ingredients
Julienne	Cutting very thin strips of food used for a garnish	Carrot, celery, raw beetroot, pepper
Brunoise	Cutting very small cubes of food (about 3 mm)	Carrot, celery, raw beetroot
Mincing	Cutting foods into very small pieces	Carrot, celery, raw beetroot, onion, leek, fresh herbs, garlic
Deboning	Removing the bones from a meat joint or poultry	Chicken breast, thighs, legs; leg or shoulder meat joints
Filleting	Removing sections of flesh from a whole fish or poultry	Whole round or flat fish; chicken breast
Segmenting	Removing segments of citrus fruits so that they do not have any membrane, skin or pith attached to them	Oranges, grapefruit

Key terms you should try to include in your answers

Caramelise/caramelisation – when sugar is heated, the colour, flavour and texture changes to a golden-brown caramel syrup

Coagulate/coagulating – the joining together of lots of protein molecules from the effects of heat, beating/whisking or acids, which causes changes to the appearance and texture of a food

Ferment/fermentation – the breakdown of substances, such as carbohydrates, by bacteria and yeasts to produce alcohol, lactic acid and carbon dioxide

Gelatinise/gelatinisation – the swelling and softening of starch granules and release of starch, when they are cooked in a liquid, which makes the liquid thicken

Palatability – the qualities of a food that make it acceptable and good to eat

Solidify – to change from a liquid to a solid

Starch granules – little 'packets' of starch that are stored in plants such as starchy vegetables (e.g. potatoes, yams, peas, beans, squashes) and cereal grains (e.g. rice, wheat, maize)

Methods of cooking food

...be able to

Cooking skills are often referred to as cooking methods. There are various methods used to cook foods. Many methods use heat, but not all, e.g. some foods are chilled or frozen.

Methods of cooking that use **heat** include:

- using water to cook foods, e.g. boiling, steaming
- using dry heat to cook foods, e.g. baking, grilling
- using oil to cook foods, e.g. frying, roasting.

Methods of cooking that use **cold temperatures** include:

- cooling
- chilling
- freezing.

Choosing suitable methods of cooking for different foods and recipes is part of the skill and creativity of a chef.

The cooking methods are also divided into **skill levels**, which are listed in the chart below. Each one is then set out in more detail, describing how they affect the sensory (organoleptic) qualities of the food (flavour, aroma, texture – see page 177), how they affect nutrients in the food and which foods are most suited to being cooked by each method. You need to know and use this information in your Unit 2 Assessment (see pages 180–200).

Cooking techniques		
BASIC	**MEDIUM**	**COMPLEX**
Basting	Baking	Baking blind
Boiling	Blanching	Caramelising
Chilling	Braising	Deep fat frying
Cooling	Deglazing	Emulsifying
Dehydrating	Frying	Poaching
Freezing	Griddling	Tempering
Grilling	Pickling	
Skimming	Reduction	
Toasting	Roasting	
	Sautéing	
	Setting	
	Steaming	
	Stir frying	
	Water-bath (sous vide)	

Basic cooking methods

Basting BASIC

Basting – means to pour or brush meat juices and/or melted fat over a joint of meat or poultry bird (e.g. chicken, turkey), while it is cooking in the oven or on a rotisserie (a long, metal skewer that is pushed into the meat or poultry), over a fire.

Suitable foods:

Meat joints, whole poultry birds

What are the effects on the nutrients in the food?	What are the effects of this method of cooking on the sensory qualities of the food?	
	• **The appearance of the food (colour, size, shape, etc.)?**	• **The palatability of the food (texture, aroma, flavour)?**
• Some of the fat that has drained away from the meat during cooking will be put back and remain on the meat.	• The surface of the meat will be shiny.	• The meat or poultry is prevented from drying out, so it stays moist and succulent (juicy).

Boiling BASIC

Boiling means cooking food in water at 100 °C.

Suitable foods:

Eggs, rice, pasta, vegetables such as carrots, potatoes, swede; joints of meat such as gammon (bacon/ham); beans, peas, lentils, vegetable or meat stock

What are the effects on the nutrients in the food?	What are the effects of this method of cooking on the sensory qualities of the food?	
	The appearance of the food (colour, size, shape, etc.)?	The palatability of the food (texture, aroma, flavour)?
• Vitamin C, B₁ (thiamine) and B₂ (riboflavin) are destroyed by prolonged heating at boiling point • Water-soluble vitamins (B group and C) dissolve into the cooking water • Over-cooking meat will make the protein less digestible • Vitamin A remains stable when cooked • **Starch granules** are softened and some starch released, which makes it easier to digest	• Pasta, rice, beans and lentils swell up as their starch granules absorb the boiling water • Green vegetables turn bright green for a few minutes, then gradually become a dark olive green if over-cooked • Red/purple fruits and vegetables are affected by acids (makes them turn a brighter red/purple) and alkalis such as bicarbonate of soda, which makes them turn blue • Egg white changes from clear to white and the yolk becomes a lighter yellow as the protein coagulates • Meat/poultry shrink in size as protein coagulates	• Pasta, rice, peas, beans and lentils become soft as they absorb the water • Vegetables become soft and tender. They may become mushy and break up if they are boiled for too long • Meat becomes tender, but will dry out if boiled for too long because the protein **coagulates** too much and squeezes out the moisture it held • The flavour of some vegetables gets stronger, e.g. carrots become sweeter • Some flavour from meat will go into the water, but if the water is used to make gravy or stock, the flavour will be saved • The flavour of stock and sauces gets stronger as the water evaporates

Chilling BASIC

Chilling means to cool food to 0 °C to 5 °C in a refrigerator, chiller cabinet or blast chiller.

Suitable foods:

Desserts, e.g. jelly, mousse, cheesecake, fruit salad, panna cotta, lemon posset; soups, e.g. gazpacho, cucumber; meat and meat products, e.g. cold meats, cooked ham, pâté, Grosvenor pie, pork pie

What are the effects on the nutrients in the food?	What are the effects of this method of cooking on the sensory qualities of the food?	
	The appearance of the food (colour, size, shape, etc.)?	The palatability of the food (texture, aroma, flavour)?
• Vitamin C is less likely to be destroyed in chilled foods	• Liquid jelly and mousses set and become semi-solid and can be moulded into different shapes	• The coldness can mask some of the flavours • Chilled and set desserts such as crème caramel and possets develop a smooth, velvety texture

Cooling BASIC

Cooling means to reduce the temperature of a hot cooked food, down to at least 8 °C, either by using a refrigerator, a blast chiller, an ice bowl or leaving the food in a cool room, so that it can be safely stored to prevent the growth of bacteria.

Suitable foods:

All foods that have been heated during cooking

What are the effects on the nutrients in the food?	What are the effects of this method of cooking on the sensory qualities of the food?	
	The appearance of the food (colour, size, shape, etc.)?	The palatability of the food (texture, aroma, flavour)?
• Nutrients, such as B vitamins and vitamin C, become more stable in cooler foods	• Melted fat in meat dishes will solidify • Melted chocolate and butter will **solidify** in sauces, ganache and frostings used on baked products	• The flavour of some foods is enhanced (increased/improved) during the cooling process, e.g. curry spices become stronger

Dehydrating (see also page 146) BASIC

Dehydrating means to remove water from a food by the heat from the Sun, an electric dehydrator or an oven. The temperature range for dehydrating is 40 °C to 48 °C.

Drying times will vary according to the type of food used and the method used to dehydrate it. Here are some average times for a variety of foods:

Apples 7–15 hours
Strawberries 5–15 hours
Potatoes 6–14 hours
Tomatoes 5–9 hours

Suitable foods:

Fruits such as apples, strawberries, apricots, cranberries, bananas; vegetables such as potatoes, courgettes, onions, beetroot, mushrooms; herbs; meat such as beef to make beef jerky

What are the effects on the nutrients in the food?	What are the effects of this method of cooking on the sensory qualities of the food?	
	The appearance of the food (colour, size, shape, etc.)?	The palatability of the food (texture, aroma, flavour)?
• There may be some loss of vitamins A, C and B during dehydration	• The food will shrink • Some fruits will go brown due to enzyme action • Some slices of fruit and vegetables will form curled shapes	• The flavours intensify (becomes stronger) as the water evaporates • The texture may become chewy

Freezing BASIC

Freezing means to reduce the temperature of a food until it has frozen to between –18 °C and –24 °C.

Suitable foods:

Frozen desserts such as, ice creams, sorbets (puréed fruit, sugar and water frozen and churned until smooth), granita (similar to sorbets, but with a flakier texture), semifreddo (similar to a frozen mousse); meat and meat products, fish, poultry, cakes, pastries, some desserts, breads, milk, many fruits and vegetables, soups, some sauces.

What are the effects on the nutrients in the food?	What are the effects of this method of cooking on the sensory qualities of the food?	
	The appearance of the food (colour, size, shape, etc.)?	The palatability of the food (texture, aroma, flavour)?
• Vitamin C is prevented from being destroyed if foods such as peas, beans, berries and other fruits and vegetables are frozen very soon after being harvested (see also Blanching page 153)	• Ice crystals form inside and on the outside of the food • The food becomes solid 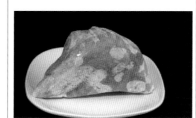	• If the food is frozen quickly, small ice crystals form, giving the food a smooth texture • If the food is frozen slowly, large ice crystals form, which can spoil the texture of the food • If frozen meat, poultry or fish is not wrapped properly in the freezer, the cold can cause proteins in them to become dry and tough, and white patches will show on the surface – this is called 'freezer burn'. The flavour may also be spoilt. • The cells inside some fruits and vegetables are damaged when ice crystals form, and when the food is defrosted, their texture will become soft, mushy and wet • Some foods, e.g. bananas and potatoes, become dark brown/black in colour in very cold conditions

Grilling/barbequing BASIC

Grilling/barbequing means cooking foods by intense radiant heat on a metal grid or grill rack, underneath a heated grill element in a cooker or above the glowing charcoal/flames of a barbeque.

Suitable foods:

Meat and poultry joints, oily fish, sausages, burgers, toppings for gratin dishes (cheese sauce), halloumi cheese, tomatoes, sweetcorn cobs

What are the effects on the nutrients in the food?	What are the effects of this method of cooking on the sensory qualities of the food?	
	The appearance of the food (colour, size, shape, etc.)?	The palatability of the food (texture, aroma, flavour)?
• Vitamin C, B₁ and B₂ are damaged by the intense heat • Fat melting out of meat, meat products and other foods reduces the energy density of the food • Over-cooking meat / poultry will make the protein less digestible	• Meat/poultry will shrink rapidly due to protein coagulating • Fat melts and drains out • Surface of meat/poultry develops a golden-brown colour	• Juices from meat and poultry are squeezed out and develop flavour on the surface • Food develops a smoky flavour from the burning charcoal • If cooked too rapidly, meat and poultry can become dry and chewy due to protein coagulating and squeezing out water • Flavour gets stronger as water evaporates

Skimming BASIC

Skimming means to take off a layer of foam or fat from the surface of liquids that are being cooked (boiled).

A slotted spoon (one with holes or slots cut out) should be used for skimming foam from the surface and a solid spoon for removing liquid fat.

Suitable foods:

Jam, marmalade, boiled lentils, meat, poultry or fish stock, broths and soups

What are the effects on the nutrients in the food?	What are the effects of this method of cooking on the sensory qualities of the food?	
	The appearance of the food (colour, size, shape, etc.)?	The palatability of the food (texture, aroma, flavour)?
• If fat is skimmed off, it will reduce the energy value of the dish	• Removing the grey foam will allow a soup, such as consommé, to become clear	• The foam is edible and should not affect the flavour of most dishes if it is not removed • The removal of a layer of melted fat prevents the dish from being oily in texture

Toasting BASIC

Toasting means cooking starch-based foods with dry heat from a grill or flame.

Suitable foods:

Bread, buns, crumpets and other starch-based products, nuts, seeds

What are the effects on the nutrients in the food?	What are the effects of this method of cooking on the sensory qualities of the food?	
	The appearance of the food (colour, size, shape, etc.)?	The palatability of the food (texture, aroma, flavour)?
• Starch turns to dextrin (a type of carbohydrate formed when starch is heated by dry heat)	• Food develops a golden-brown crust	• Flavour gets stronger • Crust adds texture to the food

Medium cooking methods

Baking MEDIUM

Baking means cooking foods in a hot oven.

Suitable foods:

Cakes, breads, biscuits, cookies, scones, pastries, potatoes, pizzas, desserts

What are the effects on the nutrients in the food?	What are the effects of this method of cooking on the sensory qualities of the food?	
	The appearance of the food (colour, size, shape, etc.)?	The palatability of the food (texture, aroma, flavour)?
• Gases from raising agents expand with the heat and make mixtures rise • Protein coagulates • Added sugars melt and form a syrup that softens the **gluten** (protein found in flour) • Added sugars eventually **caramelise** • Fat will melt • Starch granules absorb water and/or melted fat, swell and **gelatinise** • Alcohol produced by yeast in bread doughs evaporates in the heat of the oven • Yeast is killed by the heat • Gluten, egg proteins and starch set and form a framework around the gas bubbles inside baked products	• Baked foods containing raising agents rise and expand before setting in the heat of the oven  • Starch in the outside crust of baked goods turns to dextrin and turns a golden-brown colour • Caramelised sugars add golden-brown colour	• Risen food sets and develops a tender, open/crumbly/spongy texture inside  • A crust develops on the outside • Caramelised sugars add flavour

Blanching MEDIUM

Blanching means to place food that is going to be frozen, into boiling water for a short time (a few seconds to a couple of minutes depending on the food), removing it, and placing it into very cold/iced water to cool rapidly.

Suitable foods:
Vegetables ready for freezing, such as peas, sweetcorn, green beans, broad beans, asparagus

What are the effects on the nutrients in the food?	What are the effects of this method of cooking on the sensory qualities of the food?	
	The appearance of the food (colour, size, shape, etc.)?	The palatability of the food (texture, aroma, flavour)?
• Blanching helps to prevent the loss of some vitamins such as B group and vitamin C	• Blanching causes the green colour of vegetables to become very bright	• Blanching destroys the natural enzymes in vegetables that cause a loss of flavour

Braising MEDIUM

Braising means sealing in hot oil, then cooking slowly in a covered dish with a little liquid.

Suitable foods:
Meat, poultry, tagines, vegetables, e.g. carrots, fennel, red cabbage

What are the effects on the nutrients in the food?	What are the effects of this method of cooking on the sensory qualities of the food?	
	The appearance of the food (colour, size, shape, etc.)?	The palatability of the food (texture, aroma, flavour)?
• Starch granules absorb water and gelatinise • Protein coagulates • Meat tenderises • Vegetables tenderise • Fat will melt	• The colour of red meat becomes brown • Meat/poultry shrink in size as protein coagulates • Red cabbage becomes a deep red/purple colour • Sauces become glossy (shiny)	• Meat, poultry and vegetables become tender • Food cooks slowly and absorbs flavours from stock, vegetables, herbs and spices that are added to it

Deglazing MEDIUM

Deglazing means to remove the brown, strongly flavoured sticky residues that get left on the bottom of a frying pan or roasting tin when meat or poultry is fried or roasted. Deglazing is done by dissolving the residues in a liquid such as water, wine or stock.

Suitable foods:
Meat, poultry, fried onions

What are the effects on the nutrients in the food?	What are the effects of this method of cooking on the sensory qualities of the food?	
	The appearance of the food (colour, size, shape, etc.)?	The palatability of the food (texture, aroma, flavour)?
• No significant effects	• The residues colour the dissolving liquid to a golden-brown colour	• The residues are formed from the liquid inside the cells of meat and have a distinctive, rich, slightly salted flavour, which improves the flavour of gravies, stocks and sauces

153

Frying MEDIUM

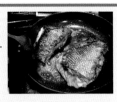

Frying is often called pan frying and means to cook food in a shallow amount of melted fat or oil.

Suitable foods:

Meat, fish, poultry, eggs, vegetables, e.g. potatoes, onions, mushrooms, peppers; fruits, e.g. pineapple, apple, nuts

What are the effects on the nutrients in the food?	What are the effects of this method of cooking on the sensory qualities of the food?	
	The appearance of the food (colour, size, shape, etc.)?	The palatability of the food (texture, aroma, flavour)?
• High temperatures can destroy some vitamins such as B group and C • Protein sets (coagulates), and carbohydrate will gelatinise	• Food develops a golden-brown colour • The oils in nuts and seeds melt and are released • Meat browns and fat and juices are released from it	• Flavour gets stronger • Oils are released and add texture and flavour • Fat in meat melts and drains out • Proteins in meat coagulate and squeeze out juices from the meat, and add to its flavour

Griddling MEDIUM

Griddling means to cook food, with or without fat, on a metal surface, which is heated underneath, and sometimes has raised lines which give the food a distinctive appearance.

Suitable foods:

Meat steaks, sausages, burgers, fish, poultry, some vegetables, e.g. corn on the cob, aubergine slices, kebabs, satay chicken, pancakes

What are the effects on the nutrients in the food?	What are the effects of this method of cooking on the sensory qualities of the food?	
	The appearance of the food (colour, size, shape, etc.)?	The palatability of the food (texture, aroma, flavour)?
• High temperatures can destroy some vitamins such as B group and C • Protein coagulates, and carbohydrate will gelatinise	• Food develops a golden-brown appearance, marked by lines if the griddle has them • Meat and poultry will shrink	• Meat and poultry tenderise • Outside surface may become crisp • Flavours develop and intensify with the heat

Pickling MEDIUM

Pickling is a method that is used to preserve food by stopping the growth of microbes. There are two methods:

• Food is covered in vinegar and put in a sealed container.

• Food is **fermented** in brine (salt and water), plus other flavouring e.g. garlic, mustard, chilli pepper, herbs. Harmless bacteria ferment natural sugars in the food and produce lactic acid that preserves it and gives flavour.

Store pickled foods in a cool, dry place for several weeks to develop flavour and texture.

Suitable foods:

Examples that are pickled in vinegar: cabbage, gherkins, onions, hard-boiled eggs, gherkins, onions, apples, beetroot, ginger

Examples that are fermented in brine: cabbage (to make sauerkraut and kimchi); barley, rice and soya beans (to make products such as miso and tempeh); fish to produce fish sauce; soya to produce soy sauce

What are the effects on the nutrients in the food?	What are the effects of this method of cooking on the sensory qualities of the food?	
	The appearance of the food (colour, size, shape, etc.)?	The palatability of the food (texture, aroma, flavour)?
• Some vitamins and minerals are easier for our bodies to absorb • Natural bacteria in the gut are more able to produce vitamin K and some of the B vitamins • Some sugars and starch in fermented foods are broken down during fermentation	• Pickled foods usually keep their colour • Some fermented foods may go brown. If the whole batch goes brown and smells 'off', do not eat it	• Pickled vegetables often develop a crisp, crunchy texture. • Fermented cabbage (sauerkraut) develops a soft texture – it should not be slimy. • Pickled foods develop a range of flavours and are usually sour / acidic and tangy to eat

Reduction MEDIUM

Reduction means simmering a liquid, e.g. a stock or sauce, to evaporate the water in it, until its flavours have intensified (become stronger) and the texture has thickened. The final liquid is called a reduction.

Suitable foods:

Stocks: Meat, poultry or fish bones – when the stock goes cold, it becomes a jelly due to the gelatine in the bones.

Salt is not added to stock, because the reduced liquid would become too salty.

Sauces: e.g. Espagnole sauce – made from tomato purée and brown stock and thickened with a roux (fat and flour), then reduced in volume by at least one third. Add salt after reducing the liquid when making sauces.

Stews/gravies: The liquid is reduced by one third to concentrate the flavours and thicken the texture. Add salt after reducing the liquid.

Glazes: e.g. meat stock is reduced in volume by three quarters, until it will coat the back of a spoon. Add salt after reducing the liquid.

Balsamic vinegar is reduced until it has a syrupy texture and is poured over fruits, desserts and vegetables.

What are the effects on the nutrients in the food?	What are the effects of this method of cooking on the sensory qualities of the food?	
	The appearance of the food (colour, size, shape, etc.)?	The palatability of the food (texture, aroma, flavour)?
• Prolonged simmering will damage some B vitamins and vitamin C	• Sauces and gravies develop a shine and a rich colour	• Flavours and aromas intensify, and the texture thickens

Roasting MEDIUM

Roasting means cooking food in fat or oil in the oven.

Suitable foods:

Meat and poultry joints; root vegetables; some fruits, e.g. plums; nuts

What are the effects on the nutrients in the food?	What are the effects of this method of cooking on the sensory qualities of the food?	
	The appearance of the food (colour, size, shape, etc.)?	The palatability of the food (texture, aroma, flavour)?
• Fat used in roasting adds to energy density • Fat used adds fat-soluble vitamins A, D, E, K • Vitamins C, B$_1$ and B$_2$ are affected by the heat • Over-cooking meat/poultry will make the protein less digestible	• Red meat turns brown; poultry turns a creamy/white colour • Onions, parsnips, carrots become golden brown due to caramelisation of sugars • Colours of vegetables get stronger • Vegetables shrink as water evaporates from them • Skin on poultry and fat on meat, e.g. pork, becomes golden brown • Juices from meat and poultry are squeezed out and develop into a golden-brown glaze in the roasting pan • Meat/poultry shrink in size as protein coagulates	• Vegetables/fruits tenderise inside and develop a crisp outer texture • Juices from meat and poultry are squeezed out and develop flavour on the surface • Skin/fat on outside of joints of meat/poultry become crisp • Over-cooking causes meat/poultry to dry out and become difficult to digest

Sautéing MEDIUM

Sautéing means frying food gently in a little oil in order to soften the food and develop flavour.

Suitable foods:

Onions, leeks, peppers, meat/poultry and vegetables used as a base for soups and stews, celery, carrot, butternut squash, sweet potato, courgette

What are the effects on the nutrients in the food?	What are the effects of this method of cooking on the sensory qualities of the food?	
	The appearance of the food (colour, size, shape, etc.)?	The palatability of the food (texture, aroma, flavour)?
<ul><li>Vitamins C, B_1 and B_2 are affected by the heat</li><li>Over-cooking meat/poultry will make the protein less digestible</li><li>Fat/oil used for sautéing adds to the energy density of the food</li><li>Fat/oil will add some fat-soluble vitamins (A, D, E, K)</li><li>Starch granules are softened and some starch released, which makes it easier to digest</li></ul>	<ul><li>Onions, parsnips, carrots become golden brown due to caramelisation</li><li>Red meat turns brown; poultry turns creamy/white colour</li><li>Meat/poultry shrink in size as protein coagulates</li></ul>	<ul><li>Caramelised vegetables taste sweeter</li><li>Flavour gets stronger as water evaporates</li><li>As meat and poultry cook, protein coagulates and shrinks and juices are squeezed out and form flavour on the surface</li></ul>

Setting MEDIUM

Setting is a method that causes a liquid (often warm or hot) to become solid when it has cooled down, or when heat coagulates protein in the liquid.

Suitable foods:

Items set with gelatine: jellies, savoury and sweet mousses, cheesecakes, panna cotta
Items set with egg protein: egg custards, crème caramel, crème brûlée, quiches, flans
Items set with gelatinised starch: blancmange, cornflour custard

What are the effects on the nutrients in the food?	What are the effects of this method of cooking on the sensory qualities of the food?	
	The appearance of the food (colour, size, shape, etc.)?	The palatability of the food (texture, aroma, flavour)?
<ul><li>Heat may affect some B vitamins and vitamin C in items set with gelatine, egg protein or gelatinised starch.</li></ul>	<ul><li>Items set with gelatine and gelatinised starch can be set in a variety of shapes in a mould</li></ul> 	<ul><li>Items set with gelatine have a jelly texture and can be firm enough to cut into slices. If the gelatine is over-heated when being prepared, it may form lumps when it goes into the mixture and fail to set it properly</li><li>Items set with egg, e.g. egg custard, must be cooked gently to avoid coagulating the egg protein too quickly, which may cause the mixture to become lumpy</li><li>Items set with gelatinised starch must be stirred constantly during cooking, to avoid the formation of lumps in the mixture</li></ul>

Steaming (MEDIUM)

Steaming means cooking food in the steam rising from a pan of boiling water beneath.

Suitable foods:

Green vegetables, e.g. broccoli, cabbage, spinach, kale, Brussels sprouts; white fish; dim sum dumplings; sponge puddings; rice

What are the effects on the nutrients in the food?	What are the effects of this method of cooking on the sensory qualities of the food?	
	The appearance of the food (colour, size, shape, etc.)?	The palatability of the food (texture, aroma, flavour)?
• Loss of water-soluble vitamins (B group and C) is reduced because the food does not come in direct contact with boiling water • Some foods can take a long time to cook, so more vitamin C may be destroyed as a result • Protein is unlikely to be over-cooked by this method so is more digestible • Starch granules are softened and some starch released, which makes it easier to digest	• Green vegetables turn bright green for a few minutes, then gradually become a dark olive green if over-cooked • Fish shrinks slightly and separates into flakes of muscle as the protein coagulates • Sponge puddings rise and set, but do not develop a golden crust because the starch they contain does not turn to dextrin in moist heat  • Dim sums swell as the starch granules in the flour gelatinise, and the filling coagulates and sets • Rice grains swell as the starch granules they contain gelatinise	• Food cooks gently and is unlikely to be over-cooked • Foods become tender and develop a soft, moist texture that is easy to digest

Stir frying (MEDIUM)

Stir frying means frying food for a short time in a wok at a high temperature, using very little oil and stirring all the time.

Suitable foods:

Finely cut vegetables and other foods, e.g. peppers, onion, mushrooms, courgettes, pak choi, spring onions, bean sprouts, mange tout peas, bamboo shoots, root ginger, seafood, fish, meat, poultry, nuts, tofu

What are the effects on the nutrients in the food?	What are the effects of this method of cooking on the sensory qualities of the food?	
	The appearance of the food (colour, size, shape, etc.)?	The palatability of the food (texture, aroma, flavour)?
• Starch granules absorb oil and soften • Protein coagulates • Fruit and vegetables soften	• Colours of vegetables get stronger • Vegetables shrink as water evaporates from them • Meat/poultry/seafood shrink in size as protein coagulates	• Quickness of stir frying helps to preserve the flavours of the vegetables • Vegetables soften a little but stay quite crisp • Meat/poultry/fish cook quickly so must be cut into small pieces in order to be tender and cooked right through

157

Water bath (sous vide) MEDIUM

Sous vide means 'under vacuum'. It is a cooking method where food is placed in a plastic bag that is sealed in a vacuum (the air is removed from the bag). The bag is placed in a water bath and cooked at a very precise temperature. It is also known as Low Temperature, Long Time (LTLT) cooking, because the food is cooked at a lower temperature than in an oven or under a grill, and for a much longer time. This means that the food cooks very evenly all the way through and stays moist and tender, with a good flavour and aroma because it cooks in its own juices.

Suitable foods:

Meat (especially tougher cuts, such as neck or leg, which become tender); eggs; vegetables, especially carrots; fish, e.g. salmon

Sous vide pan with temperature controller

What are the effects on the nutrients in the food?	What are the effects of this method of cooking on the sensory qualities of the food?	
	The appearance of the food (colour, size, shape, etc.)?	The palatability of the food (texture, aroma, flavour)?
• The low temperatures will help to prevent destruction of group B vitamins and vitamin C	• Food is evenly cooked all the way through • Meat is less likely to shrink	• Food retains moisture so is juicy and succulent • Aromas and flavours are kept inside the vacuum bag, so the food has a stronger flavour and aroma than if cooked another way • Tough cuts of meat have a lot of connective tissue that surrounds the muscle fibres they contain. As the meat slowly cooks in its own juices, some of the protein in the connective tissue changes into gelatine, which frees the muscle fibres and makes the meat tender

Complex cooking methods

Baking blind COMPLEX

Baking blind means to bake a pastry base for a pie or flan in the oven, without a filling. The pastry is lined with baking paper, and weighted down with ceramic or dried baking beans, which are removed when the pastry is cooked.

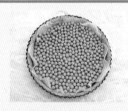

Suitable foods:

Sweet and savoury flan and pie pastry bases

What are the effects on the nutrients in the food?	What are the effects of this method of cooking on the sensory qualities of the food?	
	The appearance of the food (colour, size, shape, etc.)?	The palatability of the food (texture, aroma, flavour)?
• Heat damages B group vitamins • Starch is more digestible because of the baking process	• The pastry base sets during baking and has a light golden colour	• Without a filling, the pastry base becomes crisp, which means it is less likely to go soggy when the filling is added

Caramelising (COMPLEX)

Caramelising is a method where white sugar crystals are gently heated until they melt into a syrup, which then boils. Water is formed and it evaporates, making the syrup become very hot (160–170 °C) and thick. Gradually, the colour of the syrup changes from clear to golden brown. If boiled for too long, the syrup will burn and become bitter.

Suitable foods:

Granulated or caster sugar; onions and shallots; apples and pears

What are the effects on the nutrients in the food?	What are the effects of this method of cooking on the sensory qualities of the food?	
	The appearance of the food (colour, size, shape, etc.)?	The palatability of the food (texture, aroma, flavour)?
• Sugar is a carbohydrate and after caramelising, it still provides the body with energy	• Sugar syrup changes from colourless to a transparent golden-brown colour – it becomes 'caramelised' • Onions contain natural sugars, and these will caramelise when chopped onions are sautéed in oil. The onions develop a golden-brown colour	• The syrup sets into a toffee and forms long strands when a spoon is pulled out of the caramel • Vegetables and fruit become sweet

Deep fat frying (COMPLEX)

Deep fat frying means frying food in a deep pan of very hot oil, so that the food is fully immersed (covered) in the oil.

Suitable foods:

Coated/battered fish, scotch eggs, chicken joints and pieces, battered vegetables (tempura), spring rolls, doughnuts, churros, seafood, fritters (e.g. apple, pineapple, corn), poppadums, onion bhajis, falafels, potato croquettes, potato chips/fries

What are the effects on the nutrients in the food?	What are the effects of this method of cooking on the sensory qualities of the food?	
	The appearance of the food (colour, size, shape, etc.)?	The palatability of the food (texture, aroma, flavour)?
• Oil used in deep frying increases the energy density of the food, especially if the oil is not hot enough when frying starts as it will be absorbed by the food • Vitamin C and some B vitamins are damaged by the heat • Over-cooking meat/poultry will make the protein less digestible	• Meat/poultry shrink in size as protein denatures and coagulates • Fish shrinks slightly, becomes opaque and separates into flakes of muscle as the protein in it coagulates • Fried foods containing starch and sugars develop a golden-brown colour	• Foods develop a crispy texture on the outside, especially if the food is coated with egg and breadcrumbs or batter • Vegetables tenderise and develop a crisp coating

Emulsifying (COMPLEX)

Oil and water do not mix – they will separate out into two layers with the oil on top. Emulsifying means either keeping drops of oil or fat suspended in a liquid (water) and preventing them from separating out, or keeping drops of water suspended in an oil or fat and preventing them from separating out. This is done by adding an emulsifier, e.g. lecithin (found in egg yolk or soya).

Suitable foods:

These foods are emulsified: mayonnaise, Hollandaise sauce, butter, vegetable fat spreads

What are the effects on the nutrients in the food?	What are the effects of this method of cooking on the sensory qualities of the food?	
	The appearance of the food (colour, size, shape, etc.)?	The palatability of the food (texture, aroma, flavour)?
• Due to the oil content, emulsified foods are energy dense	• The oil and water stay mixed, so the mixture has the same colour throughout	• The texture is smooth throughout

Poaching (COMPLEX)

Poaching means cooking food in a shallow pan of water, wine or other liquid at just under boiling point, with only a few bubbles showing.

Suitable foods:

Chicken, fish, eggs, fruit, e.g. pears

What are the effects on the nutrients in the food?	What are the effects of this method of cooking on the sensory qualities of the food?	
	The appearance of the food (colour, size, shape, etc.)?	The palatability of the food (texture, aroma, flavour)?
• Vitamins C, B$_1$ and B$_2$ are affected by heat, but the damage will be less than in boiling as the temperature is just below boiling point for poaching • Water-soluble vitamins (B group and C) dissolve into the cooking liquid, and will be lost when the liquid is poured away	• Egg white changes from clear to white and the yolk becomes a lighter yellow as the protein coagulates • Fish shrinks slightly and separates into flakes of muscle as the protein coagulates	• Fish and poultry become tender • Fish is less likely to be over-cooked because the temperature of the water is just under boiling point and it is easy to see when the protein has coagulated • Some flavour from poultry and fish will go into the water, but if the water is used to make gravy or stock, the flavour will be saved • The time needed to poach fruit, e.g. pears in wine and spices, allows the flavours from the poaching liquid to be absorbed by the fruit

Tempering (COMPLEX)

Tempering is a technique that is used to stabilise an ingredient, so that it doesn't change in any way; e.g. when a cold ingredient is added to a hot ingredient, such as adding cold fresh cream to a hot soup. This is because if cold and hot ingredients are mixed, one or other of them may react by curdling, becoming hard or lumpy, or splitting.

Tempering increases the temperature of cold ingredients very slowly, so that they will mix with hotter ingredients without being changed. This is usually done by adding a little of the hot ingredients to the cold ingredients and mixing thoroughly – this allows the cold ingredients to 'get used to' the hotter ones.

Chocolate is tempered to make sure it cools and hardens with a shiny surface. The chocolate is melted in a bowl over hot water and then stirred or spread onto a cold slab and moved around with a metal spreader, until it is smooth and has cooled to 31–32 °C for dark chocolate and 30–31 °C for milk chocolate.

Suitable foods:

Sauces, ice cream, pastry cream, custard, soups, chocolate and recipes where cream is added to form a sauce at the end of the cooking time, such as in some curries, meat and fish dishes

What are the effects on the nutrients in the food?	What are the effects of this method of cooking on the sensory qualities of the food?	
	The appearance of the food (colour, size, shape, etc.)?	The palatability of the food (texture, aroma, flavour)?
• No significant changes	• Tempered chocolate has an even colour and shiny surface when set	• Sauces and other dishes should be smooth, with no curdling or lumps • Tempered chocolate should have a smooth texture and break with a 'snap'

The number and types of skills used in different recipes/dishes

Many recipes/dishes are a mixture of basic, medium and complex skills. The more complex skills a recipe uses, the more skilful a person needs to be to complete it to a high standard. To illustrate this, here are two recipes for cakes – one more complex than the other – showing the skills used in each:

Name of **complex** recipe	Complex preparation, knife and cooking skills used	Medium preparation, knife and cooking skills used	Basic preparation, knife and cooking skills used
Whisked chocolate and orange sponge fruit gateau	• Whisking eggs and sugar (aeration) • Piping whipped cream decoration • Melting chocolate using bain-marie • Tempering chocolate for ganache filling	• Weighing ingredients • Folding flour and cocoa into eggs and sugar foam • Baking • Slicing orange for decoration	• Sieving flour
Name of **basic** recipe	Complex preparation, knife and cooking skills used	Medium preparation, knife and cooking skills used	Basic preparation, knife and cooking skills used
All-in-one jam sandwich cake	None	• Baking • Weighing ingredients	• Beating all ingredients together • Sieving flour

For your Unit 2 Assessment, you will need to list which skills you have used for the dishes you make. The way to do this is to identify the skills used to make each dish in the method given for each recipe. Here is an example to show you how:

Which skills are used to make a lemon meringue pie?

1. Identify each preparation, knife and cooking skill in the method and underline them.
2. Complete a chart, like the one shown on pages 183–88, listing each of the skills in the correct level (Basic, Medium, Complex).
3. Use the chart in your assessment report.

Method for making a lemon meringue pie

1. Preheat the oven to gas 6 / 200 °C.
2. Pastry base: prepare the pastry by by sieving the flour into a bowl, then rubbing the fat into the flour until it is like breadcrumbs. Add the water and mix to a short dough.
3. Knead the pastry lightly until smooth on a lightly floured worktop.
4. Roll out the dough slightly larger than the flan dish/tin.
5. Line the baking tin with the pastry – try not to stretch it. Trim and crimp the edge to neaten it.
6. Line the pastry with baking paper and put some baking beans on top.
7. Blind bake the pastry for 15 minutes – remove the baking beans and bake for a few more minutes, if necessary, until the middle is crisp.
8. Turn the oven down to gas 1 / 40 °C.
9. Make the filling: zest and juice the lemons. Measure the water. In a small pan, carefully blend the cornflour, water, sugar, egg yolks, lemon zest and juice together so that there are no lumps.
10. Heat the filling and stir all the time until the mixture boils and thickens.
11. Pour the filling slowly into the baked pastry case and leave to cool while you make the meringue.

12. Make the meringue: Place the egg whites in a clean, dry, grease-free bowl. Whisk the egg whites until very stiff.
13. Whisk the caster sugar in a tablespoon at a time until the mixture is thick and glossy.
14. Pipe the meringue on top of the lemon filling using a large star nozzle.
15. Place the pie in the oven and bake for approximately 30 minutes to 1 hour until the meringue is lightly browned and crisp. Check it regularly to make sure it is cooking evenly.

Name of recipe	Complex skills used	Medium skills used	Basic skills used
Lemon meringue pie	*Preparation:* • Whisking egg whites • Piping meringue topping • Crimping pastry edge	*Preparation:* • Measuring water for pastry and sauce filling • Weighing ingredients • Rubbing in butter to flour for the pastry • Mixing in the water to form a dough • Kneading the pastry dough • Rolling out the pastry	*Preparation:* • Zesting lemons • Juicing lemons • Blending cornflour into liquid for sauce • Sieving flour for pastry
	Knife:	*Knife:*	*Knife:* • Trimming the pastry
	Cooking: • Baking blind (pastry)	*Cooking:*	*Cooking:* • Boiling the sauce filling • Cooling the filling

Activity: Identify the skills used

Identify the preparation, knife and cooking skills used in the following methods for a variety of recipes.

Complete the skills chart for each. Use the chart on pages 146–148 to help you.

1. Apple and apricot nutty crumble

Method:
1. Heat oven to gas 5 / 190 °C (180 °C fan ovens).
2. Peel, core and slice the apples. Open the tinned apricots and drain off the juice into a jug.
3. In a pan, stew the apple slices gently in the juice from the apricots until tender.
4. Put the apples into the ovenproof dish with the drained apricots.
5. Rub the butter or margarine into the flour until it looks like breadcrumbs, and then stir in the bran or oats, sugar, seeds and chopped nuts.
6. Sprinkle the crumble mixture over the fruit.
7. Place the dish on a baking tray and bake at gas 5 / 190 °C for 20 minutes until crisp on top.

Name of recipe	Complex skills used	Medium skills used	Basic skills used
Apple and apricot nutty crumble	*Preparation:*	*Preparation:*	*Preparation:*
	Knife:	*Knife:*	*Knife:*
	Cooking:	*Cooking:*	*Cooking:*

2. Leek and bacon tray bread

Method:

1. Heat oven to gas 5 / 90 °C (180 °C fan ovens).
2. Sieve the flour and salt into a bowl.
3. Add the dried yeast to the flour and mix well.
4. Rub the butter into the flour.
5. Add the beaten egg and warm milk to the flour, mixing it to form a stretchy dough.
6. Knead the dough until it is smooth (approx. 5 minutes), then leave it to prove in a warm place until it has doubled in size.
7. Filling: slice the leeks, place them in a colander and wash them thoroughly. Heat the oil in a frying pan and sauté the leeks until they are soft but not browned. Leave to cool slightly.
8. Knead the risen dough again; roll it out to fit a greased and lined Swiss roll tin, bringing the dough up the sides to create a space for the filling to go in.
9. Place the leeks on top of the dough and arrange the chopped bacon on top of the leeks.
10. Whisk the eggs, cream and milk together. Add the chopped basil leaves and season with salt and pepper.
11. Carefully pour the egg mixture over the leeks.
12. Bake the tray bread for 30–35 minutes until the filling has set and the dough is a golden-brown colour round the edges.

Name of recipe	Complex skills used	Medium skills used	Basic skills used
Leek and bacon tray bread	*Preparation:*	*Preparation:*	*Preparation:*
	Knife:	*Knife:*	*Knife:*
	Cooking:	*Cooking:*	*Cooking:*

3. Vegetable lasagne

Method:

1. Pre-heat oven to gas 4 / 180 °C.
2. Peel the onion and garlic.
3. Dice the onion, pepper, courgette, aubergine and tomatoes.
4. Mince the garlic.
5. Heat oil in a pan; add the onion and garlic and sauté until softened.
6. Add the aubergine, pepper, courgette and tomatoes.
7. Season and add the herbs. Simmer for 20 minutes.
8. Steam the spinach for a few minutes until softened, drain and squeeze out any water. Place in a food processor with the ricotta cheese and egg and blend until smooth. Season with black pepper and grated nutmeg.
9. Make the cheese sauce by melting the butter in a pan, add the flour and cook for 1 minute. Remove the pan from the heat and gradually add / blend in the milk to make a smooth liquid. Re-heat and stir until the sauce has boiled and thickened. Add half the cheese and stir well.
10. Lightly grease a lasagne dish. Place half of the vegetable mixture in the dish and add a layer of lasagne sheets. Add the spinach mixture, then lasagne sheets, then the rest of the tomato mixture. Finish with lasagne sheets.
11. Top the lasagne with cheese sauce and sprinkle with the remaining cheese.
12. Bake in the oven for 45–50 minutes until golden and tender.

Name of recipe	Complex skills used	Medium skills used	Basic skills used
Vegetable lasagne	Preparation:	Preparation:	Preparation:
	Knife:	Knife:	Knife:
	Cooking:	Cooking:	Cooking:

4. Fruit trifle

Method:

Sponge

1. Heat the oven to gas 5 / 180 °C.
2. Grease and line a Swiss roll tin.
3. Place the eggs and sugar in a bowl and whisk at medium speed until the mixture is light, thick and creamy, and leaves a visible trail for at least 5 seconds when the whisk is removed.
4. Sieve the flour twice and fold it very gently into the mixture with a metal spoon until there is no visible flour – do not beat it or use a whisk, as the air will come out.
5. Pour the mixture into the tin and tip it until the mixture spreads evenly into the corners.
6. Bake for approximately 10 minutes, until well risen, spongy to the touch and starting to shrink away from the edges of the tin.
7. Leave the sponge to cool, then cut it into squares. Spread one surface of each sponge square with jam and place in the bottom of the serving dish. Sprinkle with the fruit juice and scatter the defrosted fruit on top of the sponge squares.

Custard:

8. Place the milk and vanilla essence in a small pan and slowly bring to just below boiling point on a low heat.
9. Place the egg yolks, cornflour and sugar in a bowl and blend them together.
10. Whisk in the hot milk and vanilla, and then pour the liquid back into the pan.
11. Cook over a gentle heat, stirring constantly, until the custard starts to thicken, *being careful not to allow it to boil*.
12. Cook gently for two minutes until the custard is a thick pouring consistency. Pour the custard into a cold bowl to prevent further cooking. Cover the bowl with damp parchment paper to prevent a skin forming on the custard and allow it to cool.
13. Spoon the cooled custard onto the fruit in the trifle bowl, spreading it to the edges with a palette knife.

Topping:

14. Whisk the cream until it nearly holds its shape, then spoon half of it on top of the custard and carefully spread it to the sides of the bowl.
15. Whisk the remaining cream until it holds its shape. Pipe swirls of cream around the top of the bowl and decorate with fruit, flaked almonds, grated chocolate, etc.

Name of recipe	Complex skills used	Medium skills used	Basic skills used
Fruit trifle	Preparation:	Preparation:	Preparation:
	Knife:	Knife:	Knife:
	Cooking:	Cooking:	Cooking:

Important temperatures in catering

There are a number of important temperatures in catering you should know and use in your practical assessment production plan:

Food production stage:	Food delivery to kitchen
Safe temperatures:	Refrigerated foods: **0 °C to 5 °C**
	Frozen foods: **–22 °C to –18 °C**
Notes:	If a higher temperature, do not accept the food.

Food production stage:	Food storage – high-risk foods (milk, butter, cream, yogurt, cheese, meat, meat products, fish, seafood, poultry)
Safe temperatures:	Refrigerated / cold store foods: **0 °C to 5 °C** (England and Northern Ireland); **up to 8 °C** (Wales and Scotland)
	Frozen foods: **–22 ° to –18 °C**
Notes:	Check refrigerator and freezer temperatures every day.

Food production stage:	Defrosting frozen meat, poultry, fish or seafood
Safe temperatures:	**0 °C to 5 °C**
Notes:	Defrost on a tray (to prevent drips) in the refrigerator or cold store.

Food production stage:	Cooking high-risk foods
Safe temperatures:	Core temperature: **minimum 70 °C for 2 minutes** to destroy any pathogenic (harmful) bacteria
Notes:	Use a food probe that has been checked (calibrated) for accuracy by placing it in ice to check that it reads 0 °C or just under; then placing it in boiling water to check that it reads 100 °C.

Food production stage:	Cooling cooked foods
Safe temperatures:	The food should reach **5 °C or cooler within 1½ hours** to prevent the growth and multiplication of bacteria
Notes:	Food will cool down quickly in a blast chiller or well-ventilated room away from the heat of the kitchen.
	Foods such as cooked rice can be cooled quickly by rinsing in very cold water.
	Foods such as meat sauces can be poured into large shallow trays. The large surface area helps them to cool quickly.

Food production stage:	Blanching
	Food is blanched to soften it, or to partially cook it, or to remove something from it e.g.:
	• Nuts can be blanched to remove their skins, e.g. almonds, hazelnuts
	• Vegetables, such as fresh peas and beans, are blanched to destroy natural chemicals called enzymes, which would cause vitamin, colour, texture and flavour changes to the vegetables during storage.
Safe temperatures:	Vegetables can be blanched in boiling (**100 °C**) water for a few minutes.
	They are then rapidly cooled (refreshed) in iced water and chilled until needed later.
	They can be reheated quickly, ready for service.
	Potato chips / fries can be blanched in hot oil (**130 °C**) to cook the inside of the potato. They are then drained, and later fried in hotter oil (**190 °C**) to make the outside really crisp.
Notes:	Blanching destroys enzymes and bacteria on the surface of vegetables and keeps their bright colour, texture and vitamin content.

Food production stage:	Reheating cooked and chilled foods
Safe temperatures:	Core temperature: **minimum 70 °C for 2 minutes** in England, Wales and Northern Ireland; **minimum of 82 °C** in Scotland
Notes:	Cooked foods should only be reheated **once** to prevent the growth and multiplication of bacteria.

Food production stage:	Hot holding – keeping cooked food hot for service
Safe temperatures:	**Minimum 63 °C**
Notes:	This temperature prevents the growth and multiplication of bacteria.

Food production stage:	Cold holding / chilled foods displayed for service
Safe temperatures:	**0 °C to 5 °C**
Notes:	This temperature prevents the growth and multiplication of bacteria.

Activity: Which is the correct temperature?

Match the correct temperature information to the correct food production stage.

Cooking high-risk foods

0 °C to 5 °C

Core temperature: minimum 70 °C for 2 minutes

Cooling cooked foods

Core temperature: minimum 70 °C for 2 minutes (England, Wales and Northern Ireland); in Scotland minimum 82 °C.

Hot holding – keeping cooked food hot for service

Refrigerated foods should be: 0 to 5 °C
Frozen foods should be: –22 °C to –18 °C

Checking the temperature of high-risk foods when they are delivered to the kitchen

Core temperature: minimum 63 °C

Cold holding/chilled foods displayed for service

0 °C to 5 °C

Storing high-risk foods in a refrigerator, cold store or freezer

Defrosting frozen meat, poultry, fish and seafood

The food should reach 5 °C or cooler within 1½ hours

Refrigerated/cold-store foods should be:
0 to 5 °C (England and Northern Ireland); up to 8 °C in Wales and Scotland
Frozen foods should be: –22 °C to –18 °C

Reheating cooked and chilled foods

General advice on presenting food

1. **Have all the ingredients ready and cooked before starting to put the food on the plate.**
2. **Choose a suitable plate / serving platter:**
   - Not too big.
   - Not too small.
   - White or black plates will show off the colours of the food.
   - Plates and platters are made from a variety of materials, e.g. wood, ceramic/china, slate, stone (e.g. granite), stainless steel, banana leaves, bamboo stems, etc.
   - If the food is hot, the plate should be warmed.
   - Cold food should be served on a cold plate.
   - Wipe the edges of the plate with a clean cloth or fresh piece of kitchen paper to remove food drips and spills before serving.

Remember!

The first sense that people use when choosing and enjoying their food is sight.

Good presentation of a dish will make people want to choose it and they will enjoy eating it.

There are no set rules about how food should be presented – this is down to you. Be creative!

3. **Place the ingredients on the plate/platter:**
   - Not too much – the plate should be a frame around the food.
   - Do not have food hanging over the edges of the plate.
   - Have one ingredient as the focal point of the plate, e.g. the protein / main food (e.g. meat, fish or vegetarian main). This is often placed to one side of the dish, rather than directly in the centre, with the rest of the foods around it like this:
   - Foods such as potatoes and meat balls, are often served in odd numbers (e.g. 3, 5, or 7) as it makes it look like there is more food on the plate.

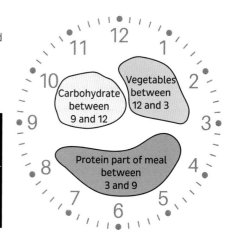

4. **Be creative:**
   - Make use of the natural colours and shapes of foods.
   - Combine different textures, e.g. smooth sauces with crunchy chopped nuts; crispy vegetables and soft purées.
   - Decorate plates creatively with sauces:

– Use caramelised sugar to make decorations:

– Make chocolate decorations, e.g. chocolate leaves, swirls, squares, etc.
– Chocolate shapes can be drizzled or piped onto non-stick silicone baking paper and allowed to cool and set, then lifted off and used as decorations. Keep shapes cool until used.
– Spread melted chocolate onto non-stick silicone baking paper and allow it to cool and set at room temperature, then cut out shapes, e.g. squares or triangles, using a sharp knife or metal cutter. Keep shapes cool until used.
– Dip fresh fruits into melted chocolate and allow to set.

5. Use garnishes and decorations

– Use garnishes and decorations that complement the other ingredients and add flavour and texture to the meal – do not use too many.

– Place the garnishes and decorations carefully on the plate to add to the creativity of the meal.
– Flowers from these plants are edible: basil, borage, calendula (marigold), chervil, chives, lavender, nasturtium, pansy, rose, sage. Any flowers that are used for food must be clean and **must not** have been sprayed with pesticides, fertilisers, or be contaminated with urine or faeces from animals.

There are various tools that are designed for serving food creatively, including:

Silicon plating wedge

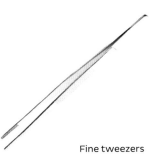

Precision spoon

Fine tweezers

Ring mould

Plastic squeeze bottle

Portion control

Portion control means serving a portion of food that is always the same size each time.

The number of portions that a recipe makes is usually called its **yield**, e.g. a large cheesecake may yield 16 portions.

Portion control is essential to make sure that a catering business makes a profit. If just a small amount of extra food is regularly given to customers when they are served, over a period of time the business will struggle to make a profit and may even lose money.

The amount of food that is given in a portion to customers will depend on:

- The type of customer – do they need large portions? Are they builders working on a nearby building site; or are they elderly people who may have smaller appetites?
- The type of business – e.g. roadside cafés that tend to sell 'hearty' (larger) portions compared with a fine dining restaurant where portions tend to be smaller
- How much the food costs the restaurant to buy
- The quality of the food – better-quality food tends to have less waste and gives more portions
- The knowledge of the food buyer and the chef about what to buy and the number of portion sizes needed and expected to be made from different recipes.

In this picture of a meal of chicken casserole and vegetables, the portion size is too large so the plate is overloaded, and it would be difficult to pick up and serve as the food comes right to the edge of the plate. It also looks messy, which spoils the presentation.

How to make sure that portion sizes are controlled

- Train the kitchen staff to use the correct serving equipment to make sure sizes are always the same.
- Make sure that each recipe clearly shows how many portions it will yield.
- Use portion control equipment that is designed to serve a fixed amount of food, e.g.:

Serving scoop for mashed vegetables, ice cream

Scoops to serve chips/fries

Healthy food-portion controller

Double-sided cake marker – each side gives a different number of portions

Accompaniments

Accompaniments (also called side dishes or 'sides') are extra food items that are served with a starter, main course or dessert.

Accompaniments are used to:
- add to the flavour of the dish
- add extra colour
- give a contrasting (different) texture, e.g. moistness, crunch, creaminess, shortness, to the dish
- add extra bulk to the dish, which makes it more satisfying to eat.

There are some basic rules for accompaniments:
- The ingredients, colours and textures should be different from those in the dish.
- The flavour of the accompaniment should not be stronger than the dish it goes with.
- The accompaniment should use different cooking methods from the dish.

Here are some examples of accompaniments:

Breads: croutons, crusty bread, bread sticks, flatbread, brioche, focaccia, corn bread, challah, baguette (French stick), ciabatta, pita, rye, soda, toast, tortilla.

Salads: green (lettuce, rocket, herb, watercress, etc.), bean, tomato and basil, coleslaw, Waldorf, Caesar, beetroot and red onion, couscous, potato, pasta, corn, pepper, mixed fresh fruit, mixed dried fruit.

Dips: blue cheese, jalapeno, salsa, hummus, guacamole, pesto, aioli, mayonnaise.

Preserves /sauces: chutneys, pickles, piccalilli, mint sauce, apple sauce, horseradish sauce, chilli sauce, jams, jellies, seafood sauce, tartare sauce, gravy, roux sauce, custard.

Fruits and vegetables: lemon/orange/lime slices/wedges, vegetable sticks, fresh herbs, edible flowers, fruit compote, fruit coulis, spiralised vegetables, French fries, potato wedges, spring rolls, dahl, aloo.

Biscuits: tuilles, sponge fingers, biscotti, amaretti, shortbread, sables, cookies, melting moments, ginger snaps, brandy snaps, macaroons.

Activity: Making meals look appealing to patients in hospital

Look at the dinner menu for a hospital ward where people are recovering from operations.

Suggest some ways in which the chefs can present the dishes creatively and some accompaniments that could go with each main course, so that the patients want to eat them.

Starter
Cream of mushroom soup with brown bread roll

OR

Hummus and crackers

Main course
Fish pie topped with mashed potatoes

OR

Meatballs in tomato sauce with spaghetti

Dessert
Apple crumble and custard

OR

Cheddar cheese and biscuits

When you are preparing, cooking and presenting the two dishes for your Unit 2 Assessment, you need to demonstrate (show) that you know, understand and are able to:

- follow correct personal safety practices
- follow correct food safety practices
- follow correct personal hygiene practices
- use equipment and facilities (the workspace and kitchen) safely and hygienically.

Much of this information has been covered in Unit 1 of the course, and the following chart gives a summary of what you **should** and **should not** do when storing, preparing and cooking food:

Activity	Examples of what you should do	Examples of what you should not do
Personal safety practices (also the safety of other people working in the kitchen) 	• Wear non-slip, low-heeled shoes with backs when working in the kitchen • Wear an apron and sleeves that protect you from splashes of hot food and liquids • Use step ladders or a purpose-made step stool to reach items on high shelves • Wipe up any spills of food or liquids from the floor as quickly as possible • Keep long hair tied back and long sleeves rolled up when using equipment such as electric mixers	• Wear high-heeled or slip-on shoes with no back • Wear a thin, short top without an apron, where your skin is exposed to heat and splashes of hot food or liquids • Wear loose, long sleeves that may dangle in food or flames; wear long hair down • Stand on chairs or worktops to reach items, e.g. ingredients or equipment from high shelves • Remove safety guards from machines • Leave items on the floor or electrical leads trailing where they can be tripped over • Leave bags or other items on the floor where people will walk
Food safety practices 1. Storing food / ingredients 	• Store high-risk foods (e.g. fresh chicken, meat, fish, dairy foods) covered, in a refrigerator • Make sure high-risk foods do not touch or drip onto other foods • Keep cooked and raw foods separate • Store low-risk foods in a cool, dry place • Protect all foods from flies and dust/dirt contamination • Wash soil from vegetables	• Leave high-risk foods at room temperature • Leave high-risk foods uncovered • Put dirty vegetables next to other foods
2. Preparing food 	• Use the correct coloured chopping board (if available) for different foods • Keep raw and cooked foods separate • Throw rubbish and food scraps away regularly • Wash hands after handling high-risk foods and using the rubbish bin	• Use the same chopping board and knife for raw and cooked foods without washing them thoroughly in between • Lick fingers while preparing food • Fail to wash hands regularly

Activity	Examples of what you should do ✓	Examples of what you should not do ✗
3. Cooking food	• Use a food probe to check the core temperature of high-risk foods • Make sure high-risk foods are cooked all the way through • Check that chilled food is cold enough • Use a clean spoon to taste food to check for flavour • Use clean food tongs to move or turn food over during cooking	• Guess the temperature of cooked food • Serve under-cooked high-risk foods • Keep food that is meant to be chilled at room temperature • Taste food from a spoon then put the spoon back into the food without washing it first • Use unwashed food tongs that have already been used for raw food to pick up or turn cooked food
Personal hygiene practices	• Wear a clean apron/chef's jacket • Tie long hair back • Have short, clean nails • Wash hands regularly • Cover cuts and sores • Cough or sneeze away from food and into a tissue	• Wear nail varnish • Wear false nails • Wear jewellery • Cough or sneeze over food • Wipe your nose with your hand or sleeve • Touch face and nose while preparing food • Wear long hair loose
Using equipment	• Use equipment correctly, following the manufacturer's instructions • Use oven gloves to put food into and take it out of the oven/grill • Use very hot, clean water and detergent for washing equipment • Use safety guards • Carry sharp knives with the blade pointing down, at the side of your body • Wash sharp knives and other sharp objects carefully, one at a time • Keep and use electrical equipment away from water • Wipe food splatters off unplugged electrical and other equipment before storing it away	• Treat equipment roughly or incorrectly • Allow pan handles to stick out when using the hob • Use cold, greasy/dirty water to wash equipment • Put sharp knives and other objects into washing up water where they cannot be seen • Handle electrical equipment with wet hands • Put equipment away dirty
Using the facilities (workspace and kitchen)	• Clean as you go to keep the workspace tidy and organised • Move around the kitchen carefully – never run • Clean the workspace ready for the next person to use	• Run from one part of the kitchen to another • Leave the workspace untidy and dirty

Key learning

- To **review** means that you look at all aspects of something (e.g. an activity, a report, a plan, etc.) with the aim of making changes and improvements to it, if they are needed.
  - A **review** is usually presented as a written report.
  - It should include **positive** feedback, with specific examples of how and why something was good and how something can be improved, in a supportive and encouraging way.

- To **evaluate** means that the activity, report, plan, etc. is given a value, using criteria/statements that are set out by, e.g., a mark scheme.

  For example, the practical work that you carry out for the Unit 2 Assessment will be evaluated against the criteria set out in the course specification and mark scheme.

You will **review** and **evaluate** the dishes you choose to make for the Unit 2 Assessment, and how well you work in a practical situation to make the dishes. You will review the good parts of your work and suggest how you can make improvements to other areas of it.

What you have to do

Review and evaluation are used in hospitality and catering, e.g. a review of customer feedback about a new menu that has been tried out in a restaurant, to see if any dishes could be improved or need to be replaced by others.

Two chefs review a menu following customer feedback

When you have completed your Unit 2 Assessment, you will be asked to write a **brief review** of the dishes you chose and made, and how well you worked during the practical assessment.

The following two sections set out the points you must include in your review and give examples of what you could write or talk about.

In this section of your review of the dishes you made, you need to write or talk about the planning, preparation and cooking of them, as shown in the following chart.

Points to consider	What it includes	Examples of what you could write or talk about (NB: these examples refer to more than one practical assessment)

Dish selection	• Did your dishes show a range of basic, medium and complex skills?	• In my assessment, I used a good range of techniques:
		  – 3 basic, 7 medium and 3 complex preparation techniques
		  – 3 basic, 2 medium and 2 complex knife techniques
		  – 3 basic, 4 medium and 2 complex cooking techniques
		
		Study tip
		You could list the specific skills that you have used here in a chart (see pages 183–188)

	• Did your dishes meet the requirements of the Unit 2 Assignment Brief (see page 181)?	• I had to produce two dishes for a main evening meal, and I chose one main course and one dessert dish.
	• Did the nutrients provided by your dishes meet the needs of the customers?	• The main course has protein in three types of beans, rice, and tofu, which will be suitable for the customer who is vegan. • I served fresh-fruit salad (which contains vitamin C in the oranges, kiwi fruit and strawberries) to go with the dark chocolate mousse (which contains iron in the chocolate). The vitamin C helps iron to be absorbed in the body. This is important for the teenage girl, to help prevent anaemia.
Dish production	• Did you follow the production of the dish in a logical order in your production plan?	• Most of my production plan was in the correct order, but some of the timings I planned were not long enough, e.g. it took longer for the potatoes to boil so they were soft enough to be mashed, so I carried on to the next part of the plan and went back to the potatoes once they were ready.
	• Did you have any problems during the production of the dishes?	• I had the heat too high when I was making the cheese sauce and this meant that there were some lumps in the cooked sauce, so I used an electric hand blender to break them down to make a smooth sauce.
Health and safety	• Did you store your ingredients correctly?	• I put the fresh chicken and cream on a tray in the refrigerator at the start of the assessment. • I washed the potatoes thoroughly to get rid of any dirt and stored them away from other foods.
	• Did you clear up regularly?	• I tried to clear up regularly, but I got a bit behind near the end of the assessment, so I missed one session of clearing up on my production plan.
	• Did you use the correct chopping boards for different foods?	• I used a brown board for the potatoes and fruit, but I realised that I should have used a green one for the fruit.

	• Did you use a food probe to check cooked dishes?	• I used a food probe to check that the chicken dish was thoroughly cooked (it was 88 °C, which is a safe temperature for cooked high-risk foods).
	• Did you work safely with knives, heat, equipment?	• I used oven gloves and made sure that the pan handles on the hob were not sticking out. • I carried the sharp knives from the rack with the point down at my side.
	• Did you work carefully to keep other people safe?	• I was in a hurry and spilt some cream on the floor, so I cleared it up with kitchen paper and a little washing up liquid to stop the floor being slippery.
Hygiene	• Were you dressed hygienically to work in a kitchen?	• I wore a clean apron and tied my long hair back. I was not wearing nail varnish.
	• When did you wash your hands?	• I washed my hands regularly, especially after I handled the raw fish and eggs, and put some rubbish in the bin.
	• Did you cover any sores/cuts on your hands?	• I accidentally cut my finger when preparing the vegetables, so I washed my hands, put on a plaster, and wore a plastic glove for the rest of the session.
	• Did you cough or sneeze over the food?	• When I was sieving the flour, I sneezed but I turned my head away from the food. It would have been better if I had sneezed into a tissue, but I didn't have one.
Improvements you could make	• Selection of dishes	• I was pleased with my choice of dishes, especially the dessert, where I used three complex techniques, but when it was finished, it looked rather plain. I could have served it with something colourful, such as slices of fruit, to make it more appetising.
	• Organisation of your workspace • Clearing up	• I tried to work neatly and I organised my workspace well at the start of the assessment. It got a bit messy near the end of the assessment though, because I was rushing to finish, so in the future, I need to clear up more often earlier on, to prevent a build-up of things on the workspace.
	• Mise en place	• I should have prepared the quiche tin, lining paper and baking beans during mise en place, because I had to do it when I had made the pastry, which cost me some time.
	• Preparing dishes	• I think I could have decorated the mousse more neatly, by putting fewer pieces of fruit on the top, as it was rather crowded. • I should have checked for any holes in the pastry case and patched them, because the quiche leaked a little bit during baking, which caused it to stick to the baking tray.
	• Use of equipment	• I used several pieces of equipment, including an electric hand blender, electric whisk, bain-marie and mandolin. The hand blender was very useful for making my lumpy sauce smooth, but it meant I had another item to wash up, which I hadn't planned.

Sensory (organoleptic) qualities of your dishes	• Appearance of dishes	• The dishes had good colours, e.g. the chicken pie had a golden-brown crust and I served it with colourful vegetables. • The red, green and dark blue of the fruit decoration showed up well against the chocolate-brown colour of the mousse, and the whipped cream rosettes gave it a neat and nice appearance. I think it would have looked better with fewer pieces of fruit though, as you would have seen more of the mousse.
	• Flavour and aroma of dishes	• The sauce for the chicken pie filling had a good flavour, due to heating up the milk for the bechamel sauce with celery, bay leaves, onion, peppercorns and mace before making the sauce. This, and the flavour from the mixed herbs, was taken up by the chicken. The creamed potato and sautéed leek looked nice, but it was a bit bland, so I should have checked the seasoning and added more before I presented the dish. The chocolate mousse had a rich chocolate flavour and aroma and the fruit, especially the raspberries, went well with it.
	• Texture of dishes	• The chicken in the pie was tender. The sauce was smooth, and this went well with the shortness of the pastry. The mousse was smooth and creamy, which went well with the crisp, shortbread biscuits I made to go with it.
Presentation of your dishes	• Appearance	• I made sure that the plates and serving dishes were clean and dry. • I served the food carefully and neatly and tried not to put too much on the plate, but I think I put too much potato with the chicken pie and vegetables.
	• Temperature	• The plate for the main course was warmed. The plate for the dessert was chilled.
Food and other waste	• Food waste	• There was some food waste – mostly vegetable and fruit peelings, and I had some whipped cream left over, so I froze that in a covered box.
	• Recycled waste	• I was able to recycle some of the food packaging (cream pot, plastic tray from the fresh fish), but some of the plastic packaging from the vegetables could not be recycled.

Reviewing own performance

In the review of how well you worked during the Unit 2 Assessment, you should identify your personal strengths and weaknesses in the following points.

Points to consider	What it includes	Examples of what you could write about (NB: these examples refer to more than one practical assessment)
Decision making	• How the production of the dishes was planned and carried out	• I was pleased with the production plan I wrote in Assignment Task 2, and most of the plan worked well. However, there were a couple of problems, which meant I had to make a quick decision on what to do during the practical session: 1. In the production plan, I was going to make the bread rolls halfway through the practical session, but before I started, I realised I had not allowed enough time for the dough to rise. So, I decided I would make the dough first, which did put some of my other timings out, but I managed to catch up with my plan. I had thought that I would make different shaped rolls, to show my skills, but that would have taken too much time, so I chose to make them all one shape (a knot), and was pleased with the result, as they all looked neat. 2. I realised I would now have the bread rolls and the crème caramels in the oven at the same time, but they are cooked at different temperatures. As the bread rolls take less time to bake than the crème caramels take to set, I decided I would bake them first, then turn down the temperature of the oven and let it cool quickly by leaving the door slightly open for a few minutes, before I put the crème caramels in.
Organisation	• Time, workspace, equipment, ingredients, clearing up	• **Time** – Most of the timings I planned were OK, although it took me less time to chop some fruit and make my cake mixture than I planned. I didn't realise how long it takes for water to boil in a pan on the hob, or how much it cools down when you add the cold vegetables to it, which meant that my vegetables took longer to be cooked than I planned for. I should have boiled the water in a kettle, which would have taken less time. • **Workspace, equipment and ingredients** – I set out my ingredients on a tray on one side of me and the equipment on the other side. This worked well for most of the session, but my workspace became a bit untidy towards the end, so I stopped what I was doing and cleared it up, which meant I could complete the presentation of the dishes in a tidy space. • **Clearing up** – I planned several clearing up sessions throughout the assessment, and this really helped me to manage my workspace and meant that I didn't run out of equipment such as spoons, knives and bowls, which were needed several times.

| **Planning** | • The advantages and disadvantages of the dishes and how they meet specific needs | • **Advantages** – The main course I chose (fish pie) needs a range of basic, medium and complex preparation, knife and cooking skills (mashing, skinning, chopping, peeling, dicing, filleting, boiling, sautéing, baking, poaching), which would help me to gain marks. It was suitable for the specific needs of young children, i.e. it provided a range of nutrients from fresh foods (fish, vegetables and dairy foods) and was easy for them to eat, because of its soft texture, which fitted the requirements of the assignment brief.

The dessert I chose (strawberry mousse) also needs a range of basic, medium and complex preparation, knife and cooking skills (puréeing, folding, mixing, piping, chilling, setting). It was suitable for the assignment brief because young children would like the colourful fruit used for decoration and the soft, smooth texture of the mousse.

• **Disadvantages** – It was quite difficult to remove all the little bones from the fish when I filleted it, so this could be a problem when little children eat it.

The mousse contains raw whisked egg whites, to provide air bubbles that make the mousse light, and I realised after I made it that it is not advisable for young children to have raw egg, for food safety reasons. The eggs I used were very fresh though, and I had kept them in the refrigerator. |
| **Time management** | • How effective the production plan was | • I tried to plan the production of my dishes in a logical order, so that things that took the longest to make (i.e. the bread rolls and panna cotta) were made first. This worked well, because the bread dough had plenty of time to rise, which meant that the baked rolls were light and well risen, and the panna cotta was set in plenty of time for me to decorate it carefully and neatly.

• I had a lot of work to do, and on my production plan, it looked like I could complete everything in the time allowed. However, I did not allow enough time to spend on the presentation of my dishes, so they were not as neat and creative as I wanted them to be. It would have been better to have prepared some of the garnishes during mise en place at the start of the practical assessment, so that I had them available to use when I presented my dishes, rather than trying to chop the herbs and slice the fruits in the last few minutes. |

Introduction

This section of the book will explain and guide you through the different stages for planning and carrying out the Unit 2 Assessment.

You will be given an **assignment brief (AB)** and a set of **assignment tasks (AT)** that you will carry out at school/college.

The Unit 2 Assessment is your chance to show your knowledge, your practical, organisational and creative skills, and understanding of the hospitality and catering industry.

The Unit 2 Assessment

- You will have **12 hours** to complete the Unit 2 Assessment.
- You are not allowed to have any more time than this.
- Your teacher will tell you how and when the 12 hours will be divided into different sessions.
- You are expected to use what you have learned from the following topic areas in **Unit 1** to complete the assignment tasks (see below) for the Unit 2 Assessment, i.e.:

Unit 1 Topic area	Section of Unit 1	Page
The operation of the front and back of house	1.2.1	29
Hospitality and catering provision to meet specific requirements	1.2.2 1.2.3	47 47
Health and safety in hospitality and catering provision	1.3.1	55
Food safety	1.3.2 1.4.1 1.4.2	69 73 73
Preventative control measures of food-induced ill health	1.4.3	85

- You will also use the knowledge and skills you have gained from the following topic areas of **Unit 2**:

Unit 2 Topic area	Section of Unit 2	Page
The importance of nutrition	2.1.1 2.1.2	114 145
Menu planning	2.2.1 2.2.2	128 141
The skills and techniques of preparation, cooking and presentation of dishes	2.3.1 2.3.2 2.3.3	145 167 172
Evaluating cooking skills	2.4.1 2.4.2	174 175

- You will need to **read the assignment brief** and **assignment tasks** very carefully so that you understand clearly what you need to do.
- During the Unit 2 Assessment sessions, you must work on your own, without help, and must not discuss or show your work to any other students.
- Always **check your work** to make sure you have done everything that you have been asked to do.

What you need to do to complete the Unit 2 Assessment

The assignment brief

The assignment brief sets the scene for what you must do for the Unit 2 Assessment. It will describe a hospitality and catering scenario, i.e.:

- The **hospitality and catering business**, e.g. in-house caterer in a hotel, independent high street café, outside caterer
- The **place**, e.g. café, community centre, restaurant, hospital kitchen
- The **event** being catered for, e.g. lunch menu, special occasion, buffet
- The details of **two specific groups of customers** being catered for (e.g. young children, elderly people, vegetarians).

You will be given instructions to produce **two dishes** (plus **accompaniments** – see pages 141–143) to cater for the specific needs of these two customer groups (i.e. one dish plus accompaniments for each group of customers).

Once you have been given the assignment brief, you will start and complete **four assignment tasks**. These are set out below, in the order in which you will do them.

Assignment task 1: (*2.1 – The importance of nutrition*)

You must write your answers to part a) and part b) (see below).

Recommended time: **up to 2 hours**

What you must do:

a) 2.1.2 Read and carefully think about which dishes plus accompaniments you will suggest for each of the two customer groups given in the assignment brief.

Explain how each dish you have chosen meets the nutritional needs of each customer group, using your knowledge and understanding of macronutrients (protein, fat and carbohydrate) and micronutrients (vitamins and minerals).

b) 2.1.2 Explain how the cooking methods used will affect the nutrients in the dishes you have chosen.

Assignment task 2: (*2.2 – Menu planning*)

Part a) You must produce a written report.

Recommended time: **up to 1 hour**

What you must do:

2.2.1 Discuss the factors which affected your choice of dishes, e.g. cost; portion control; nutrients; customer needs; equipment available; basic, medium and complex skills you will demonstrate; time of day; time available; environmental issues; season of the year; sensory (organoleptic) qualities.

Part b) You must produce a production plan for making your chosen dishes.

Recommended time allowed: **2 hours**

2.2.2 Write a production plan to show the order in which you will make your chosen dishes and accompaniments.

You should include:

- An ingredients list with how much of each ingredient you will need
- An equipment list of what you will use to prepare, cook and present the dishes
- How you will show that you are working with health, safety and hygiene in mind
- Contingencies (see pages 141–143) you have planned in case you have a problem when you are preparing, cooking and presenting your dishes
- Quality points you will show when you are preparing, cooking and presenting your dishes
- Sequencing and dovetailing (see page 141) the production of your dishes (the order in which you will do things)

- Timings for the preparation, cooking and presentation of your dishes
- Mise en place (how you will set up and organise your workspace, equipment and ingredients before you start producing your dishes)
- Cooking methods you will use
- How you will cool dishes that need it
- How you will keep food hot (hot holding)
- How you will present the dishes
- How you will store your ingredients.

Assignment task 3: (*2.3 – The techniques of preparation, cooking and presentation of dishes*)

Practical cooking session: An observation record will be completed by your teacher as you make your dishes.

Recommended time: **up to 3½ hours**

What you must do:

a) 2.3.3 Show your teacher how you can:
- work safely using equipment when preparing, cooking and presenting food
- handle food safely and hygienically when preparing, cooking and presenting food.

b) 2.3.1 Prepare the dishes using a variety of basic, medium and complex preparation and knife skills.

c) 2.3.1 Cook the dishes using a variety of basic, medium and complex cooking methods/skills.

d) 2.3.2 Present your dishes in a way that meets the needs of the customer groups in the assignment brief, showing your skills in:
- creativity
- garnish and decoration
- portion control
- accompaniments to the dishes.

Assignment task 4: (*2.4 – Evaluating cooking techniques*)

Part a) You must produce a written report or a voice recording.

Recommended time: **up to 1¾ hours**

What you must do:

2.4.1 Assess the production of the dishes you made.

Think about how you planned, prepared, cooked and presented the dishes, describing what was successful and anything you could have improved. When doing this, include the following points:
- The dishes you selected and made
- The sensory and other qualities of what you made
- Improvements you did make or could have made
- How you presented the dishes
- How well you followed health, safety and hygiene rules and practices
- The amount of food waste produced.

Part b) You must write a report.

RRecommended time allowed: **1¾ hours**

What you must do:

2.4.2 Review how well you worked during the practical session.

You should identify any of your strengths and weaknesses, in the following areas:
- How well you made decisions when choosing the dishes and making them
- How well organised you were when making the dishes
- How well you planned the assessment, including the advantages and disadvantages of the dishes you chose and how well they met the specific needs of the customers in the assignment brief
- How well you managed your time throughout.

Here is a reminder of the basic, medium and complex preparation, knife and cooking skills that are covered in Unit 2:

Preparation techniques

BASIC	MEDIUM	COMPLEX
Beating	Creaming	Crimping
Blending	Dehydrating	Laminating (pastry)
Grating	Folding	Melting using bain-marie
Hydrating	Kneading	Moulding/unmoulding/
Juicing	Mixing	shaping
Marinating	Puréeing	Piping
Mashing	Rubbing-in	Whisking (aeration)
Melting	Rolling	
Proving	Skinning	
Shredding	Toasting (nuts/seeds)	
Sieving	Weighing and measuring	
Tenderising		
Zesting		

Knife techniques

BASIC	MEDIUM	COMPLEX
Chopping	Baton	Julienne
Peeling	Chiffonade	Brunoise
Trimming	Dicing	Mincing
	Slicing	Deboning
	Deseeding	Filleting
	Spatchcock	Segmenting

Cooking techniques

BASIC	MEDIUM	COMPLEX
Basting	Baking	Baking blind
Boiling	Blanching	Caramelising
Chilling	Braising	Deep fat frying
Cooling	Deglazing	Emulsifying
Dehydrating	Frying	Poaching
Freezing	Griddling	Tempering
Grilling	Pickling	
Skimming	Reduction	
Toasting	Roasting	
	Sautéing	
	Setting	
	Steaming	
	Stir frying	
	Water-bath (sous vide)	

For the rest of this section, an example assessment will be set out and worked through, with example answers given for each assignment task. Suggestions as to how you could set out your answer for each task are also given. Your teacher will also give you guidance on this.

Example assignment brief

Cookswich Community Centre, which is in a large town with a multi-ethnic population, has opened a purpose-built café and catering kitchen. The café caters for the numerous groups who use the centre each week, at various times of the day and evening and at weekends.

In addition to drinks and snacks, the café produces lunches and suppers, as well as catering for occasions such as special meetings and social events. All the food is produced by the café chefs in their well-equipped kitchen next to the café. They also provide work experience for students at a nearby catering college.

As a trainee chef from the college, you have been asked to plan, make and present one dish* that will be served on the menu for lunch for the **new parents' social group** and another dish* that will be served in the evenings for members of the **senior citizens' board games and supper group**.

*The dish can be a starter, main course or dessert.

Study tip

You could set out the options for dishes you might choose, in the form of a mind map.

Assignment task 1

Example answer

a) Chosen dishes and how each one meets the nutritional needs of each customer group

For the young parents' group, I am going to make a main course dish. Here are the dishes I have thought about making:

Vegetarian – roasted vegetable, ricotta and spinach lasagne, roasted vegetable pasta bake, vegan shepherd's pie, lentil and bean curry, goat's cheese and onion tart, vegetable moussaka

Fish – fish pie, seafood risotto, fish cakes, salmon en croute

Main course dish

Meat/poultry – sweet and sour chicken, chicken and leek pie, lamb meat balls in tomato sauce, lamb tagine, stuffed chicken breast with savoury rice, beef curry, beef pasties

Dairy foods – broccoli and cheese quiche flan, cauliflower and leek au gratin, ricotta and spinach stuffed cannelloni in cheese sauce, cheese scotch eggs

I have chosen to make:

Roasted vegetable, ricotta and spinach lasagne

Served with homemade coleslaw

The young parents' group will include women and men from different ethnic groups and some of the women may be breastfeeding their babies. As young parents, their bodies may still be growing and developing, so they will need plenty of nutrients and energy to allow this to happen, as well as cope with the needs of a baby. Therefore, it is important that they eat a balanced diet containing plenty of fresh fruit and vegetables to give them:

-   a variety of vitamins, minerals and fibre
-   protein from plant foods such as beans, seeds and grains, and/or animal foods including meat, poultry, fish and/or dairy foods
-   carbohydrate from wholegrain rice, pasta, couscous and bread, and potatoes and other starchy vegetables such as yams and plantains.

They should only eat a limited amount of high sugar, high-salt and high-fat foods, such as snacks and takeaway foods.

The bones and teeth of young adults are also still developing, and they need to reach peak bone mass so they are as strong as possible. It is important that they have enough calcium (the main mineral needed for strong bones and teeth), which is found in dairy foods, green leafy vegetables, canned fish, some nuts, enriched plants milk drinks and flour, as well as vitamin D (from dairy foods, oily fish, vegetables spreads and eggs in their diet and exposure to sunlight so it can be made under the skin) to help absorb the calcium in the body. This is important for the mothers who breastfeed their babies, as they will need enough calcium and vitamin D for their needs and the needs of the baby through their milk.

A good account of the nutritional needs of this group of people and linked well with the additional needs of being a young parent.

All the women in the group will also need to make sure they have enough iron and vitamin C in their diet to prevent them from becoming anaemic, due to blood loss during a period.

The roasted vegetable, ricotta and spinach lasagne will meet the nutritional needs of the young parents as it provides:

-   a range of vitamins and minerals from the vegetables, milk, cheese and eggs
-   protein from the ricotta cheese and cheese and milk in the sauce, and the egg in the pasta
-   fat from the cheese and milk and from oil used for roasting the vegetables
-   carbohydrate from the pasta and starch in the roasted vegetables and fibre from the vegetables
-   calcium provided by the milk, cheese and flour in the pasta and sauce and some from the vegetables
-   vitamin D from the cheese and milk
-   iron found in the spinach and flour in the pasta and sauce
-   vitamin C from the raw cabbage and apple in the coleslaw which will be served with the lasagne.

The list of nutrients provided by the dish is clearly set out and detailed.

For the senior citizens' board games and supper group, I am going to make a dessert. Here are the dishes I have thought about making:

Dessert

Chilled – fruit or chocolate mousse, panna cotta, cheesecake, trifle, tiramisu, fruit and cream gateau, pistachio and lemon roulade, custard tart, lemon tart

Hot – apple pie, red berry crumble, spiced fruit steamed pudding, raspberry and white chocolate brioche pudding, queen of puddings, sticky toffee pudding

I have chosen to make:

Pistachio and lemon roulade

Served with a red berry compote

The members of the senior citizens' board games and supper group will be older adults, who need to eat a balanced diet, as with younger adults, to stay healthy and remain active. They especially need:

- the B group vitamins to help prevent memory loss
- calcium and vitamin D to help maintain the strength of their bones and teeth
- vitamins A, C and E (e.g. from green leafy vegetables, fruits, nuts and other vegetables) to keep their eyesight healthy
- vitamin C and iron, because not having enough of these can lead to scurvy and anaemia, which is quite common in older people, so it is important that they also include foods that contain these in their diet, e.g. iron from red meat, lentils, dark green leafy vegetables, wholemeal bread, eggs, dried apricots and cocoa; and vitamin C from fresh fruit and vegetables.

The specific nutritional needs of this age group have been given in very good detail.

Body systems, such as blood circulation and digestion, start to slow down in older people, and often their appetite gets smaller. This means that they often prefer to eat smaller amounts of food, so it is important that any food they do eat has as many nutrients in it as possible, as well as fibre to prevent constipation.

The pistachio and lemon roulade served with red berry compote, will meet the nutritional needs of the older adults as it provides a range of nutrients and energy:

- Protein is provided by the nuts and eggs in the sponge and lemon curd and some in the cream filling.
- Carbohydrate is provided by the flour and sugar in the sponge and the nuts.
- Fat is provided by the cream filling, the egg yolks and the nuts.
- Fibre is provided by the nuts and the berries in the compote.
- Some iron is provided by the eggs and the flour in the sponge and the red berry compote.

The list of nutrients provided by the dish is detailed.

- Lemon curd will provide some vitamin C to help the body absorb the iron.
- Calcium is provided by the flour and cream filling.
- There is some vitamin D in the cream.
- Some B vitamins are provided by the eggs, flour and cream filling.

b) How the cooking methods used in the chosen dishes will affect the nutrients

Roasted vegetable, ricotta and spinach lasagne

Served with homemade coleslaw

- The oil used for roasting the vegetables can help the body absorb the vitamin A they contain.
- The protein in the cheese on the top of the lasagne may become toughened with the heat of the oven and be less digestible.
- Some of the vitamin C in the spinach will be damaged by heat when it is boiled.

Pistachio and lemon roulade

Served with a red berry compote

- Some of the B vitamins in the egg, nuts and flour of the sponge will be damaged by the heat of the oven during baking.
- Some of the vitamin C in the red berry compote and lemon curd will be damaged by the heat when it is simmered.

Assignment task 2
Example answer

Part a) I chose the two dishes for the following reasons:

- **Cost:** The lasagne is not very expensive to make because it uses vegetables and no meat. The most expensive items are the ricotta and cheddar cheeses. The ingredients in the salad and coleslaw can be varied to suit what is most economical to make. The most expensive ingredient in the pistachio and lemon roulade are the pistachios, and if the café wanted to reduce the cost, they could use less expensive nuts such as hazelnuts or pecan nuts instead. I am going to make a small amount of lemon curd, which should cost less than buying a whole jar. The red berry compote can be made using frozen fruits. At the times of the year when fresh fruits are not in season or are expensive, frozen ones will be a cheaper option.

- **Portion control:** The lasagne would be made in a large catering tray in the café, so that it can be portioned by the chef. It would be a good idea to offer large and small portions at different prices to suit the appetites of the young parents. The roulade can easily be divided into equal sized slices and the compote can be served using a ladle, so that the same amount is given for each serving. Both will help with portion control and also for the dessert to be profitable for the café.

- **Equipment available:** I will be able to make the dishes in the food room, as there is enough special equipment that I need, e.g. a pasta rolling machine, Swiss roll tin for the roulade, a roasting tin for the vegetables, an ovenproof glass dish for the lasagne, a bain-marie for the lemon curd, food processor to grind the nuts, electric hand mixer, and sharp vegetable knives.

- **Skills:** I will demonstrate the following basic, medium and complex preparation, knife and cooking skills when making these two dishes, set out in the chart below:

Preparation skills

BASIC	MEDIUM	COMPLEX
Juicing the lemons for the lemon curd	Folding the flour and nuts into the whisked egg and sugar mixture	Melting using bain-marie the butter and sugar for the lemon curd and cooking it over the bain-marie to cook the eggs and thicken the curd
Zesting the lemon rind	Measuring the milk for the lasagne sauce	Whisking (aeration):
Sieving the flour for the roulade	Weighing the ingredients for the roulade, lemon curd, pasta dough and lasagne sauce	- the eggs and sugar to make the sponge for the roulade
	Mixing the pasta dough	- the double cream to aerate the roulade filling
	Kneading the pasta dough	
	Rolling the pasta dough for the lasagne sheets	

The skills have been very clearly set out.

Knife skills

BASIC	MEDIUM	COMPLEX
Peeling the vegetables for roasting	Deseeding the pepper	Mincing the garlic
Chopping the vegetables for roasting, the spinach and the coleslaw ingredients	Dicing the onion, pepper, tomatoes and courgette	
Trimming - the crisp edges of the baked roulade - the lasagne dough into sheets to fit the dish		
Shredding the cabbage and carrot for the coleslaw		
Blending ingredients for cheese sauce for lasagne		

Cooking methods/skills

BASIC	MEDIUM	COMPLEX
Boiling the spinach for the lasagne	Roasting the vegetables for the lasagne	
Cooling: - the roulade before filling - the lemon curd after cooking - the compote before serving	Baking: - the roulade - the lasagne	

Analysis and evaluation are detailed and include a wide range of factors that have influenced and justified the choice of dishes.

- *Time of day:* Batches of the lasagne could be made and frozen in advance at the stage before it needs to be baked in the oven, which would be a good use of the time for the chefs. Before it is frozen, the lasagne will need to be chilled to 0–5 °C within 90 minutes of being cooked. When it is defrosted for service at the young parents' group lunch, it will need to be baked to a minimum core temperature of 70 °C and held at a minimum of 63 °C for service. The roulade is best made and served on the same day because the sponge may become dry if it is kept too long. If it is made in the morning or afternoon before the senior citizens' board game group in the evening, it will need to be kept chilled and served at 0–5 °C.

- *Time available:* I have a lot to do, but I should be able to make these two dishes and their accompaniments in the 3½ hours available if I am well organised, which I will show in my production plan in part b) of this task.

- **Environmental issues:** Some of the vegetables for the lasagne and fruits for the compote could be organically produced and bought when they are in season from local farmers and producers. This means that fewer food miles will be needed to transport them. The café tries to buy and use misshapen vegetables and fruits to prevent them from being wasted. It also donates any unsold food to local charities to provide food for poor families and homeless people.

- **Organoleptic qualities:** I chose the lasagne because it is a popular choice for many people, especially those who want to eat less meat. The dried herbs and garlic add flavour to the vegetables, and roasting the vegetables makes their flavour stronger, because the water is driven out of them. The texture of the lasagne is mostly soft and smooth, and the salads that are served with it add crisp and crunchy textures. The lasagne is colourful because of the vegetables and bright green layer of spinach and ricotta cheese in the middle layer. The salads include a range of colours, and the coleslaw can be made with purple cabbage and red onions to add more colour.

  I chose the roulade, because it has a range of textures, i.e. the spongy layer with the nuts on the outside and the filling which is creamy and smooth. The nuts give the sponge a light green colour and add flavour and this goes well with the deep red/purple colours of the compote.

Part b) Here is my production plan for the two dishes:

Production plan for:
Roasted vegetable, ricotta and spinach lasagne
Homemade coleslaw
Pistachio and lemon roulade
Red berry compote
Time: 09.00 – 12.30

Quantities of commodities (ingredients) needed:

Roasted vegetable, ricotta, and spinach lasagne (Serves 4–6 people)

1 tbsp olive oil	Pasta:
1 medium onion	250 g strong plain pasta flour
1 clove garlic	3 medium eggs
1 yellow pepper	Semolina flour for dusting
1 courgette	Parsley for garnishing
200 g butternut squash	
400 g fresh tomatoes	Homemade coleslaw
1 tsp dried mixed herbs	¼ of a small white cabbage
300 g tomato passata	1 carrot
200 g fresh spinach	4 spring onions
1 egg	1 small apple
250 g ricotta cheese	2 heaped tbsp mayonnaise
½ tsp grated nutmeg	Seasoning

Sauce:
25 g butter or margarine
25 g plain flour
300 ml milk
100 g grated cheddar cheese

Study tip

Here is an example of what a production plan could look like (your teacher may ask you to use a different layout).

Whatever layout is used, it is important that the production plan is clearly set out, so that both you and the person marking your work can follow it easily.

The plan will also be used as a guide by you when you are making your dishes, so it is important that you include vital information in it, i.e. oven and other temperatures; instructions (the method) for each stage of making the two dishes; timings and reminders about clearing up, etc.

The text for each dish is shown in a different colour as a guide to help you follow the plan. You could do this on a typed plan or use highlighter pens. You will also see that the plan has used **sequencing** and **dovetailing** (see page 141) to use the time available as efficiently as possible.

Pistachio and lemon roulade (Serves 8 people)

Sponge:
3 medium eggs
75 g caster sugar
75 g shelled pistachio nuts (not salted)
75 g self-raising flour

Filling:
150 ml double cream

Lemon curd:
2 lemons
2 medium eggs
50 g unsalted butter
225 g white sugar
To finish – 4 tsp icing sugar

Red berry compote
125 g frozen mixed berries (blackcurrants, blueberries, raspberries, redcurrants, strawberries)
20 g caster sugar

Equipment needed:	
Roasted vegetable, ricotta, and spinach lasagne and homemade coleslaw	
Roasting tin, sharp chef's knife, brown and green chopping board, grater, saucepan, mixing bowl, pasta rolling machine, ovenproof rectangular deep dish, two trays for pasta sheets, clean, damp tea towel, food processor, food probe	
Pistachio and lemon roulade	
Bain-marie, zester, juicer, mixing bowls, electric hand whisk, baking paper, Swiss roll tin, food processor / grinder, sieve, pan, heat-proof jar or bowl for finished lemon curd	

Time	Activity	Notes Key: **C** = Contingency **HSH** = Health, safety and hygiene point **QP** = Quality point
09.00	Mise en place: line Swiss roll tin with baking paper; weigh/measure ingredients, set out chopping board and knives; set up bain-marie on hob; set up electric hand whisk; set up pasta rolling machine and trays for the cut pasta sheets, organise other ingredients. Wash the vegetables.	**HSH** Place cream and both cheeses on a tray in the refrigerator, away from other foods to prevent cross-contamination.
09.15	Heat the oven to gas 5 / 190 °C (180 °C for fan oven). Make lemon curd: Place the clean jar/bowl on a tray in the oven to heat and sterilise it. Beat the eggs. Zest the lemon rinds and squeeze the juice from both. Put all the ingredients into the top of the bain-marie and place it over a pan of simmering water. Stir, until all the sugar has dissolved, and continue heating, stirring occasionally, until the curd thickens and coats the back of a wooden spoon.	**HSH** Wash hands thoroughly after handling raw eggs. **QP** If there are lumps of cooked egg white protein in the curd, strain it through a sieve before using. **C** If a bain-marie is not available, use a heat-proof bowl over a pan of simmering water.
09.25	Clear away and wash up. Throw away any rubbish and waste.	**HSH** Wash hands thoroughly after handling rubbish.

09.35	Check the lemon curd to see how well it is thickening. Make pasta dough: Beat the eggs. Sieve the flour into a bowl. Make a well in the centre and add the eggs. Gradually work in the flour with a spoon or fork until a dough is formed, then knead it for at least 3 minutes until it is silky, smooth and elastic. Cover the bowl with a plate and rest the dough in the refrigerator for at least half an hour.	**HSH** Wash hands thoroughly after handling raw eggs.
09.45	Pour the lemon curd into the hot bowl or jar and leave it to cool.	**HSH** Protect the lemon curd from dust and flies.
09.53	Clear away and wash up. Throw away any rubbish and waste.	**HSH** Wash hands thoroughly after handling rubbish.
09.58	Make roulade sponge: Process the pistachio nuts until they are very finely chopped. Whisk the eggs and sugar together in a large bowl until very thick and light and the mixture leaves a visible trail for at least 5 seconds. Very carefully fold in half of the sieved flour and half of the processed nuts. Repeat with the rest of the flour and half of the remaining nuts, save a quarter of the nuts for sprinkling over the finished roulade. Pour the sponge mixture into the greased and lined Swiss roll tin and bake for approximately 10–12 minutes.	**HSH** Wash hands thoroughly after handling raw eggs.
10.13	Clear away and wash up. Throw away any rubbish and waste.	**HSH** Wash hands thoroughly after handling rubbish.
10.20	Set up the pasta machine on the workspace with the trays nearby and the semolina in a bowl by the machine.	**C** If a pasta machine is not available, the dough can be rolled out using a rolling pin.
10.25	Remove the roulade sponge from the oven and straightaway, turn the sponge onto a sheet of baking paper sprinkled with some of the saved processed nuts and roll it up with a piece of baking paper inside. Leave on a cooling rack to cool. Increase the oven temperature to gas 6 / 200 °C (190 °C for fan oven).	**QP** The roulade should be well risen and spongy to the touch.

10.28	Prepare the lasagne:	
	Finely dice the peeled onion, butternut squash and courgette.	
	De-seed the pepper, remove the core and dice finely.	
	Chop the tomatoes into quarters and remove any tough cores.	
	Peel and mince the garlic.	
	Mix the oil with the vegetables, except the spinach and place them in the roasting tin.	
10.45	Roast for 40–45 minutes until soft – stir occasionally.	
11.00	Clear away and wash up. Throw away any rubbish and waste.	**HSH** Wash hands thoroughly after handling rubbish.
11.05	Remove the pasta dough from the refrigerator. Divide the dough into three balls – working on one at a time and keeping the others covered with the damp tea towel.	**QP** Make sure that the lasagne sheets are all the same size and thickness, so that they fit the dish properly and will cook evenly.
	Flatten each ball and run it through the thickest setting on the pasta machine. Fold the ends to the middle and repeat on the same setting another three times.	
	Lightly dust the dough with the semolina flour and repeat the rolling on the next setting down.	
	Repeat the process, each time reducing the setting on the machine until thin sheets of pasta are formed.	
	Cut each piece of rolled out pasta into four lasagne sheets (12 altogether) and lay them out on the two trays dusted with semolina.	
11.20	Boil the spinach in 4 tbsp water for a few minutes until softened. Drain and squeeze out any water. Place the spinach in a food processor with the ricotta and egg and blend until smooth. Season with black pepper and nutmeg.	
11.25	Make the cheese sauce: melt the butter, add the flour and cook for 1 minute. Remove from heat and gradually add the milk to make a smooth liquid. Re-heat and stir until thickened. Add half the cheese and stir well.	
	Lightly grease the lasagne dish with butter or vegetable fat.	
11.30	Check the roasted vegetables – stir and check that they are tender. Remove from oven and stir in the tomato passata.	

11.35	Season the vegetables and add the herbs. Place half of the vegetable mixture in the lasagne dish and add a layer of lasagne sheets. Add the spinach mixture, then more lasagne sheets, then the rest of the tomato mixture. Finish with lasagne sheets. Top with cheese sauce and sprinkle with remaining cheese. Cook in oven for 45–50 minutes until golden and tender.	
11.45	Whisk the cream for the roulade filling. Carefully unroll the roulade and spread it evenly with 4 tbsp of the cooled lemon curd, and then with the cream. Roll it up carefully and place it on a serving dish. Sprinkle the remaining nuts over the roulade and dust with the icing sugar.	**QP** Avoid over-whisking the cream by controlling the speed of the electric whisk. **HSH** Place finished roulade in refrigerator to keep chilled at 0–5 °C.
11.55	Place the frozen fruits in a small pan with the sugar, and gently simmer for 5 minutes until the fruit has softened. Pour into a serving bowl and leave to cool.	**QP** Keep the heat very low to avoid burning the fruit and to preserve some of the vitamin C.
12.05	Make the coleslaw: Finely shred the cabbage and grate the carrot. Peel and thinly slice the spring onions, including the green stems. Core the apple and chop into small pieces. Season and mix everything thoroughly with the mayonnaise. Place coleslaw into serving bowl.	**HSH** Use a green chopping board (if available). **HSH** Place coleslaw in refrigerator to keep chilled at 0–5 °C.
12.15	Clear away and wash up. Throw away any rubbish and waste.	**HSH** Wash hands thoroughly after handling rubbish.
12.25	Remove the lasagne from the oven.	**QP** Check if it is cooked by testing if the lasagne is tender with a metal skewer.
12.30	Present dishes on serving plates: Present a serving of lasagne with some coleslaw on a cold plate (the coleslaw needs to be kept cold, but the lasagne will be very hot as it has just come from the oven). Garnish with chopped parsley. Present a serving of the roulade with some red berry compote on a cold serving plate.	**HSH** Final clearing up.

Assignment task 3 (AT3) – general information

(not specifically about the example Assessment Brief in this section).

Assignment task 3 is the practical test, where you make the dishes you have planned in the previous two tasks. It will be marked by someone at your school/college – usually your teacher – while you are preparing and cooking your dishes.

The teacher will follow the mark scheme, set by the exam board, to fill out an observation record and they will judge your work against the Assessment Objectives (see page 104); in particular, how you *apply and use* your practical skills, knowledge and understanding for different parts of the task.

The following chart shows:

- examples of the things your teacher/examiner will be looking for while you are working during the practical test
- examples of what you might do in the practical test to show your skills, knowledge and understanding.

Section of AT3	What the examiner is looking for: How you use (apply) your skills, knowledge and understanding in AT3	Examples of how you might show your skills, knowledge and understanding in the practical assessment
a) 2.3.3 Working safely / food safety	**How well you carry out food safety practices, including:** • Store ingredients safely	• Put high-risk foods, e.g. meat, fish, dairy foods in the refrigerator at 0–5 °C. • Put raw fresh poultry, fish and meat on a tray in the refrigerator, away from cooked foods, to prevent cross-contamination. • Wash the soil off vegetables to prevent cross-contamination.
	• Correctly cook, keep hot, cool or chill high-risk foods	• Use a food probe to check that cooked meat, poultry and fish has a core temperature of 70 °C minimum for 2 minutes and is held hot at a minimum core temperature of 63 °C. • Pour hot, cooked food into a shallow tray, cover and leave it in a cool area to cool down as quickly as possible, to 5 °C or cooler, within 1½ hours after cooking.

	• Use correct chopping boards for the preparation of foods to prevent cross-contamination	• Chop foods on different coloured boards (if available) i.e.:
		  – Brown – root vegetables
		  – Red – raw meat and poultry
		  – Blue – raw fish and shellfish
		  – Yellow – cooked meats, poultry and fish
		  – Green – leafy vegetables, salads and fruits
		  – White – dairy foods and bakery items.

	• Thoroughly clean equipment to prevent cross-contamination	• Carefully and thoroughly wash equipment used for the preparation of raw, high-risk foods in hot water and detergent and dry it before it is used for other foods.

How well you apply hygiene practices (personal and food hygiene), including:

- Hand washing is carried out frequently

- Wash your hands before:
  - handling any food
  - transferring hands from one high-risk food to handling another food.
- Wash your hands after:
  - handling high-risk foods such as raw eggs, poultry, meat and fish
  - getting rid of waste food, food packaging and other rubbish
  - going to the toilet
  - blowing your nose or coughing into your hands.

- Standard of personal hygiene

- Wear a clean apron, make sure your fingernails are short and clean; tie back long hair; do not wear nail varnish, false nails, false eyelashes or jewellery; make sure your hands are clean.

- Workspace hygiene and management

- Frequently clear your workspace ('clear as you go'); wash up used equipment often and well; clear away rubbish and food scraps; regularly clean/sanitise your workspace.

How safely you use equipment and kitchen facilities:

- Safety of self and others is considered throughout and acted upon

- Wipe up spillages of water or food on the floor straight away.
- Keep the floor clear of trailing wires, bags and other items.
- Move around the room with care.

- Use of equipment and facilities is carried out safely and correctly

- Use the cooker hob and oven safely, e.g.:
  - Do not allow pan handles on the hob to jut out, to prevent them from being knocked off
  - Use oven gloves to put things into and take them out of the oven.
- Use electrical equipment safely, e.g.:
  - Away from water
  - Hands are dry when using electrical equipment
  - Electrical equipment is correctly cleaned and stored away after use.
- Use sharp items safely, e.g. carry knives correctly, with the blade pointing down, from the knife rack to the workspace
  - Wash up all sharp items carefully, using a washing up brush, e.g. food processor blade, mandolin, grater, sharp knife
  - Use safety guards on electrical equipment and items such as a mandolin.

b) 2.3.1
Use of basic, medium and complex preparation and knife techniques

How you apply your knowledge and understanding of preparation and knife techniques:

- Range of preparation and knife techniques used
  - You used a range of mostly complex/medium/ basic preparation and knife skills.
  - You have needed no guidance / a limited amount of guidance / a lot of guidance.

- How ingredients are handled
  - You accurately weigh/measure ingredients.
  - You correctly store ingredients.
  - You correctly heat/cool ingredients.
  - You handle and control ingredients **competently** (i.e. it is obvious/clear that you know what you are doing), **speedily** and **precisely** (carefully/ accurately).

- How processes and techniques are carried out
  - You handle ingredients/mixtures correctly, competently, speedily and precisely, e.g.:
    - bread dough is kneaded long enough to develop the gluten
    - short pastry dough is kneaded lightly to avoid toughening the gluten
    - egg whites are whisked sufficiently to trap enough air for a stable meringue
    - double cream is whipped until thick enough to pipe, but does not split
    - gelatine is correctly dissolved and added to a panna cotta to allow it to set
    - a cake mixture has sufficient air beaten into the mixture to allow it to rise.

- Knife techniques
  - Where available, you use the most suitable type of knife to cut an ingredient, e.g. a serrated knife to segment an orange; a chef's knife to chop nuts; a filleting knife to prepare raw fish.
  - You use sharp knives safely, on a chopping board effectively, speedily and precisely.

c) 2.3.1
Use of basic, medium and complex cooking techniques

How you cook the dishes:

- Range of cooking techniques used
  - You use a range of mostly complex/medium/basic cooking skills.
  - You need no guidance / a limited amount of guidance / a lot of guidance.

- How cooking techniques are carried out
  - You carry out and control cooking methods **competently** (it is obvious/clear that you know what you are doing), speedily and precisely (carefully/accurately) e.g.:
    - crème caramel is cooked at the correct temperature until it has coagulated and lightly set
    - a bechamel sauce is stirred constantly during heating, until it has boiled and thickened to a smooth, glossy sauce
    - meat is correctly cooked to tenderise it
    - green vegetables are placed into boiling water or steamed until just tender
    - chicken legs are frequently turned over during grilling to ensure even and thorough cooking
    - deep fried foods are cooked at the correct temperature and regularly turned, to ensure they do not absorb too much oil and are cooked all the way through.

d) 2.3.2 Presentation of dishes

How you present the dishes:

- Range of presentation techniques used
- Creativity, garnish and decoration

- You use a variety of presentation skills, which are carried out and controlled **competently** (it is obvious/clear that you know what you are doing), speedily and precisely (carefully/accurately) e.g.:
  - Suitable knives and techniques are used creatively to produce garnishes and decorations for dishes
  - Presentation is neat, colourful and makes use of pattern and shape
  - Ingredients used for garnish and decoration go well with each dish in terms of flavour, texture, colour, size and distribution (where they are placed).

- Portion control

- You present portions of the same dish in equal size to the others.
- The portion sizes you present are suitable for the person who will eat the food.
- You use items such as spoons, ladles, ruler, scoop, measuring jug to help with portion control.

- Accompaniments

- You serve accompaniments with each dish that are suitable in size, texture, flavour, colour, shape, ingredients used and cooking method.

Assignment task 4

Example answer

Here are the finished results of my two dishes:

Vegetable lasagne and coleslaw salad

Pistachio and lemon roulade with red berry compote

2.4.1 Review of my dishes

Selection and production:

I had to produce two dishes for the café at Cookswich Community Centre; one each for two different groups that meet there. I chose one lunchtime main course dish for the young parents' group, and one dessert dish for the senior citizens' board game supper group, which met the requirements of the assignment brief.

I was pleased with the dishes I chose; they would be suitable for the café to produce because:

- both dishes could be prepared in advance (the main course dish could be frozen in batches), which would help the chefs in the café to plan their production ready for lunchtime and evening meals
- the dishes could be pre-portioned by the chefs and served quite easily, which is important to help with the flow of customers through the café at busy times
- they allowed me to demonstrate a range of basic, medium and complex skills, which are set out in a chart, in Assignment task 2 on pages 183–84 of my assessment, i.e.:
    - 3 basic, 6 medium and 2 complex preparation skills
    - 5 basic, 2 medium and 1 complex knife skills
    - 2 basic and 2 medium cooking methods.

Organoleptic qualities of my dishes:

Colour: dishes had good colours, i.e. the layers of the lasagne sauce in the main course dish were red/orange, with a bright green layer of spinach and ricotta in the middle. The top of the lasagne was a golden-brown colour from the cooked cheese.

The pistachio nuts gave the roulade sponge a pale green colour, which went well with the yellow lemon curd, white cream and the rich red/purple colour of the fruit compote. I think perhaps I dusted the outside of the roulade with too much icing sugar though.

Flavour: The flavour of the lasagne sauce was helped by adding the dried herbs and the garlic. Roasting the vegetables made their flavour stronger, especially the tomatoes. The cheese sauce was not very strong – it would have been better if I had used a stronger cheddar cheese.

The lemon curd in the roulade went very well with the flavour of the sponge. The fruit compote was not too sweet.

Texture: The lasagne sheets I made cooked well and were tender, although in some areas of the top layer, the cheese sauce had not quite covered them and so some bits were a bit dried and crisp.

The coleslaw accompaniment was crunchy and crisp and was a good contrast to the softness of the lasagne.

The roulade sponge was light and easy to cut into neat portions when it was rolled up.

Presentation of the dishes:

I made sure that the plates and serving dishes were clean and dry.

The plate for the main course was cool because of the coleslaw, which is cold. The plate for the dessert was chilled.

I served the food carefully and neatly and tried not to overcrowd the plates. It was a bit tricky to keep the lasagne portion in a nice shape because the sauce was quite runny.

I was quite pleased with how I presented the roulade. It looked neat and was colourful.

Good and varied reasons for the selection of dishes are given and linked to the organisation and work of the chefs in the café.

The student has given an honest and appropriate review of the organoleptic qualities of their dishes.

Health, food safety and hygiene:

I put the cheeses and cream in the refrigerator at the start of the assessment.

I washed the vegetables well to get rid of any dirt on them and kept them away from other foods.

I tried to clear up often, but near the end of the assessment, I had quite a big build-up of washing up as I was busy trying to get everything finished.

Just before I presented it, I used a food probe to check that the lasagne was cooked right through (it was 85 °C, which is a safe temperature for cooked high-risk foods, i.e. the spinach, ricotta cheese and egg layer).

The roulade had been chilled to 0–5 °C.

I washed my hands regularly, especially after I handled the raw eggs, vegetables and cream and put rubbish in the bin.

Safety:

I used oven gloves to put the roulade in the oven and take it out.

I put the lasagne dish on a baking tray in the oven to make it easier to put in and take out. I made sure that on the hob, the pan handles were not sticking out.

I was careful when carrying, using and washing up the sharp knives, food processor and electric whisk that I used.

Food and other waste:

There was some food waste – mostly vegetable peelings, and I had some whipped cream left over, so I froze that in a covered box.

I was able to recycle some of the food packaging (cream and ricotta cheese pots), but some of the plastic packaging from the vegetables could not be recycled. It would have been better to have bought the vegetables loose, but I couldn't find any in the supermarket.

2.4.2 Review of my performance in producing the dishes

Choosing and producing the dishes:

I was pleased with the production plan I wrote in Assignment task 2, and most of it worked well.

I was pleased with the roulade, as the sponge rose really well in the oven, which meant that it was easy to roll up and looked good when it was filled and cut into slices.

There was one problem, which meant I had to make a quick decision about what to do. I had used the pasta rolling machine a few times before in my Food lessons at school and managed to get the thickness and size of the pasta sheets just right. However, in the assessment, the pasta dough I made was a bit too soft, so I had real problems trying to roll it through the machine. I think perhaps the eggs were too large, and this made the dough difficult to handle. I decided to roll out the dough using a rolling pin instead and dusted the work surface with plenty of semolina to stop the dough sticking. I managed to make enough lasagne sheets within the time I had planned.

Good detail given in these points, showing knowledge and understanding of food safety and hygiene.

A good and honest review of their own performance has been given and the student has successfully managed to resolve a problem that arose during the practical assessment.

Organisation of my workspace:

Time – My production plan was mostly in the correct order, but some of the timings I planned were not long enough, e.g. it took la bit longer to make the pasta and coleslaw than I planned, which meant I was rushing a bit towards the end of the practical assessment.

Workspace, equipment and ingredients – I set out my ingredients on a tray on one side of me and the equipment on the other side. This worked well for most of the time, but it did get a bit messy towards the end, so I stopped what I was doing and cleared it up a bit, which meant I could finish the presentation of the dishes in a tidy space.

Clearing up – I planned several clearing up sessions throughout the assessment, and this really helped me to manage my workspace for most of the time and meant that I didn't run out of equipment such as spoons, knives and bowls, which I used several times.

Planning the dishes:

Advantages – the vegetable lasagne and roulade used a range of mostly basic and medium and some complex preparation and knife skills, including juicing, zesting, slicing, folding in, mixing, kneading (making pasta), melting in a bain-marie to make lemon curd, whisking (aerating), chopping, peeling, trimming, shredding, blending, deseeding, dicing and mincing, all of which would help me to gain marks.

I think each dish would appeal to the group of people it was made for, as lasagne is a popular main course dish and many people are trying to eat less meat, and the roulade is a light but attractive and tasty dessert that would appeal to people having an evening meal out.

For the chefs in the café, both dishes can be prepared in advance (especially the lasagne, which can be frozen once prepared), which will help them to plan their work schedule and would be a good exercise for the trainee chef on work experience from the catering college to plan, organise and make.

Disadvantages – Making fresh pasta for the lasagne may not be a good use of the chefs' time in the café, and it would probably be better for them to buy dried lasagne sheets, which are easy to store and use. The roulade is best eaten on the day it is made, as the sponge can dry out after a few hours, so the chefs at the café would need to decide whether there are likely to be enough people who may order it for their dessert in the evening group, to prevent waste and make it profitable.

Time management:

I tried to plan the production of my dishes so that things that took the longest to make, set or rest (i.e. the lemon curd and fresh pasta) were made first. This worked well because, even though the pasta took longer to make than I thought it would, I still had enough time to use it in the lasagne, which was cooked on time.

I had a lot of work to do, and I just managed to have enough time to present my dishes neatly at the end.

Good awareness of the logistics of working in the hospitality and catering industry.

Good awareness of the need to consider possible wastage and its effects on profitability when planning a menu.

Time management and organisation are honestly reviewed and conclusions about performance are effective.